LEO STRAUSS AND THE REDISCOVERY OF MAIMONIDES

LEO STRAUSS AND THE REDISCOVERY OF MAIMONIDES

Kenneth Hart Green

THE UNIVERSITY OF CHICAGO PRESS | *Chicago and London*

Kenneth Hart Green is associate professor in the Department for the Study of Religion at the University of Toronto. He is the author of *Jew and Philosopher: The Return to Maimonides in the Jewish Thought of Leo Strauss*.

The University of Chicago Press, Chicago 60637
The University of Chicago Press, Ltd., London
© 2013 by The University of Chicago
All rights reserved. Published 2013.
Printed in the United States of America

22 21 20 19 18 17 16 15 14 13   1 2 3 4 5

ISBN-13: 978-0-226-30701-5 (cloth)
ISBN-13: 978-0-226-30703-9 (e-book)
ISBN-10: 0-226-30701-8 (cloth)
ISBN-10: 0-226-30703-4 (e-book)

Library of Congress Cataloging-in-Publication Data

Green, Kenneth Hart, 1953– author.
Leo Strauss and the rediscovery of Maimonides / Kenneth Hart Green.
pages cm
Includes bibliographical references and index.
ISBN-13: 978-0-226-30701-5 (cloth : alkaline paper)
ISBN-10: 0-226-30701-8 (cloth : alkaline paper)
ISBN-13: 978-0-226-30703-9 (e-book)
ISBN-10: 0-226-30703-4 (e-book)   1. Strauss, Leo. 2. Maimonides, Moses, 1135–1204—Influence. 3. Philosophy, American—20th century. 4. Jewish philosophy—To 1500. I. Title.
B945.S84G74 2013
181'.06—dc23
2012033255

♾ This paper meets the requirements of ANSI/NISO Z39.48-1992 (Permanence of Paper).

For Sharon

"LOVE IS ONE SOUL DWELLING IN TWO BODIES."
ARISTOTLE

"Every person . . . who trains in wisdom, . . . [and] who discovers joy in virtue, celebrates a festival their entire life. To be sure, such people are only a tiny number; they are like embers of wisdom kept smoldering in our cities, in order for virtue not to be altogether smothered and to disappear from our race."

PHILO JUDAEUS OF ALEXANDRIA

"There are different kinds of these people: first those who seek the right path. When one of them rejects anything as false, he will be lifted towards a better symbol which is nearer to the truth and is not open to that objection; and if he is satisfied with it, he will be left where he is. When that better symbol is also rejected by him as false, he will be lifted to another rank, and if he is then satisfied with it, he will be left where he is. Whenever a symbol of a given standard is rejected by him as false, he will be lifted to a higher rank, but when he rejects all the symbols as false and has the strength and gift to understand the truth, he will be made to know the truth and will be placed into the class of those who take the philosophers as their authorities. If he is not yet satisfied with that and desires to acquire philosophical wisdom and has himself the strength and gift for it, he will be made to know it."

ABU NASR AL-FARABI

"I am the man who when the concern pressed him and his way was straitened and he could find no other device by which to teach a demonstrated truth other than by giving satisfaction to a single virtuous man while displeasing ten thousand ignoramuses—I am he who prefers to address that single man by himself, and I do not heed the blame of those many creatures. For I claim to liberate that virtuous one from that into which he has sunk, and I shall guide him in his perplexity until he becomes perfect and he finds rest."

MOSES MAIMONIDES

"It seems that all great things first have to bestride the earth in monstrous and frightening masks in order to inscribe themselves in the hearts of humanity with eternal demands."

FRIEDRICH NIETZSCHE

"Maimonides . . . was a truly free mind."

LEO STRAUSS

CONTENTS

ACKNOWLEDGMENTS | ix

ONE | The Unanticipated Maimonides | 1

TWO | Strauss and Irony: *Bypassing the Maimonidean Scholars* | 17

THREE | Maimonides and the Free Mind | 42

FOUR | Untying the Literary Knots: *Maimonides the Poet* | 54

FIVE | Why the Moderns Need the Medievals | 66

SIX | Absorbing and Surpassing the Alternatives | 105

SEVEN | The Maimonidean Revolution: *Western Tradition as Reason and Revelation* | 126

ABBREVIATIONS | 167   NOTES | 171   INDEX | 205

ACKNOWLEDGMENTS

I WOULD LIKE TO ACKNOWLEDGE THOSE WHO HELPED me to formulate and refine the ideas that brought about this book. It is a distinct pleasure to recognize the friendship of Martin D. Yaffe, who generously shared his knowledge and wisdom in conversations too numerous to count. I am also grateful to three good friends—Clifford Orwin, Arthur Fish, and Norman Doidge—for scores of discussions that sparked myriad clarifying thoughts on this topic.

I would like to express my appreciation to those intrepid students (graduate and undergraduate) who have come along with me and engaged in the study of Maimonides' *The Guide of the Perplexed* in a seminar that I have been teaching for the past twenty years or so at the University of Toronto. I am grateful to all of them. Moreover, Erik Carlson of the University of Chicago Press deserves special mention for his superlative copyediting, which went much beyond the call of duty. I also owe a debt to the anonymous readers of the University of Chicago Press, who made various substantial suggestions for the improvement of the present book. And I am grateful to Martin D. Yaffe and Evan Lowe, both of the University of North Texas, for their dedicated and carefully considered production of the index.

Sincere thanks are due to the Social Sciences and Humanities Research Council of Canada for its generous support during the years that I did research on Strauss's works on Maimonides, which was also of immeasurable help in the composition of this book.

Last but not least, I would like to say a word about the dedication: it is an expression of gratitude to my wife Sharon, whose intelligent listening and critical responses have assisted me in avoiding the worst pitfalls and helped me to move toward the light.

ONE

The Unanticipated Maimonides

LEO STRAUSS'S MODERN EXPLORATION OF THE DISTANT domain of Moses Maimonides' medieval Jewish philosophic thought, almost entirely lapsed from modern consciousness, was akin to embarking on a voyage of discovery. For however much the name of Maimonides may still have been revered by some, it is undoubtedly the case that the realm of thought in which this thinker dwelled was—in contemporary philosophy as well as in contemporary Jewish thought—an almost-forgotten, lost, neglected, or unknown domain: Strauss had to be immoderately daring from the start just to assert its contemporary relevance.[1] What was Strauss searching for? In the greater scheme of things, Strauss seems from his youth to have been driven to embark on his travels in search of nothing other than "enlightenment." Or rather, we might say that what this search was moved by was the same thing asked about by Immanuel Kant and Moses Mendelssohn in a famous 18th-century contest of essays: What is "enlightenment"? They both assumed, as did Strauss, that this is the highest concern of the rational mind, but such concern must also be set in the context of human life comprehensively encompassed.[2] Each believed that, in addressing this question, it was possible for him to truly know the essential answer, which Strauss also wanted to know but which with regard to the available arguments he was not fully persuaded by. In the wake of two previous but unsatisfying efforts (focused on Benedict Spinoza and Hermann Cohen), for several reasons Strauss turned to Maimonides for help in answering this question, as improbable as that choice may have been to most contemporary scholars and thinkers. To be sure, prior to Strauss's setting sail on his own, he prepared for his journey by training in the skills needed to navigate the lands and the waters he would traverse, however unwitting he may have been of the challenges he would need to confront in his journey. Hence, he assumed the modest guise of a modern historical scholar and used only such humble tools of art as a modern critical student conventionally employs to penetrate the unknown and unpredictable country of the past.[3] Though not yet a captain directing his own ship with the bold insight and wise expedition he would subsequently distinguish himself by, even so he already employed the tools of his science for plotting a course of travel with a peculiar verve. Thus, his works even as an apprentice scholarly navigator are, almost from the beginning, characterized by their rigorous historical exactness and their honed philosophic incisiveness. Yet originally he aimed at the advancement of knowledge about Maimonides only in a limited sphere. At his point of departure, Strauss wished to test the claims made about Maimonides by his philosophic critics (such as Spinoza), asking whether they instead created prospective modern prejudices. And likewise Strauss wished to test the claims made about Maimonides by his philosophic defenders (such as Cohen), asking whether they instead created retrospective medieval legends.[4] But in so doing, like some unwitting Christopher Columbus, Strauss courageously rediscovered a veritable lost continent of thought. Thus, to adapt to Strauss himself the suggestive language which he utilized to characterize an unanticipated "spiritual" possibility contained in the modern study of the thought of the past: he embarked on a journey whose end was completely hidden from him, and he returned to the shores of the present another man from the one who had originally departed from them.[5]

The unplanned result of his lifelong search for the "real" Maimonides, which he conducted both as a scholar of Jewish thought and as a student of Western philosophy, was the uncovering of an entirely different history of Western thought, and the further uncovering of an entirely different Maimonides. This is the veritable lost continent of thought that Strauss rediscovered. The idealized defense of Maimonides proffered by Cohen, and the distorted criticism of Maimonides promulgated by Spinoza, both proved defective, forced, and unsatisfactory: they did not do justice either to the subtle thought of Maimonides or to his complex soul, and hence to his obvious contradictions.[6] And greater than their scholarly deficiencies, neither Cohen nor Spinoza seemed equipped, as philosophic thinkers, to deal adequately with the crises of the present.[7] Paradoxically, or just peculiarly to some, Strauss discovered in Maimonides a philosophic thinker who—although Strauss never embraced the purely "medieval" aspects of the thought of Maimonides—seemed better able to help him think through, and so to resolve, the most difficult of our modern dilemmas. This is surely a paradox and a peculiarity, one that must utterly astound us as a claim, stranger than any other, made by Strauss about Maimonides! How can it be? But to begin with the simplest, and yet somehow also the deepest point, Maimonides had not made the most common error of the moderns, from Machiavelli to Heidegger, while he also anticipated several of the key critical thoughts in which modernity was rooted.[8] By the most common error, I mean to say that Maimonides—although as unyieldingly committed to the power of human reason as were any of the moderns—never attempted to get around, by clever devices of the mind, *the* fundamental Western conflict. This is the conflict, according to Strauss, between what he characterized as "Jerusalem and Athens," framed also as the critical dialogue between the Hebrew Bible and Greek philosophy, or what others, like Matthew Arnold and Isaac Husik, preferred to call "Hebraism and Hellenism."[9] It is fundamental because it is a conflict about the one eternal truth, or "the one thing needful." For once Strauss examined the great modern thinkers, he concluded that this is perhaps their most common or repeated error, which leads to almost a theological-political determinism concealed in modern thought: the several cognitive attempts to settle or force the theological issue, which required simplifying it, and hence distorting it—besides the often regrettable, or at least ambiguous, political impact and moral repercussions made by such attempts.[10] Strauss seems to have discovered the unavoidable and even irreducible character of the tension between "Jerusalem and Athens" for modern Western philosophy in Nietzsche's notion of the "superman": at the high point of Nietzsche's philosophy, his supreme goal for man in the future unites or even synthesizes Jerusalem and Athens ("the body of Caesar" with "the soul of Christ"), i.e., he who is the harshest analyst and the most ferocious critic of the biblical legacy consciously cannot and will not fully renounce its legacy, even if Strauss thinks he did not resolve the tension adequately.

What is the almost theological-political determinism of modern thought, according to Strauss, repeats itself in almost generation in different forms. It may be walked through in the following series of steps. Modern thought arose from a horror both at the spiritual illnesses with which biblical religion, or rather Christianity, was beset (and with which, as a result, Europe was afflicted) and at the fierceness with which it resisted honest rational diagnosis and cure by its own wisest doctors of the soul.[11] By those spiritual illnesses, I refer to bloody wars and unending political grabs for power papered over by didactic debates about theological dogma; hostility to reason and critical thought as threats to religious faith; messianic pretensions and utopian claims that cannot be sustained or achieved in this world; gratuitous cruelty toward other human beings, often manifested in the persecution of "heretics" or Jews, under the cover of a high-minded devoutness about and a sincere fidelity to the true faith (what Machiavelli dubbed "pious cruelty"); a single-minded stress on the otherworldly, which monomania allowed the theologians and the believers to make little of all that is wrong with this world, i.e., of the remediable defects in the human situation, dismissed as the merely transitory present life. Whatever its flaws in intention or execution, the power and greatness of modern thought (which Strauss certainly appreciated) lay in its being seemingly the first noble effort to seriously confront and correct the remediable defects of the present life as they, in a certain measure, originated in the political conceptions of biblical religion and the theological virtues associated with those conceptions. Modern thought, rooted in and shaped by a revamped conception of philosophy and science, attempted to offer a solution to the severe problems in premodern Western political life caused by biblical religion: it devised the bold strategy of attempting to bury *the* fundamental conflict by repressing it, and so pretending that it had been resolved, with the hope that this would cause "Jerusalem" as a difficulty to wither away, containing the wild beast by training it to keep itself in the bonds of secular politics and natural morality. This containment policy usually involved disposing of "Jerusalem," either by claiming to "refute" it, and so to relegate it to the past, or by claiming to contain it in versions of rational moralism, which made it safe and unthreatening but often missed its unique and most forceful truth claims or suppressed its deepest theological and moral impulses.[12]

Modern thought made a promise to use human reason in order to reshape the human soul and to remold human nature, constructing political conditions which will direct human energy to productive channels and counteract harmful impulses. It also pledged to conquer nature, or the threatening forces in the world in which human beings dwell, for the sake of the relief of man's estate, i.e., to make his life better in matters of essential human well-being. And it was likewise concerned to account for everything that happens by laws of fixed necessity; at the very least, this had as its purpose to prove the sufficiency of reason, and thus to render revealed religion superfluous. The essential strategy of modern thought—radical in intention, though often moderate in execution—was to tame biblical theology: captured like a wild lion of the jungle, it would be put in the cage designed by science, and it would be domesticated through the focus on morality.[13] In other words, the original answers offered by biblical theology, in response to deep questions which agitated the human soul, were to be submerged and repressed rather than refuted, and as a result—such was the hope of modern thought—laid to rest. But as we have been taught by modern thought in a different context,[14] the repressed returns in all sorts of unacknowledged ways, shapes, and forms. Curiously, Maimonides already seems to have anticipated the difficulties with the modern strategy. To be sure, he too focused on the needs of human nature and the human soul which had not been adequately addressed by traditional religion, and which he likewise regarded as mostly rational.[15] Yet in his medieval "philosophic" version of this modern strategy he refused to ignore, and never attempted to set aside,[16] those aspects of human nature and the human soul that had been judiciously addressed and wisely met by biblical theology. Instead, Maimonides insisted on a direct confrontation with the key issues in the higher conflict between reason and revelation; he resolved *the* conflict through a judicious wisdom, attempting to imitate and advance the biblical model, as he comprehended it. In other words, Maimonides was not unsympathetic to most of those modern criticisms and defenses of reason, but he must have been convinced in advance that this "method" of repression would not work: the human soul is more complex or contradictory, and simultaneously less directable or malleable, than modern thought was wont to claim.[17] Thus, though not in any sense opposed in principle to everything the modern thinkers dreamed of accomplishing or to everything they hoped to improve or had actually improved of the human situation, especially as the medieval era knew it, this was very often not as well ordered as rational minds knew that it can be. Besides, Strauss respected what has been genuinely discovered by the boldness and originality of modern science, even if it was frequently discovered to be deficient in its comprehension of the human dimension, or what was once known as the "soul." Rather, Strauss was impressed with Maimonides for his not lacking any of the enthusiasm of the moderns for human reason, and for his certainty about our need to embrace it for the sake of human dignity and human perfection in the fulfillment of our nature.[18] But he also grasped, as they mostly did not, the frailty of reason as a substitute for religion in political life, never mind what its absence from morality and psychology yields as an access to the human soul.[19]

Likewise Strauss was impressed with how Maimonides seemed to comprehend in anticipation the defectiveness of the modern strategy for the human individual. Even though the dignity of man in his individuality is claimed as one of the special virtues of the modern turn, Maimonides recognized that this would leave him stripped bare of the spiritual protections, the moral advancements, and the educational preparedness which are the special products of biblical religion. These are its special gifts to the human individual, if the legacy of biblical religion is judiciously appropriated. The defectiveness of the modern strategy as it surfaced through history lay in its aim—pursued by diverse "methods" of art, and developed at different stages in modern thought (which superficially might seem to resemble those of its medieval "philosophic" predecessors)—to settle the issue of religion finally and forever by "quieting" the human need for God as the eternal source. For to "resolve" the challenge of religion—especially biblical religion—and thus to settle it in favor of science and rational morality, is merely to put it to sleep by attempting to theologically repress or deny the deeper conflict in the soul of each human being, even in those of higher human type, i.e., the most "spirited," and most "erotic," human beings. For man's deepest desire, his desire for eternity, cannot be resolved by denying that desire, or by repressing the traditional answers provided to the great question which this desire arouses, i.e., how to make contact with eternity, how to appropriate it, or even how to "achieve" it.[20] Instead, Maimonides perceived that the "religious" needs of the higher type must be directly addressed, and reconciled with the needs, both higher and lower, of this type as a human being among human beings. In other words, if the deeper questions in each soul were not confronted and answered, then the religious needs of man as an individual, and especially the higher types, would just reappear in another form, for they must have satisfaction. As "autonomous" higher desires, they can neither be purged in the sense of eradicated or neutralized nor satisfied by being diverted to the lower urges from which they are believed to have originally emerged, according to most streams of modern thought. There might be such reappearances perhaps through collective delusions unwittingly embraced, and probably in guises designed by those clever enough to manipulate human need, even those needs of the purer sorts—of the high-minded, and even of the philosophically disposed.[21]

Thus, Maimonides begins with an analysis of the soul, of what its proper character and contours are, and of what deeper needs it has. His analysis presupposes a correlated synoptic diagnosis of the temptations to which the human soul is prone and the regimen which prevents it from succumbing to those temptations, as these are graphically but often deceptively generated by the misdirected desires of the soul, i.e., the ever-powerful imagination. For Maimonides set the problem of the imagination in the very heart of the human situation, since its power raises the question about what man most essentially is. Strauss encountered in Maimonides, with his seriousness and balance about the imaginative capacity and about the deeper needs of man, a thinker who seemed better equipped (with sounder views about the essence of human beings in actual life) to deal with man in full than the modern thinkers. For the modern thinkers tended either to underestimate (like Descartes), or to overestimate (like Heidegger), the power of the imagination in the human soul, and in so doing to devise visions of what man is and can be which do not accord with his true nature. Maimonides dealt with the deepest human desire, i.e., for eternity, by directing it toward *the* truth, which he wished to identify with God, though not so as to diminish man's desire as needfully achieved, or rather served, through a permanent, irremovable, and ever-deepening *search* during the length of a human life, which is why it is best grounded in God. Truth, like God, is to be loved, although it is known ultimately by the cognitive faculty while aided by the imaginative faculty; it is thus facilitated mainly by what is conceived as science; and yet it is both prepared and completed by scripture and its poetry. This last element helps to keep man from succumbing to the highest mind-numbing delusion, which tempts him to believe that his ascending thought has issued in a simple attainment of *the* truth. Truth is also like God in that, to remain truth, it must be constantly desired and yet loved from a distance. This is because the love of truth, as blended with or in the end not even distinguishable from the love of God, is a force that man is never able to fully satisfy if he is to remain man. Man desires the infinite, but *to be* infinite is only for the divine. What man can do is to make progress toward truth (satisfying in and of itself) as an itinerary toward God. Thus, Strauss discovered in Maimonides a thinker who knew that perhaps *the* fundamental problem for the ancients, the medievals, and the moderns is the question of the human soul, which at the deepest level proves itself unchangeable: what defines it, what it truly wants, and what it can be or do. This medieval thinker showed a keen if skeptical awareness of history (which, along with science, is the pride of the moderns), but he recognized that this dramatic and powerful human unfolding in events and actions—which changes some of the highest things and which shows man malleable in some key aspects of his nature—itself demonstrates man's malleability as subordinated to and limited by a deeper human need which is unchangeable, i.e., for the eternal.

However, Strauss's approach to Maimonides' or to any other thinker's thought and teaching in terms of his grasp of the "human soul" is just the sort of thing that makes us dubious about the relevance of the "medieval" Maimonides, and about the usefulness of Strauss's modern approach to him. We are still not prepared to use this sort of word, such as "soul," in ordinary language. As we suspect, this word seems to threaten the return of everything that premodern thought seemed mired in, which is precisely what modern thought promised to rid us of. Strauss rejected this suspicion about the "soul" as a guide to man because it supposedly leads to the essential premodern fault, since he noticed that the numerous modern attempts to describe man in its absence, as pure materiality or body alone, from Machiavelli to Freud, basically prove themselves deficient because they are compelled to depend on a "self-evident" truth, which is both unacknowledged and not self-evident. This supposedly "self-evident" truth involves the complexity of man as the being who contains in himself something high, which the modern thinkers believe can somehow be reduced to the material. Yet that high element of man has never been persuasively explained in such bodily terms. Thus, they cannot explain why and how great thinkers like Machiavelli or Freud do what they do on its basis. And they cannot account for why—other than as idiosyncratic need—they interest themselves in knowing the pure truth which brings no material recompense, and yet which consequently these great thinkers pass on to humanity although these are not just their own idiosyncratic truths. Hence, Strauss also discerned that the modern attempts to prescribe an ethos for man which lacks an awareness of the "soul" seem to also lack both psychological persuasiveness and moral rigor, never mind their manifesting a scientific dubiousness. This recommendation on how life is to be led is neither as compelling nor as binding on fellow human beings even as the despised "religious" teachings, however defined: something human seems to be morally missing, or is cognitively absent. As a result, these attempts did not seem to Strauss as empirical or as critical as an approach that would consider the "soul," at least tentatively or provisionally. However much Strauss acknowledged the helpful modern tendency to take "the low" seriously and to give it its proper due, he was not impressed with those modern criticisms, which tended to misconceive this dimension by attempting to dogmatically reduce "the high" to it. He believed that this dogmatic reductionism badly misses an entire dimension of the human being evident even in ordinary life, and necessary for the adequate comprehension of the complete or best human life.

Also with regard to the moderns, Strauss stresses that the typical modern thinker as an heir of Machiavelli devised a strategy for the improvement of the world on the basis of "the variability of all human things and of nature." Not only is this basis against the thought of the ancients and the medievals, but this strategy also required him by an unavoidable logic following in Machiavelli's wake to engage in the obscuration of the fuller as well as deeper significance of possible permanent things. Several examples will help to indicate what, for Strauss, such permanent things may be: moral virtue, or natural right and wrong; the soul and its proper order; the true "needs of the mind"; tragedy; philosophy or wisdom; justice; "a hierarchy of ways of life or of goods"; and something Strauss calls rather ambiguously "the supra-political." However, in thus proceeding in the absence of thinking through what such permanent things may imply about man, again the modern thinker as Machiavelli's student cannot make sense of himself: he is unable to provide "a clear account" of "his own doing." This brought Strauss to formulate a further theological-political determinism of modern thought that is repeated in almost every generation: a bold thinker arises who invents an original system of thought, often to improve the human situation, but who is unable to explain himself on the basis of his own thought in his activity as thinker. Thus, for the typical modern thinker this determinism that recurs in most modern systems reveals a fatal if unwitting flaw of blindness about what it might seem to imply about human nature if man is undoubtedly a thinking being. The argument against this approach to Machiavelli or in defense of his philosophic revolution, as Strauss himself anticipates, would seem to be that Machiavelli had to do what he did because he discovered entirely unknown phenomena. These entirely unknown phenomena required a different "method" to see these previously unfamiliar facts in an accurate light. But Strauss plainly demurs: "In fact, however, Machiavelli does not bring to light a single political phenomenon of any fundamental importance which was not fully known to the classics." In order to prove his point, Strauss significantly chooses to contrast Machiavelli with Maimonides. The former's account of the vices of contemporary Italy which brought it to ruin precisely parallels the latter's account of the sins of ancient Israel which led to or at least help to account for its demise by the oblique consequences of their "sins":

> Machiavelli declares that Savonarola, that unarmed prophet, was right in saying that the ruin of Italy was caused by "our sins," "but our sins were not what he believed they were," namely, religious sins, "but those which I have narrated," namely, political or military sins (*Prince* XII). In the same vein Maimonides declares that the ruin of the Jewish kingdom was caused by the "sins of our fathers," namely, by their idolatry; but idolatry worked its effect in a perfectly natural manner: it led to astrology instead of to the practice of the arts of war and the conquest of countries.

However, what Strauss is saying is not that Machiavelli and Maimonides operate entirely on the same wavelength. Instead, this parallel leads Strauss to ask the related question about whether it is as hard as it was once thought to be to remake human nature, and his tacit answer seems to be that we have learned this may not be impossible—but it may not be so easy to live with the consequences. "Modern man as little as premodern man can escape imitating nature as he understands nature." The features of human nature which were radically transformed by Machiavelli, and as a result by modern philosophy in its unfolding conception as followed the fundamental thought of Machiavelli, are delineated by Strauss in such terms as it is possible to apply with equal facility to Nietzsche, perhaps his last serious student:[22]

> Moral virtue . . . is dependent on society and therefore subject to the primary needs of society. It does not consist in the proper order of the soul. It has no other source than the needs of society; it has no second and higher source in the needs of the mind. . . . That moral virtue is a qualified requirement of society is infinitely clearer to him than that it is a requirement of philosophy or of the life of the mind. As a consequence he is unable to give a clear account of his own doing. What is greatest in him cannot be properly appreciated on the basis of his own narrow view of the nature of man. . . . He does not give an account of how the stability of human excellence . . . is compatible with the variability of all human things and of nature. . . . [He does not understand] the moral-political phenomena in the light of man's highest virtue or perfection, the life of the philosopher or the contemplative life. . . . Solutions of the political problem which are altogether satisfactory to the good citizen prove to be inadequate solely because they make men oblivious of man's highest perfection. . . . He denies that there is an order of the soul, and therefore a hierarchy of ways of life and of goods. . . . Man is not by nature ordered toward fixed ends, [and so] he is as it were infinitely malleable. . . . Man is not by nature ordered toward goodness, or . . . men can become good and remain good only through compulsion [and so, as one must conclude,] civilization or the activity which makes men good is man's revolt against nature.

The reverse of these fundamental conceptions—which is yet able to take them into account and to give them a better comprehension in the proper view of human nature—could be attributed to Maimonides, as Strauss suggests. Strauss was interested in restoring the reverse of these conceptions not for any dogmatic reasons, never mind theological ones, but as of greater helpfulness for the adequate comprehension of man than anything put on offer by Machiavelli or by his multifarious modern "students." Strauss was not less concerned with the political than was Machiavelli or even Maimonides as he construes him, but he believed we have need of a more complex view of man precisely because of the perceived disappointments and debacles of modern thought in directing modern man. Whether Strauss is right to do so is one key question; whether it is possible to do so is the other key question. Both can perhaps be reduced to a single answer, which may be better apprehended through Strauss's focus on Machiavelli himself: while the science on which Maimonides' view might rest may be antiquated, the empirical facts have not changed, i.e., the empirical facts about the nature of man. Indeed, it is only possible to do what Strauss attempted to do if the essential nature of man has not changed. What might suggest it has done so is the thesis of historicism and the consequent belief in applying progress to the fundamental nature of man, which are both dubious and doubtable propositions, to say the least. The best counterevidence against what Machiavelli argued for about man, i.e., *the* empirical fact, as it were, is Machiavelli himself. I shall repeat the key lines because they reiterate an idea constantly replicated by Strauss in order to bolster his criticism of the moderns: "That moral virtue is a qualified requirement of society is infinitely clearer to him than that it is a requirement of philosophy or of the life of the mind. As a consequence he is unable to give a clear account of his own doing. What is greatest in him cannot be properly appreciated on the basis of his own narrow view of the nature of man." Machiavelli himself, like Maimonides, is a thinker of profundity and of a deeply moral sensibility who, so to speak, makes a spontaneous historical appearance rather than providentially or as determined by previous historical events. Their emergence stems from a sense of moral duty—while fully devoted to the life of the mind, which their political action did not diminish—to legislate for their respective societies. To state the contrast in the starkest possible terms: Maimonides can make sense of Maimonides on the basis of his own philosophy; Machiavelli cannot.

Only Nietzsche among the moderns attempted to answer the question about man by proceeding from a truly different ground, i.e., by his thinking of man in terms of sheer "will to power." He wished both to better establish the modern project and to surpass it, by honestly avoiding anything of the Platonic-Maimonidean—and, if Strauss is right, also even the unwittingly Machiavellian—frame of reference on man, this being the grounding belief in the mind of man as somehow something separate in the universe. The cogency of Nietzsche's thought would seem to depend on whether he was wise as well as correct in attempting to let "the will to power" substitute for or combine both "*eros* and the pure mind," as he puts it about Platonism, i.e., wise in the sense of being able to account for himself and those like him through it. Is his philosophy able to adequately make sense of man and his nature in its manifold types and ranks of virtue, and especially of those whom he himself calls the "philosophic legislators," or whom Maimonides and Machiavelli both called "prophets," a type of soul in which both the "armed" and the "unarmed" are encompassed? The fundamental question, then, is as his contemporary Nietzschean (or "postmodern") opponent might put it, whether Strauss himself believed that there is something called "the pure mind." We are acquainted with his apparent belief in "the free mind": is it perhaps for him the condition of the "the pure mind"? This is, it seems to me, what needs to be answered if one is to know whether Strauss himself believed in the "possibility of philosophy." Thus, it is not so much whether he allowed for "the noetic perception of pure form," which Stanley Rosen maintains is the fundamental issue, since "the noetic perception of pure form" is dependent on "the pure mind." Something like "the pure mind," i.e., the autonomy of the high or whether man's higher ability to think is not *merely* an arbitrary or accidental product of his lower urges sublimated, is *the* fundamental issue. This, I would suggest, is because "the pure mind" is the condition of the possibility of "the noetic perception of pure form," although the two may become known through one another, in that the *experience* of intellection—or, to employ Rosen's mode of expression—of intuition, is first for us. But what is first for us may not be what is first truly. It seems to me that "the free mind," as the condition of the "the pure mind," is *the* issue if Strauss's recovery of Maimonides is to be seen and judged in the right light: is man capable of this truly free sort of thinking, which puts his mind beyond the control of being determined by his historical conditions?[23]

In a similar vein, Strauss did not regard the endeavor to comprehend the "mind" of Maimonides, if not also to glimpse his "soul" through it[24]—i.e., his unity in excellence of intellect and heart—as an irrelevant distraction, an unattainable fantasy, or a derivative misconception.[25] For Strauss, this is a question that every scholar asks, or at least assumes, about the human being which he is studying, whether he admits it or not, and whether he is aware of it or not. What he asks is whether the human being he probes is a great-souled man, considering himself worthy to engage in great actions, and ultimately moved by high motives, or whether he is a small-souled man, thinking himself unworthy of great actions, and ultimately moved by low motives.[26] Similarly, doing justice to the complex soul of Leo Strauss is something one might address, however obliquely, by considering *how* his mind is revealed in applying itself to Maimonides, i.e., in the manner of his approach. Indeed, we could say that this very problem might be called the major deficiency in most attempts, by both friends and enemies, to convey and capture the subtle thought and dialectical complexity of Strauss himself, as it is communicated in almost everything he wrote as a mature scholar and thinker.[27] For they usually treat Strauss in a rather one-sided fashion (according to their specific preferences), rather than attempting to appropriate Strauss's enormous range and powerful depth as a thinker. For he manifested undoubted signs of being himself great souled, as made known through his students, who testify to his words and conduct as a teacher as not only most impressively enlightening them, but also able to enlarge their vision in both mind and heart of what it is to be a human being irrespective of historical epoch, even while he never ignored the unique elements in the philosophic and religious thought, and in the political and moral life, of our historical era. As can still be experienced, he leaves signs to his readers of being great souled through what he artfully wrote in his books and essays, for as a thinker who made himself a master of the literary arts he wrote most compellingly to reflective contemporary readers and addressed their own deepest needs and perplexities, which were always his point of departure as a teacher and as a writer. Indeed, what remains for the present and the future to judge him by as a thinker are the numerous and quite diverse things which he wrote. As I would suggest, they form a unity because they offer a focused instruction in what the wisest and the best among the great authors of the past, who transmit their thought to us, have conveyed for our benefit as regards the enlargement of our minds and the deepening of our souls. Among his other achievements, he helped modern readers to recognize Maimonides as one of the great authors, which was readily acknowledged by serious medieval thinkers (of whatever religious tradition or philosophic affiliation), but which modern thought since Spinoza has had great difficulty with. In substantial measure due to Spinoza, we tend to dismiss any attempt to credit Maimonides as a truly great thinker or writer as in the simplest sense unfeasible for those of us who have been enlightened by modern science and history.[28] I believe it will be fully demonstrated to anyone who is serious about reading the book for which this is a companion volume—bringing together as it happens to do Strauss's most significant essays and lectures on Maimonides, which show forth their power to endure as well as to still freshly challenge us—that henceforth he made such a dismissal impossible.

Thus, if there is a key to the thought, and indeed the "soul," of Leo Strauss, then I would suggest that this is to be located in his search for the "unknown" Maimonides. For Maimonides' previously concealed side, which was first uncovered by Strauss, made him one of the greatest figures in the history of Western thought, according to the thorough rethinking of Maimonides to which Strauss devoted himself. This thoroughly rethought—and entirely original—Maimonides as Strauss uncovered him struck almost everyone as a complete surprise: it was one of the great scholarly discoveries of the 20th century. As usually happens in response to great discoveries, however, some were disposed to expunge it as perhaps a perverse invention of Strauss's own mind or even of his imagination—which they might have been able to do if it did not rest on such solid textual ground. It especially surprised those who had been trained to see Maimonides through the seemingly clear-sighted eyes of Spinoza, who, however, looked at only some of the man, and even at that from an oblique and light-bending angle, as if he dwelled in a different dimension, bent beneath the surface of the water. It may not have come as such a surprise to those who were accustomed to viewing Maimonides through the rose-tinted glasses of tradition and of Cohen. However, they colored him, and hence distorted his thought, according to lenses which corrected and shaded the vision, but not according to the man as he made himself visible to the "enlightened," i.e., as he had wanted to be glimpsed by those who would read him carefully. Indeed, as Strauss recognized, he had gone to great trouble in his books to ensure that they would be able to do this.

Among the attributes of mind that elevated Maimonides and made him great, in Strauss's view, are several worth stressing at the very start, even though this comprehension emerged for him only gradually. Curiously Strauss was impressed by those forceful yet subtle attributes of mind that he had astonishingly discovered for himself in Maimonides, although he had previously associated these solely with modern thinkers of audacity like Spinoza, who were committed to being unyieldingly rational in their thought. Cohen had certainly taught Strauss to take Maimonides seriously as an original thinker, and to give him his due as if he was capable of greater freedom and power of thought than any other modern thinker had credited him with. The only one, besides Cohen, to approach this seriousness about Maimonides as a veritable contemporary thinker (for both philosophy and Jewish thought) was Solomon Maimon, but he still was obliged to ultimately relegate Maimonides to the thought of the pre-Kantian past, albeit even while he was willing to acknowledge him as a thinker of profundity in that past. However, this astonishment about Maimonides' bold and unconventional attributes of mind as it occurred step by step to Strauss, which had not been noticed by him at first, was mitigated somewhat, once Strauss further gradually recognized how much the obscurity of these very attributes of thought was due to the efforts of Maimonides himself in covering his own boldness and unconventionality. Indeed, as Strauss was astounded to uncover (in the fashion of a modern detective putting together clues to unravel the crime), it was Maimonides himself who had for some reason engaged in an enormous and artful labor not to let what were the greatest of his "spiritual assets" appear to plain sight: intellectual courage in facing the most difficult and subtle issues; audacity of artifice in literary expression; profundity of cognitive penetration; utmost careful study and thorough immersion in philosophic and scientific thought; single-minded attention paid to what religion teaches about the human soul, what truths may be derived from it, and how it can best serve the needs of man in society; statesmanlike skill and rhetorical art as both political leader and philosophic teacher. These character traits and achievements must be put alongside his unprecedented genius as a codifier of the law, a commentator on scripture, and a pastoral counselor to the spiritually troubled and perplexed in his era.

Although Maimonides defended the essential cognitive integrity of revelation, based on his love of truth he also manifested an unwillingness at a deeper level to compromise in the slightest with revelation if the truth as scientifically decided by reason required him to relinquish a religious dogma, however revered by tradition, save if he was impressed with its essential theological disposition, unconditional moral usefulness, or unavoidable political necessity. This was so, as Strauss perceived, even if he did not always announce that relinquishment in plain sight, and even in certain cases if he continued to formally retain it as a religious dogma for those who still needed it. He also kept his mind steadily focused on the decisive issue on or around which a matter turns; for he had a clear-eyed determination to think through consistently, and to unyieldingly wrestle with, the deepest concerns and highest issues in the conflict between Judaism and philosophy: he manfully faced the flash points, although how he resolved the conflict on a specific issue or concern was not always done on the surface. (But as Strauss was also compelled to acknowledge, he never neglected to leave obscured clues and hidden maps for serious students to follow his path to the depths, in which depths he was wont to bury the treasure of true knowledge.) As it happens, most of these concerns and issues were also characteristic of Christianity, which, like Judaism, rests on the Hebrew Bible, on whose exegesis Maimonides focused concentrated energy of thought. And likewise, the interpretation of the theological substance derived from a more or less shared monotheistic faith and revealed scripture—such as creation, prophecy, providence, etc.—pertains just as much to Islam. As a result, it occurred to Strauss that what Maimonides did with this fundamental conflict, as an undaunted thinker whose profundity of thought was recognized not just by Jews or even just by religious thinkers, amounted to something useful, if not essential, to Western civilization in its several forms, but especially as constituted by the conflict of revealed religion with philosophy.[29]

∽ TWO ∾

Strauss and Irony
Bypassing the Maimonidean Scholars

IN ORDER TO MAKE GREATER SENSE OF STRAUSS'S PERsistent focus on Maimonides and how Maimonidean thought was so helpful to him, it is essential to perceive that Strauss made the encounter between Jerusalem and Athens the pivot of his own thought. However much this issue may have been put in the shadows by contemporary thinking, the tension between reason and revelation—Hebraism and Hellenism, or Greek philosophy and the Hebrew Bible—remained of the greatest moment, and even urgency, for him, and he refused to circumvent it.[1] Strauss emphasized that this historic encounter has been both an elevated dialogue between equal conversation partners and an unbroken confrontation and even quarrel between rivals and opponents, depending on historical circumstances. This dimension of confrontation and quarrel had also to be considered honestly and seriously, because it is—at least in a certain measure—responsible, according to Strauss, for the contemporary crisis of *modern* Western civilization that we are compelled to pass through, to face, and to deal with. In other words, the mutual dislike and discord of which the two sides, Jerusalem and Athens, are capable is as much the cause of our most pressing dilemmas, which we must try to resolve, as is the mutual affinity and accord for which they seem to have the potential, based on what it is of their teachings that they share. This possible basis for agreement of the two poles in the West has received greater respect in different eras; in our modern era of aggressive humanism with a decidedly secular bent, however, the stress has been laid mainly on their disagreement. Strauss neither dismisses nor too little appreciates modern humanism or secularism; he recognizes that they may well have contributed something worthwhile and even essential, and hence may play a role in the modern West which is undoubtedly necessary. But as he also seems to think, they are not sufficient on their own. As this would seem to imply, at least about the two contending sides who conduct the Western argument, a balance of forces and a dynamic tension is healthier in the mind than a single dominant view or form of thought in complete control. Maimonides is so helpful because he was able to recognize and appreciate both their common ground, and likewise just as much their significant differences. In certain key respects he was able to teach them how to preserve friendly relations, while never allowing this consequential collegiality to obscure for him that certain issues will remain on which they cannot be reconciled. Maimonides can still teach us much, according to Strauss, about the basis on which we can learn to live with our differences—though it may require a certain amount of tightrope walking.[2] For however difficult it may be to master such an art and whatever challenges it may present to leading a courageous, wise, and decent human life, Strauss seems to think that there is something in what Maimonides knew which is of the utmost significance, if not to man as man, then certainly to Western man as Western man, and hence also to the Jew as Jew (and those like the Jew, i.e., the Christian and the Muslim), never mind to the philosopher as philosopher. Indeed, this art of tightrope walking, of balanced tensions which is dialectical thinking and the life it requires, needs urgently to be known, and its "true roots" to be comprehended and implemented, in modern Western life for its very future survival as the West.[3]

Thus, what truly made for the unsurpassed greatness of Maimonides, in Strauss's fifty-year search,[4] was not just his magisterial will, his free mind, and his courageous heart in the face of the fundamental conflict: it was his willingness not just to confront but also and especially to think through deeply and yet fairly the most difficult issues, and hence to stand astride the fault lines. Maimonides was devoted to both reason and revelation; he promoted the dialogue between them, and hence he adhered to a certain notion of their potential compatibility or harmony, though not of their "synthesis." But he also kept his strength of mind, and hence his courage for steady and balanced scrutiny: he never avoided a confrontation between them when and where he thought it called for by intellectual honesty and by the exigencies of truth. Creation versus eternity was the most famous case, but other issues brought him face to face with the conflict (such as prophecy and providence, to each of which topics Strauss devoted an essay in the companion volume). Strauss was impressed with Maimonides' ability to face these differences with complete candor (if not always by a simple statement on the surface, or as plainly evident to everyone), even while he never surrendered his love of truth, never compromised in his sense of honesty, and never weakened in his commitment to both sides of the debate or the dialogue. As Maimonides insisted, we must examine the issues, dispassionately but honestly, so as to decide whether debate or dialogue is called for, depending on the case being considered and the need which debate or dialogue will serve. To assume the proper attitude of mind to the two great antagonists, as Maimonides held it in view, is to require a supremely nonpartisan or unbiased thoughtfulness, which Strauss attempted to emulate, a genuine open-mindedness and willingness to deliberate fairly, based on a virtue which both sides claim as their special possession: the love of truth. To be victorious by force is to win the battle but to lose the war. Consequently, it was for Strauss the clarity, depth, honesty, and thoroughness of the actual effort, and the excellence of the cognitive achievement resulting from it, that characterized Maimonides' attempt to resolve the great confrontation of mind and soul, and the highest spiritual tension, which defines and animates the West, even if the ultimate resolution is not always simple, or (to repeat) always made to appear on the surface. Maimonides is for Strauss an exemplar of what we must still try to achieve as thinkers, i.e., as philosophers confronting theologians, and as theologians confronting philosophers, which mutual confrontation he defined as the very secret of the vitality of the West.[5] In other words, in the decisive respect Maimonides is just as instructive as any modern thinker, if not greater than most modern thinkers, because he unlike most of them takes both Jerusalem and Athens seriously and endeavors to give an account of human beings seen in light of both such human possibilities. This decisive respect implies, for Strauss, the achievement of the justice and wisdom that both antagonists claim to strive for and to attain: the two sides will have to be wise and just in mind toward one another, even though in the midst of an unresolved spiritual struggle. They will be fortunate to attain something which even approximates to the serene ability to consider fairly, and hence to judge with almost transcendent balance, which Maimonides achieved, as demonstrated by his various books and letters. To imitate him is to imply that thought on this great debate will have to be pursued by almost a "method" of mind which is Maimonidean, as Strauss rediscovered it, in which thinking is done as if from both sides, i.e., in the manner of a skilled and artful dialectical agility, but in which one lives with the issues in one's own soul and one has to resolve them so as to do justice to oneself. We moderns, according to Strauss, would do well to try to learn from him, insofar as it is possible for us to resemble his cognitive and moral achievement in our admittedly different historical circumstances.

Whether Strauss concluded that this heroic achievement had entirely triumphed in the effort to reconcile completely and adequately on any specific issue the two great Western antagonists, the two poles of the Western soul, was not the decisive matter in Strauss's assessment.[6] This would seem to be because it is almost against their mutual love of truth to claim to triumph totally and conclusively in *knowing* the other's fundamental error, which seemingly can never be attained. This is because the true philosopher is he who says, I know that I do not know; he resembles the believer who possesses true knowledge of God, which is the case only if he knows he can never truly know God or His will. Instead, putting aside whether, in principle, one is permitted to deem any such effort a total success or (as is unavoidable) a partial failure, nevertheless Strauss regarded Maimonides (especially in *The Guide of the Perplexed*) — though admittedly Maimonides held a brief for one side as against the other — as even still "probably the greatest analyst" of the "fundamental difference" between those two permanent Western spiritual poles or cerebral antagonists. Because of his view of their primary accord on some of the most fundamental moral issues, he was not ultimately disposed to view theirs as a merely ethical opposition. Indeed, Maimonides' thinking helped Strauss in that assessment by his subtle endeavor to demonstrate that despite the slightly different moral principles of "Jerusalem" (represented by the Hebrew Bible) and "Athens" (represented by Plato and Aristotle), this is *not* the great divide which separates them.

Likewise Strauss stood opposed to his friend Gershom Scholem, who contended that "Jerusalem" is better represented by the Jewish mystics in its effort to argue against the philosophers. Scholem achieved this position by rendering "Jewish philosophy" and "Jewish mysticism" quite divergent things. Although Strauss undoubtedly learned to respect the enormous cognitive powers of the Jewish mystics by studying the magisterial works of Scholem, he nevertheless concluded — based on Scholem's own research — that this divergence did not prevent the mystics from remaining dependent on the deeper thought of Maimonides, and this cannot be entirely separated from reliance on philosophy itself. In Strauss's view, it was the philosophic groundwork laid by the great Jewish thinker that served as the basis from which they launched their own flights of mystical thought. Moreover, Strauss added to this philosophical and historical judgment about "Jewish philosophy" and "Jewish mysticism" a mostly — but not entirely — ironic assertion: it is possible that "Maimonides was the first Kabbalist." This quasi-ironic remark reveals that Strauss's criticism of Scholem was leveled from two angles: the Jewish mystics remain dependent, for the defensible *grounding* of their belief, on the fundamental thought of the Jewish philosophers; further, serious doubts persist about the proofs provided to demonstrate the solidity of "mystical experience" in the form of an intuition of God as genuine knowledge, for such proofs remain dependent on the philosophers. As Strauss crystallizes his point,

> But what philosophy is, is as controversial as any other philosophic subject.... There is indeed no reason why one should not define philosophy as the attempt to replace opinions about God, world, and man by genuine knowledge of God, world, and man. It is controversial, nevertheless, whether there is direct experience of God — or more specifically, mystical experience — which supplies genuine knowledge of God as the first cause of all beings, and it is obvious that the manner in which this question is answered determines completely the precise meaning of philosophy.

Thus, the essential point made by Strauss in his tacit defense of Maimonides against the damning criticism of the Jewish philosophers mounted by Scholem is that it is not adequate to allow the "Jerusalem and Athens" issue to be decided by the difference between philosophy and mysticism. This curiously reflects not merely a defense of philosophy, but also an argument in favor of the Hebrew Bible, whose core teaching, Strauss suggests, is not best preserved in its mystical form.[7]

Moreover, returning to the philosophic debate about Maimonides' position, it should be observed that while Strauss thought that no one should avoid considering carefully Spinoza's powerful criticism of the Maimonidean achievement, nor should anyone regard this bold modern criticism as somehow surpassed or irrelevant, he still seemed to think that this great Western debate about *the* truth is not as deeply or as comprehensively penetrated by Spinoza as it was by the original figure whose thought he criticized, however much Spinoza had been taught by him.[8] Indeed, even if Spinoza's criticism of his "teacher" seemed to imply that a radical break had occurred in the bond connecting them, Strauss wondered whether this link was quite as negligible or as readily dissolved as Spinoza suggested. However this may be, in any case it is against the Maimonidean standard, as to intellectual labor and expressive art, that every subsequent effort must be measured;[9] in this weighing, Spinoza (with his "demonstrated" truths) lacks neither the requisite reflectiveness about nature nor as complete a sagacious thoughtfulness about the human situation. However far we may rightly move as moderns from accepting

Maimonidean thought in its antiquated philosophic or scientific aspects, or in its obsolete medieval features, he remains the highest criterion (perhaps precisely because he makes the Hebrew Bible so pivotal for his endeavor) against which the claims of each and every competitor claiming victory are still judged, whether a Pascal or a Descartes, a Kierkegaard or a Hegel.[10] In other words, we must continue to look to him and his thought if we would see what an adequate and complete modern resolution of the debate by us must surpass—or even just equal. And it has been the unfortunate fate of Maimonides and his thought to have been eclipsed, if not forgotten, due to Spinoza's criticism, which almost completely dominated opinion until Strauss embarked on his voyage of rediscovery—to be sure, pointed in the right direction by Cohen. Even while modern scholars like Salomon Munk seemed to have detected *something* precious or worthwhile hidden beneath what is obsolete on the surface, it was Strauss's good fortune to have been able to recover its buried treasure in the very spot designated as already searched and declared wanting by Spinoza: Maimonides' interpretation of the Torah as exegetically original. Maimonides recovers in it evidence of a genuinely consistent thought to the point of profundity, while Spinoza provides proof only of a delirious, agitated, and impassioned imagination, since thought can only be properly elaborated in the mode of "(geometrical) method."

It may be worthwhile to pause for a moment in order to consider what, according to Strauss, was wrong with Munk in spite of his possession of great historical knowledge about the medieval Muslim philosophic milieu in which Maimonides wrote. Certainly Strauss credits Munk's scholarly attainments insofar he recognized the value of a certain sort of precious treasure, which Maimonides managed to bury beneath what is obsolete on the surface of Maimonides' *Guide*. But why did Munk completely misconstrue the deeper meaning of Maimonides' thought? This misconception, showing his dependence on moderate historicism, diminished his achievement on the philosophic level because, for all his historical knowledge, his saw Maimonides in light of modern thought, and not as he viewed himself. Strauss makes several comments that illuminate the misconception on which Munk proceeded toward Maimonides and the *Guide*. I would suggest that the following remark best encapsulates or at least summarizes this serious misconception: "For Munk and for those others who have followed him, the doctrine of Maimonides and the *falasifa* is an Aristotelianism contaminated or corrected by neo-Platonic conceptions. This opinion is not false, but it is superficial." The reason Strauss regards this notion as superficial is that it assumes Maimonides and the *falasifa* merely accepted the doctrines which they received on authority, as it were, rather than adopting only those doctrines whose purposes drove them and those questions which caused them to search for answers. But to perceive them as answers, one must comprehend the nature of the questions which directed them, and hence grasp the character of the perplexity in which their thought is grounded. There were, Strauss maintains, no fundamental questions and then no essential answers to them which were unknown to the greatest ancient thinkers, and so also to the greatest medieval thinkers. The modern thinkers, in other words, did not know anything completely novel in terms of the most elementary issues; they just did different things with the knowledge, and they did so motivated by different "historically situated" purposes. As Strauss suggests, Munk's misconception is based on the belief in progress; he shows the pitfalls of scholars who succumb to "the facile delusions which conceal from us our true situation": this amounts in sum to the single belief "that we are, or can be, wiser than the wisest men of the past." Munk's impressive scholarly labors follow in the wake of philosophers like Spinoza, not to mention Hegel, who assure us of our modern superiority, but whose thought leaves us vulnerable to such things as the workings of evil in human affairs, as was supposed to have been surpassed by modern progress, and with which Strauss claims the medieval thought of Maimonides better prepares us to deal.[11]

As a result, all those who "believe" in some version of Spinoza's philosophic system as the high point in modern thought, if only as to systematic perfection, maintain the defectiveness of Maimonides as a thinker almost as an article of faith. In some basic respects, it still defines (at the very least through Hegel) the essential character of the modern philosophic attitude toward the Maimonidean dialectical approach (with several interesting exceptions, such as Jean Bodin, Gottfried Wilhelm Leibniz, and especially Gotthold Ephraim Lessing). For though as moderns we cannot help but sympathize with some aspects of Spinoza's criticism of Maimonides as a medieval (since his celestial science seems so remote), Strauss helps us to perceive those elements of Maimonides' thought which transcend the medieval-modern divide. Indeed, Strauss helps us to perceive a Maimonides who stands beyond and surpasses any criticism we have been disposed to accept as a final judgment against him, precisely because we have not begun to comprehend properly what he was actually thinking about human beings: the way in which he approached the human intellect, how highly he esteemed it, and how far he wanted mindfulness to stretch itself; the peculiar manner by which he expressed his thought, and the reasons for it; how much he directed his focus to the human things; and the unusually mixed form in which he presented the educative thrust and literary parry of his views, at one moment doing so most directly, and at another moment doing so as obliquely as possible. Did anyone prior to Strauss even imagine a Maimonides in which this sort of question had been asked, never mind that adequate answers had never been proffered?

Of course, this is not to suggest that Maimonides was somehow entirely unknown to modern scholars; but Strauss gave modern scholars a completely different map in order to navigate and circumambulate what he claimed was the previously uncharted, huge territory of the mind called by the name of Maimonides. To achieve this feat (and switching for a moment from a discovery-by-sea to a discovery-by-land metaphor), Strauss bypassed the overland trails, and instead burrowed beneath the calm surface of the landscape that almost everyone took for granted, so as to uncover a teaming, purposeful, and vital underground world. To continue the metaphor, Strauss viewed familiar ground afresh, ground on which generations of modern historical scholars had trod, settled, and toiled in a safe clearing of the woods. But they had ceased to notice irregularities in the surrounding landscape and on the ground itself, which should have suggested hidden depths and unknown regions, calling for a search-and-discover mission. In contrast with his predecessors as well as with his contemporaries, Strauss boldly cut his own path through the forest of tradition and traveled undaunted along unused textual byways, undeterred by "sensible" scholarly warnings about safe travel. The criticism has been leveled at Strauss, now as well as then, that he invented these unused byways, or exaggerated the measure of autonomy which Maimonides had allowed himself in thinking through the Jewish and philosophic traditions, even though such critics may even be willing to admit that he did this in an entirely untraditional manner.[12] Simultaneously, he avoided the familiar routes and the impasses to which they had led, to which he too would have been led if he had allowed himself to be guided by established intellectual signposts. Instead of doing this, he decided to make his own way and to follow his own path through disused terrain, which permitted him to uncover a figure somehow missed or ignored by generations (if not centuries) of modern scholars, who thought that they knew all of the essential contours in the Maimonidean landscape. To be sure, Strauss uncovered a perplexing, unanticipated, and thoroughly unconventional Maimonides, who concealed while he revealed, and who revealed while he concealed: Strauss offers us a perplexing guide to the perplexities, as much as (or even greater than) this is a guide that resolves our perplexities.[13] He seemed to think that in order to grasp Maimonides' *Guide* in its full originality, profundity, and power, it is needed to restore to full awareness the perplexities that drove him. Indeed, it is perplexities which have been forgotten or obscured by subsequent developments, especially in the unfolding stages of modernity—but not solely, since this disregarding had already been in progress in the post-Maimonidean medieval era—even though this realm is still as relevant as ever if one wants to progress in thinking. Likewise is this the case if one wants to penetrate the conflict between "Jerusalem and Athens" as a still unresolved dialogue that represents eternal truths about the human mind and human nature, and not just historically situated, relative concepts.

In a letter Strauss compared in its favor the *Guide* with *Thus Spoke Zarathustra* of Nietzsche, as if Maimonides' subtlety and irony (especially with regard to the Bible) had already surpassed Nietzsche in anticipation.[14] Indeed, if the contemporary crisis of Western thought was brought on by Nietzsche, this judgment offers us a clue to what Maimonides made possible for Strauss: he gave Strauss the hint to the beginning of the possibility of surpassing Nietzsche. He did so by turning in a direction which *both* pursues philosophic thinking as far as humanly possible *and* takes the Bible seriously while not needing to read it as it literally appears. This is done not by either simple rejection or by fierce criticism, but by allowing subtle (or not so subtle) irony to distance the reader who is in tune with the writer from the rejected portions of the text. It is this art of constructing a distance between the reader and the Bible that makes Maimonides known as an "esoteric" writer. It also leaves the Bible—suddenly regarded as, in its deepest layer, a form of thinking—free to raise doubts about such thinking as is not connected with its own premises. Even if altogether appealing as a possibility, it still seems paradoxical that Maimonides could be regarded as doing better than Nietzsche what he ventured to do so uniquely as a thinker and writer, since what is most evident in present-day attitudes of mind (or, what Strauss also prefers to dub the "third wave of modernity") would seem to prove that Nietzsche is in the decisive respect the dominant thinker of our contemporary era, even if we do not like this fact, or even if we value Nietzsche's thought as great but still do not regard it as the highest possible thought.[15]

Another aspect of the judgment in the aforementioned letter is that, once Strauss perceived the potential of irony as proof of the capacity of any thinker not to be subject to the beliefs of his own era (even as to its seemingly definitive but actually never-completed science, while not rejecting what is truly objective and known), he was starting to liberate himself from the dominance of Nietzsche as the thinker of the contemporary era: he no longer needed to render history the supreme category. What he perceived through Maimonides instead is that the true thinker knows the limits of contemporary thought (whatever it may be), and hence of history; he is not beholden to the thought of his contemporary era because he knows it is unfinished and thus he also knows it cannot form the basis for his own thinking, however much it may pretend to absolute finality or masterful conclusiveness. The true thinker's distance from contemporary beliefs (whether scientific, religious, or political) is based on the *priority* of thinking which accepts the world as it is while it raises questions about it; and so it also leaves the scientific, religious, or political worlds as they are, while enjoying an ironic distance from them as problems for thinking. Indeed, even biblical thought seems to proceed on the same basis of the free mind, although it moves in a different direction.[16] Yet is this claimed perception closer to an assertion, and hence is it not for Strauss merely to render a paradox sharper rather than clearer? Is the "free mind" the genuinely knowable truth of man in the world? For if not, this still will not leave us sure that Maimonides as thinker and writer can be superior to any contemporary thinker of our highest esteem. The paradoxical country in which he landed should not obscure the greatness of the discovery. And like every great discovery, it at first managed (and continues) to provoke fearful surprise, consternation, and resistance as much as it elicited augmented possibility, recognition, and gratitude.

That this was Strauss's intention, or at least his expectation, with regard to what would follow from the appearance in print of his discovery of a radically different and untraditional Maimonides, is evident from a letter he wrote to his friend Jacob Klein, of 16 February 1938. He was alerted to the "dynamite" potentially contained in his discovery by a passing comment of Nahum Glatzer, according to whom, if the house of Judaism were deprived [*entzieht*] of Maimonides as the chief grounding [*Grundlage*] of the faith, this might threaten its collapse; he even asserted, according to Strauss's report, that Maimonides was of greater significance in terms of substance for supporting present-day Judaism than the Hebrew Bible. (He compares it with present-day Catholicism: "in a certain respect," Thomas Aquinas is of greater significance than the New Testament.) As this comment by Glatzer seems to imply, it is not so much the law code of the *Mishneh Torah*, however brilliantly conceived it is as a complex, subtle, and artful work, that makes Maimonides so sustaining for present-day Judaism, but rather the *Guide* and related works, since these are equipped to present a complete and proper *theological* response to the challenge of philosophy and science. Though Strauss was obviously alerted to a public difficulty by Glatzer's warning, it did not deter him from a private willingness to characterize his "hunch" about Maimonides, that he "was a 'philosopher' in a far more radical sense than is usually assumed today and really was almost always assumed, or at least was said." He wondered whether it is being less than "responsible" to discuss this directly, as indeed whether it is wise to ventilate the entire nature of being a philosopher (or "the problem of Socrates"), and hence of esotericism in such a context, i.e., "the relationship between thought and society." As a result, he addressed the subject by turning to "some strategically favorable, non-Jewish object," a safe, ancient author who was usually dismissed as a lightweight, Xenophon, to confront the question. But if as a matter of decency, and with due respect for its social and political impact, one is unable to fully articulate Strauss's concerns and how they bear on Maimonides, then there is still no doubt about one thing—that this was and will remain for him a deeply moral issue. In fact, Strauss seems to believe that anyone who is not attentive to the moral issue of discussing in public matters which Maimonides limited to the private sphere is not truly able to penetrate Maimonides' book (if this is also not true for him about any truly serious author and book). As Strauss plainly states:

> No historian who has a sense of decency and therefore a sense of respect for a superior man such as Maimonides will disregard light-heartedly the latter's emphatic entreaty not to explain the secret teaching of the *Guide*. It may fairly be said that an interpreter who does not feel pangs of conscience when attempting to explain that secret teaching and perhaps when perceiving for the first time its existence and bearing lacks that closeness to the subject *which is indispensable for the true understanding of any book*. Thus the question of adequate interpretation of the *Guide* is primarily a moral question. [Emphasis added.]

At the same time, there is one mitigating factor in this moral conundrum of his seeming to expose that which the author wished to keep secret. Indeed, in several places Strauss indicates that this factor is a priority for him as a modern scholar and thinker. It is the threat to freedom of thought in contemporary society, which seems to justify the revealing discussion in which Strauss is engaged: "Freedom of thought being menaced in our time more than for several centuries, we have not only the right but even the duty to explain the teaching of Maimonides, in order to contribute to a better understanding of what freedom of thought means, i.e., what attitude it presupposes and what sacrifices it requires." Hence, Strauss makes no attempt to vindicate himself on the mere ground that he is perhaps the rediscoverer of authentic Maimonidean thought; instead, as he presents it, he needs to justify his own discussion of this rediscovery in terms of both moral concerns, i.e., "decency" or the duty of conscience, and of just political imperatives, i.e., the right of free thought and the key role it plays in ordering modern Western civilization.[17]

Like almost every great discoverer, Strauss was able to do what he did because he took almost nothing for granted. Of course, one also should not discount the element of the accidental, occasional, or fortuitous, which undoubtedly played a role in his happening on this key side of Maimonides that, for several "good" reasons, had hitherto tended to be disregarded, even though it had been highlighted plainly enough by Maimonides. In this sense, Strauss had also had the "good luck" that he was the first who was willing to perceive what no one else wanted to notice. Indeed, he decided to make a critical examination even of what "everyone is assumed to know" about Maimonides.[18] Thus, he gave reasons to doubt whether Maimonides was so "obviously" an Aristotelian, at least in the ultimate sense, as is accepted by the dominant modern scholarly consensus, pointing instead to vital elements of Maimonides' thought which led Strauss to regard him as primarily a Platonist. For his view that Maimonides was more of a Platonist and less of an Aristotelian than was conventionally asserted by modern scholars, Strauss was undoubtedly aided by the clue given to him on this point by Hermann Cohen. It was Cohen who first insisted that Maimonides was a Platonist rather than an Aristotelian, especially in his ethical teaching, highlighting that Maimonides embraced the transcendent Good, i.e., morality, and not worldly happiness (*eudaimonia*), as the proper end of the truly human life. But for Cohen this "Platonism" of Maimonides expressed itself as something legitimate for modern man mainly through modern neo-Kantianism as rational and autonomous morality, though supported of course by modern science. In Cohen's view, this is the predominant means to transcendent Good made immanent so far as is rationally possible. Strauss took a different route; he recognized the priority of politics to morality in Maimonides as the most encompassing guide and necessary key to all things human. He maintained not only that Maimonides shared his view that political philosophy is the queen of the sciences but, as he also stressed, this standpoint on political philosophy was shared by both Plato and Aristotle, and this conception was brought together in the unifying view of Farabi which Maimonides seems to have endorsed. And while Cohen never attempted to deny the connection between morality and politics (for which Strauss respected him), Strauss criticized the unconditional priority that Cohen awarded categorically to rational and autonomous morality. As a result of this, Cohen obscured the "sufficiency" of politics in the thought of Maimonides, for whom it is merely supported by morality and religion. In order to illustrate this point, Strauss's criticism emphasized the deficiency of Cohen's view which, in Strauss's assessment, made it possible for Cohen to censor and distort the simple and unprejudiced facts about politics: his progressive moral project for modern man enabled him to adjust the facts, to selectively deny them, or to characterize them as he wills them, inasmuch as they do not conform with what he judged the predetermined telos of history. That philosophic flaw might seem to have manifested itself most obviously (i.e., historically) in Cohen's unwillingness to consider how powerful anti-Jewish prejudice was in Germany, and to miscalculate its volatile political potential (not to mention his irately dismissing the sober analysis of the political Zionists), with dire consequences for the Jews.[19]

Similarly, Strauss wondered whether it is "self-evident" that Spinoza was the deeper thinker than Maimonides—and he was able to wonder this, in a certain measure, because he asked whether we merely regard it as self-evident since the former was a modern (and hence our antecedent), and the latter was a medieval (and hence obsolete for us). While in no sense slighting the power of Spinoza as a philosopher, Strauss asked himself (following careful study of both thinkers) whether Maimonides as a thinker did not manifest a greater profundity and a wiser reflection on God, man, and the world than his wayward "disciple." Strauss also did not judge what was in their thought by allowing himself to be unduly impressed by Spinoza's determined modern "systematic" method (in his *Ethics*) as against Maimonides' reticent medieval "scriptural" style (in his *Guide*); he regarded it as sounder to compare the *Guide* with Spinoza's *Theological-Political Treatise*; indeed, it is from this work, he concluded, that the *Ethics* proceeds, rather than vice versa.

And Strauss also probed whether Maimonides—as a clear-sighted and even eagle-eyed thinker, committed to consistent and even radical reasoning no matter how much its conclusions may stand in opposition to certain tenets of Judaism[20]—truly accepted certain fundamental "orthodox" views which he seemed to espouse even though they compromised rational thought. Strauss asked himself, then, if there were any grounds to wonder whether—at a deeper level, and contrary to appearances that Maimonides himself cultivated— he refused to endorse *any* views as unqualifiedly true just because tradition (whether philosophic or religious) seemed to require this sanction, and yet (in spite of hints to the contrary) kept his counsel about what he personally acknowledged, not regarding it as necessary to let the multitude of his potential readers know what he thought in his own mind (letting those hints—as "words to the wise"—be sufficient to educate those who were able to comprehend by themselves). As Strauss perceives it, Maimonides is not disposed to celebrate "the follower of authority," but rather wishes to cultivate the "genuine man of speculation," i.e., someone who thinks for himself, whatever the results. Of course, even if the "man of speculation" thinks for himself and reaches whatever results he will, he need not announce or promulgate those results in public. Indeed, he tends (as a student trained by Maimonides) to keep those results private, if he judges that they do not need to be revealed. This will especially be the case if the results of thinking contradict what useful "authority" teaches, or if prudent judgment determines that, while what "authority" teaches is wrong and so cannot be designated as useful, this truth is beyond being absorbed correctly by contemporary society, and so (since the truth still trumps authority) it can only be stated or taught obliquely. Strauss in fact suggests that the true Maimonidean, in being a "man of speculation," is one who also "acts as a moderate or conservative man." In other words, the "genuine man of speculation," like Maimonides himself, is not dominated by the need to acquire at any cost a reputation as a philosopher, or even fame as a great philosopher (although he may desire this, if it is at a reasonable cost and if it advances the cause of thinking in society); it must often suffice for the "genuine man of speculation" that he knows what he knows. Seen in this light, it may be possible to comprehend the implication of Strauss's perplexing comment about Maimonides, that he "brought the greatest sacrifice," which enabled him to "defend the Torah against the philosophers as admirably as he did in his Jewish books." This "greatest sacrifice" to which Strauss refers is neither the "*sacrificium intellectus*," nor the sacrifice of moral excellence, nor the sacrifice of his Judaism, which are all to construe him much too imperfectly.

To grasp the deeper significance that Strauss attributes to this comment, it may be helpful to consider Nietzsche's statement on the philosopher's distinct *need* for fame: "The boldest knights among these addicts of fame, those who believe that they will discover their coat of arms hanging on a constellation, must be sought among the *philosophers*." Nietzsche regarded the philosophers as hungrily in search of eternal fame (rather than fleeting celebrity) through what they write. They hope that this art in the form of books will earn a lasting name for themselves and their teaching, which to him seemed a somewhat legitimate and a somewhat compromised motive. Yet he too was fully aware that this is not quite as simple as he stated it in the previous passage, for as he also says, "Plato is remarkable: an enthusiast of dialectic, i.e., of such circumspection." Their teaching is not ultimately to be equated with their thought. They aim to change human life through the many, but primarily to change human minds through only the few. Even Maimonides, who seemed to be the most circumspect of men, is not quite so resistant to change as he might appear on the surface; he too had a markedly revolutionary aspect beneath the surface. Even if he was the gradualist par excellence, his complete intention to transform human minds was scarcely so limited. Hence, Strauss never remained entirely happy with the designation of Maimonides as a "conservative," as is evidenced by this arresting statement that he made to Scholem in one of their last letters, of 19 March 1973: "[Maimonides'] conservatism is only the foreground, albeit the indeed indispensable foreground of something very very different." In other words, it is the duty of the true thinker, according to Strauss's view of Maimonides, to ground himself in conservative prudence, restraint, or moderation with regard to his actions or his relations with nonthinkers in most circumstances, which usually involves a certain disavowal of the search for fame, but to be as radical as the situation calls for in the realm of thought. The political situation may on occasion even produce in him a need to present his ideas to the world, depending entirely on circumstances and good judgment, in dramatic and even fiery fashion, but this rare imperative must be judged with the prudence that Maimonides presumes the great thinker will possess. Depending on what is occurring historically, there may even be an occasional need for revolutionary action, and hence a willingness to express himself with greater audacity, to stray from his natural habitat in the private realm, and so even to court public opinion. However restrained he was in most respects, the books of Maimonides show him as a thinker of excellence who believed that his era was passing through a grave intellectual decline (as in retrospect we can recognize as true) and thus called for courageous and forthright action, which he then did in his own name. In spite of this historical diagnosis, he may have always remained moderate; and yet his bold discussion of the "secrets of the Torah," and his vigorous willingness to organize and systematize the law in the name of God and science, reveal a man who thought his world was in need of serious correction, which forced him to advance his name and to act audaciously for the sake of the cause in which he believed.[21] Strauss certainly allowed it to strike him how peculiar Maimonides' procedure was, what he started to acknowledge as his very cultivated "art" as a writer. This was not something about which anyone had thought to ask concerning what it might signify, i.e., why he had chosen to make himself a literary artist (even a masterful one), rather than regarding him as someone who just happened to be a writer of books for utilitarian reasons and who acted in a compositorial fashion which was either simple-mindedly traditional or prosaically conventional. Instead, Strauss was determined to fathom why Maimonides had followed such a peculiar procedure and artistic style, rather than dismissing it (as had every modern scholar who preceded him) as an incidental expression, an optical illusion, or a mere medieval tic.

Strauss stayed with the surface and probed its strange aspects, even if it led him to refuse to accept the seemingly evident according to convention as "obvious." Thus, he also paid close attention to the literary surface of Maimonides' writings, i.e., to the forms of his books, essays, and letters, and hence to the subtly different guises in which Maimonides appeared as an author. It is not unreasonable to aver that it was Søren Kierkegaard who reminded modern thinkers and scholars that the literary guises in which a philosophic author may choose to appear are highly significant: this is something deliberately chosen, and for serious writers this is done for serious reasons. If a philosophic author must make a literary decision in his art of writing, then—for a truly philosophic author—it must be that this is never a "merely" literary decision, but must also carry weighty philosophic and pedagogical implications. This bears a unique consequence for Maimonides: Strauss analyzed his manifold talents as a writer and contrasted his achievement with that of several other great thinkers for whom the style in which they wrote basically formed a unity. Strauss's perception certainly rings true. Thus, Plato mainly wrote dialogues (although also thirteen letters survive); Aristotle composed treatises or comprehensive lectures (although some youthful dialogues, which are spoken about by ancient writers, largely do not survive); Thomas mainly wrote large theological treatises (although a substantial number of commentaries and letters are also known); Averroes mostly composed philosophic commentaries (although some small treatises, as well as large legal discourses, are preserved); Kant and Hegel both wrote systems of philosophy in elaborately constructed works (which everything else they wrote was made to subserve). Curiously Spinoza forms an interesting exception to the aforementioned "rule," if one considers only his major works: he not only wrote a philosophic "system" modeled on Euclid, but he also composed independent works on the Hebrew Bible and theology, politics, Hebrew grammar, and pure science (i.e., the rainbow), not to mention a voluminous correspondence. In comparison with the aforementioned figures, it is striking that Maimonides wrote major works in the most diverse literary forms possible, and yet to Strauss this still somehow seems to bespeak a master plan. He composed a commentary (on the Mishnah); a law code (the *Mishneh Torah*); a series of "letters" to named correspondents on discrete and discernible themes, in which he offers authoritative answers to legal or theological questions (on astrology, on conversion, on martyrdom, on messiahs and Jewish history, etc.); an exegetical-speculative book (*The Guide of the Perplexed*), which is sui generis and is not a theological treatise or a philosophic system or a dialogue (although it is often written in a second-person form of address, with responses to hypothetical queries) or merely a series of letters to a favorite student (in which literary form the *Guide* is actually framed, as a fact that Strauss was the first to notice and highlight), but an apparently amorphous interpretive work on biblical "secrets." It is also remarkable for how full it is of hints, pointers, contradictions, clues, and suggestions. As for its apparent amorphousness, even Strauss admitted at one point that Maimonides' *Guide* "was, to begin with, wholly unintelligible to me." This fog began to lift only due to a chance encounter with an enlightening remark by Avicenna on Plato's *Laws* as the key to the comprehension of revelation and prophecy. Or as he makes that same point with similar words but focused on other works, "Avicenna describes Plato's *Laws* as the standard work on prophecy. This view of the essentially political character of prophecy influences the very plan of Maimonides' *Sefer ha-Mitzvot* and of his *Sefer ha-Madda*." It is to be noted that in this literary remark Strauss is pointedly silent about the *Guide*. Strauss seems to imply by this peculiar silence that what he suggests about the *Guide*, as a book written by a most careful writer, presents a truth about Maimonides which must cause one to revise how one reads everything written by the same author.

Here it is vital to observe that Strauss was the first contemporary scholar or thinker to ask: What is the philosophic, cognitive, or intellectual cause and significance of this specific diversity of literary expression by Maimonides? What was the intention and what was the effect that Maimonides was trying to achieve by endowing one major work with the appearance of utmost order (as this was evidently attainable by him), and the other major work the appearance of utmost disorder? Now one might even go so far as to say that Strauss's scholarly works can be characterized as explorations in search of an answer to that complex question about this singular literary diversity. In fact, one might even apply the same query to Strauss: What was the purpose of the literary unity or diversity which he came to employ by choice in his own mature works? An answer to this question, which sees Maimonides' literary art in light of a view of Strauss's thought, has been offered obliquely by Allan Bloom, who contends that it was a product of the signposts philosophers quietly erect for those who are able and willing to follow them into the depths of the labyrinth of thought: "But it was always [Strauss's] instinct to look for something important in that which seemed trivial or absurd at first impression, for it was precisely by such an impression that our limitations are protected from challenge. These writings [of Maimonides] were distant from what he understood philosophy to be, but he could not accept the ready explanations based on abstractions about the medieval mind."

Strauss, it seems, chose to communicate something of significance in the form of the works which he chose to employ. Discerning what this significance is must be an element in any serious endeavor that attempts to make sense of Strauss's own thought as a deliberate unity.[22] But further on Maimonides, Strauss noticed the Jewish character of the books in which the thought of Maimonides had been communicated as something deliberately chosen. To previous modern scholars this might have just seemed an obvious fact of little value in grasping his thought, since they regarded such simple things as merely required by Maimonides' medieval historical situation. There are undoubtedly those who will dismiss Strauss's procedure so characterized, as if to say: in the medieval era, someone like Maimonides was not free to do anything other than make his philosophic reflections appear in the guise of a Jewish book. I would suggest that, with our greater historical knowledge, this is not quite so obvious, but rather was even then a matter of choice. Perhaps, as a rule—although even in these matters instructive exceptions can be located—such a book had to be generally "religious" in appearance, but it surely did not have to be so specifically "Jewish" in content. To illustrate, I would remind readers of the case of Solomon ibn Gabirol (1021–58), a Hebrew poet and student of philosophy in Spain, who was a predecessor by a century of Maimonides. His great philosophic work, known in its Hebrew version as *Mekor Ḥayyim* (Source of Life), was translated from its (lost) original Arabic into Latin as *Fons Vitae*, and was regarded for subsequent centuries of Christian scholastics as a book written by an unknown Arab author named Avicebron. Ibn Gabirol's book, with its lack of even biblical passages utilized as proof-texts, which was the generally accepted pattern, was not known by most readers to have been written by a Jewish author until the 19th century, with the correct identity of the author discovered again in 1846 by Salomon Munk through the medieval Hebrew translation of Falaquera. One may speculate about what Ibn Gabirol may have been aiming to achieve by presenting his book as he did—as a freestanding medieval neo-Platonic philosophic "treatise," although composed in the form of a Platonic dialogue, but with no discernible "Jewish" features. It certainly cannot be argued that he did this with his main prose work because he was not a very Jewish figure: in fact, some of his great Hebrew poems (and especially *Keter Malkhut*, or *The Kingly Crown*) were added to the Jewish prayer book for use in the liturgy, and he was much admired as a Jewish religious poet with a philosophic bent. One can at least be certain from this illustration that, even in the medieval era, it was possible for a Jewish author to choose not to write a "Jewish" book. And this shows that it is not an unhistorical anachronism to ask, as Strauss did in the case of the *Guide*: Why did Maimonides choose to write so "Jewish" a book on apparently philosophic issues and themes?[23]

And similarly Strauss refused to ignore the rigorous critique of philosophy that Maimonides engaged in, and even highlighted, in most of those writings, although modern scholars tended to regard Maimonides as a philosopher pure and simple, since their model of the philosopher is of the modern sort, i.e., either systematic or academic, but certainly a figure thoroughly acceptable to everyone. Why, Strauss likewise wondered, had Maimonides elected to make his thought neither a statement of autonomous philosophy (in the standard form of the separate treatise) nor a profession of traditional piety (in the standard form of the biblical commentary). Perhaps these were not "mere" authorial devices or literary features, i.e., aesthetically significant yet cognitively accidental, but rather significant clues to his thought in which essential aspects of its teaching are contained, and which Maimonides the author had fully intended to provide as hints and pointers. Thus, Strauss notes in *The Guide of the Perplexed*, a supposed work of biblical interpretation in the Midrash mode, the peculiar amalgamation of exegetical and speculative elements, which do not always fit together even though Maimonides claims that every word and sentence in this book was deliberately chosen by its author. Indeed, he depicts the character of the *Guide*'s master plan in the following terms: "The teaching of the *Guide* is then neither entirely public or speculative nor is it entirely secret or exegetic." It was, of course, not obvious to, or even considered possible by, anyone prior to Strauss that the *Guide* might be constructed according to such a master plan. But this is not even the most noteworthy point to be observed in Strauss's depiction of Maimonides' procedure in constructing his book.

Instead, it seems completely opposed to the conventional assumption about what Judaism tends to hold in regard, and what it tends to be suspicious of, as Strauss himself reminded us. For should not speculation be private or secret, as potentially dealing with things beyond the law? And should not exegesis (i.e., of scriptural texts) be public or transparent, since it actually deals with things safely limited by the law? We must consider the possibility that Strauss adopted Maimonides' own procedure, this being a deliberately planted hint or contradiction, which as careful readers we are supposed to notice and think vigorously about, precisely because of its clash with conventional assumptions. In fact, could it be the case that Strauss has followed through on the consequences of a directive he discussed in an article which appeared much previous to "How To Begin To Study *The Guide of the Perplexed*" (1963), perhaps in this latter work enacting the thrust of the former article, "Literary Character of the *Guide*" (1941)? Certainly Strauss considered himself "a historian [with] a sense of decency and . . . respect for a superior man such as Maimonides." He did his best not to "disregard light-heartedly [Maimonides'] emphatic entreaty" not to elucidate too clearly the secret teaching of the *Guide*, even if he did in some measure choose to elucidate—as had Maimonides himself, although the law forbids it. Did he adopt a revised version of this procedure as a sign, pointing to the need to acknowledge and adapt Maimonides' wisdom to our own situation? As he states,

> Consequently, one might think it advisable for the interpreter to imitate Maimonides also with regard to the solution of the dilemma, i.e., to steer a middle course between impossible obedience and flagrant transgression by attempting an esoteric interpretation of the esoteric teaching of the *Guide*. Since the *Guide* contains an esoteric interpretation of an esoteric teaching, an adequate interpretation of the *Guide* would thus have to take the form of an esoteric interpretation of an esoteric interpretation of an esoteric teaching.

On a first reading, the last portion of the last sentence makes one laugh, as if Strauss were bringing to light an absurdity. But it emerges that Strauss is serious about considering the proposition. One may suggest that this "middle course between impossible obedience and flagrant transgression" was for Strauss navigated by directing the future interpreter to search and discover the Torah's own "secrets" through exegesis of the *Guide* and its "secrets." But

Strauss also advises doing this in such a manner as to leave the "secrets" of the Torah and of Maimonides concealed for those who are not suited for their comprehension. The proof that one is fit for such comprehension is shown by one's willingness to follow the author through the search for "the beauty of those hidden treasures" which only disclose themselves in the wake of much detailed work. As Strauss colorfully characterizes such a search and what it discloses, this often occurs through chance literary encounters along the way with assorted "devils, madmen, beggars, sophists, drunkards, epicureans, and buffoons." In other words, Strauss seems to counsel us that we do not have to lose our modern freedom if we imitate Maimonides by not saying everything we think on the surface. By letting literary art (as great novelists do) convey radical things moderately, so what we may think remains declared but in safely veiled form, and meanwhile we do not damage or mislead those who will be harmed by hearing a shocking truth. Our expression remains free if slightly shielded (a modern art of writing recaptured in Kierkegaard), and yet our intention to tell the truth for those who need it is still honored.[24]

Along a similar line, Strauss also wondered why just this literary form had been chosen in any specific case: e.g., why the *Guide* was written as a letter, or a series of letters, to his favorite student: was it so that some deeper level of thought could be expressed by the artful design as a subtle message to careful readers?[25] If this was the case, might not that deeper level of thought also have been obscured by generations of commentators and scholars who had dismissed such considerations as of relatively slight significance or even as completely peripheral matters, not worthy of serious study in the effort to delineate his more or less obvious opinions? Strauss asked himself: Is it not our duty, precisely as modern historical scholars, to engage in an archaeological excavation in search of the original intention of the author, and so attempt to uncover what may have been obscured from us by our own forgetfulness (witting or unwitting) of the past, so as to disentangle what may transpire to have been purposefully tied in knots? Are we not further obligated to reconsider his works and legacy by the very weight of the tradition about Maimonides, now that (or insofar as) we can perceive how much he chose to radically remake the tradition, which compelled him to hold it even in his own mind at some distance from himself? Surely this requires us to attain something of the same distance ourselves as much as is possible for us, if we are to make a closer approach to an authentic grasp of the original thought of Maimonides, as he possessed it in his own mind and as it is accessible to us here, at least insofar as he was able by subtle art to communicate it to us in his works? Is such an original intention of the author available to us from our study of his books, if approached in the right way?

Strauss argued that, as honest archaeologists of thought and undogmatic historical scholars, we cannot settle this in advance but must consider it a possibility, suspending a decision until the work of excavation has been fully completed, and the author's language, thought, and teaching have been fully deciphered. One compares different scholarly readings with the original text and decides which conveys the best sense of the original, as competent readers can do. But as Strauss also suggested, the most difficult requirement—if we are to know whether his thought is thinkable by us—is that we must also try to think his thoughts, to retrace the philosophic path on which he walked, as much as is this is possible for each of us according to our ability: we must try to become the sort of thinkers he wanted us to be. Only then can we know if there is a fully articulated reflection of the mind of the author available to us, which as a result will force us to consider whether this is something that we can be persuaded by.[26] But aside from the details (i.e., whether this or that is an adequate reading of a book), the truly fundamental assumption of Strauss is that (in principle) thought can be adequately communicated in language, and that language can be conveyed in books which represent the thought or "mind" of the writer. This assumption will carry with it an accompanying assumption, namely, that it is possible for a competent reader to elucidate the intention of the author of a great book if he is properly engaged in the careful explication of the text, which (if it is a great book) is never entirely a relic from the past, but also makes it a message to the present. In other words, the truly fundamental assumption of Strauss—and he claims to have been taught this by Maimonides—is that the most essential truth, however difficult to recover because encrusted in layers of tradition, is not dependent on history, but is discoverable in principle irrespective of time and place. Perhaps this fundamental assumption of Strauss's cannot be proven definitively. However, it is an assumption which, it is plausible to argue, most directly resembles what has historically brought human beings closer to the truth as it has been taught by books for thousands of years—and this deserves to be entered as compelling evidence, which at least corroborates his thesis about our access to "the greatest minds" through studying the great books.[27]

Indeed, in a certain sense Strauss proceeded with Maimonides—a genuine artist among "the greatest minds" who composed two massive works of literary art which also have to be counted among the great books—like an art restorer who removes layers of accumulated grime from a painting, sculpture, or fresco so as to uncover the obscured first layer, bringing to light lost color, shape, and detail and letting us see again its original brilliance as the artist conveyed it. He went so far as to render questionable the authoritative images in which the figure of Maimonides has been portrayed, whether as formally received through tradition or as mediated by the critical-historical approach of modern scholars. Is it beyond any doubt that Maimonides is the chief pillar of religious orthodoxy, since tradition (and perhaps primarily he himself) wishes us to conceive of him in this manner? Perhaps he is deservedly so regarded, but according to Strauss we must examine again whether it was this image of himself that Maimonides had ultimately intended—and if so, Strauss asked why he projected it. Strauss seems to have subordinated Maimonides' project to the claim he made on behalf of Plato's conception of the relation between philosophy and politics. Articulated in the context of Strauss's debate with Alexandre Kojève, he used his claim for Plato in order to criticize Hegel's notion of the relation between philosophy and politics as determined by history. To be sure, this tacit claim about Maimonides' project is not a view of the whole of Maimonides' thought, but of that part of his thought which might be called its revolutionary drive, in which he may be justly compared with Plato and Farabi:

> What Plato did in the Greek city and for it was done in and for Rome by Cicero, whose political action on behalf of philosophy has nothing in common with his actions against Catiline and for Pompey, for example. It was done in and for the Islamic world by Farabi and in and for Judaism by Maimonides. Contrary to what Kojève seems to suggest, the political action of the philosophers on behalf of philosophy has achieved full success. One sometimes wonders whether it has not been too successful.

Strauss was more impressed than Kojève by the success of the Platonic philosophic revolution in history; he was less convinced than Kojève that the true lesson of this action has been fully grasped, because Hegel's approach based on a complete synthesis (rather than a Platonic dialectic) obscures the precarious nature of its own victory. Illusions about its historical significance are perhaps the most transparent sign of a certain failure, since belief in its permanent victory makes for a certain complacency about the everlastingly established status of philosophy in Western society—and that is not good either for philosophy or for society. In other words, we have need to become educated again in the truth which has to be thought through again in every generation—and especially in our era, which is convinced of irreversible progress in history. Strauss was persuaded that, in the careful study of Maimonides' *Guide*, it is possible to obtain access to perhaps the greatest teacher of this truth, especially in its relation to biblical teaching.[28]

Similarly, was Maimonides as limited in his thinking by the medieval horizon of philosophic thought, as it is assumed he must have been by most modern scholars? Thus, what if he was as capable of the political, theological, and moral criticism that we tend to identify with the thinking of the modern Enlightenment and with those who advanced its cause (such as Spinoza), even if he employed this same criticism to different effect? Likewise, was Maimonides *merely* the product of his historical era in 12th-century Spain and Egypt, with its cultural context and presuppositions, and with its theological dogmas and political prejudices? Strauss rejected the artificial constructions that most modern scholars put on medieval thinkers, insofar as this sets limits on how far their thought may have traveled, since we have progressed so much beyond them: he wished to free us of our modern tendency to merely acknowledge condescendingly that Maimonides had achieved a remarkable freedom of thought "for a medieval." As a result, Strauss rejected the modern scholarly notion of Maimonides as a "neo-Platonic Aristotelian," an amalgam constructed by Salomon Munk. Once Munk formulated his notion of Maimonides (as well as of the *falasifa*), it has ever since been accepted by almost every subsequent modern scholar, albeit with persistent quibbles and haggling about precisely how much was Aristotelianism and how much was neo-Platonism. Strauss did not deny that this mixture appears on the surface, and hence contains a certain element of fact. He merely wonders how such serious and deep thinkers could not have noticed the blatant contradictions between the two doctrines to which they appear to hold. And if they did notice it, how could they have continued to hold to the two doctrines simultaneously? Strauss's alternate approach to this fact was that, as intelligent men, they must have chosen to seem to adhere and to appear to believe in such a contradictory mixture for substantive reasons which may not appear on the surface; indeed, at a deeper level it is possible to make sense of the apparent contradiction, and to properly conceive what the fundamental issue was for those thinkers. And perhaps the most fundamental questions gripping those thinkers are What is philosophy? What is a philosopher as a human possibility? What is his proper or natural relation with the city? How is philosophy different from revealed religion? What is God according to philosophy (*quid sit deus*)? And how is the philosopher different from the statesman and the prophet?

These fundamental questions require answers that cannot be framed in the awkward modern construct of "neo-Platonic Aristotelian": they were first of all thinkers, and their thought conformed only to what they were convinced was the noncontradictory and knowable truth. They neither remained dependent on their time and place nor merely built on the historical-traditional legacy which they received, even or rather especially if they always situated (or clothed) their thought in the dominant concerns of their time and place, and spoke to their historical-traditional legacy. As thinkers the excellence and profundity of whose efforts Strauss attempts to make manifest to us, they strove for cognitive consistency even in the search for truth, never mind the consequent awkwardness of the results in their situation. The truth (noncontradictory and knowable) in which this search aimed to culminate and on awareness of which it is also in some sense based transcends the philosophic or scientific attainments of any single era but is a core human achievement which may be accomplished in any era by the rational and free mind, irrespective of the tentative results which currently predominate.[29]

Instead, Strauss wished to make us seriously consider Maimonides as a perennial thinker (turning this "historicism" around), and so bring us to an awareness of those deeper or higher dimensions in his thought which might transcend his historical period, his geographic location, his linguistic usage, and his cultural milieu—never mind his religious tenets. These possible dimensions of past thought, vastly expanded by Strauss in his novel manner of historical approach to interpreting the medieval thinkers beyond historicism, make Maimonides as much of a challenge to us here and now as he was then and there, however different our historical circumstances.[30]

~ THREE ~

Maimonides and the Free Mind

RESISTING ASSORTED DOGMAS ABOUT MAIMONIDES AND his thought (both traditional and modern), which most modern scholars take for granted, Strauss came to highlight the problematic aspects of this array of conventional images as we have been sketching them. He gave quite a different view of Maimonides, suggesting that we reconsider him as at bottom an unfettered free thinker, and hence as someone who approached all issues with a bold and unconstrained mind—ever clear, critical (if not also likewise self-critical), and hence fully self-aware. Hence, we study the deepest thinkers in every era, according to Strauss, because they attain a view of things that is never entirely limited, as most of us are, to our time and place, and hence by this rare achievement of a synoptic view they are not only able to transcend their own historical situatedness but also able to teach us on the same plane, if we study them properly, whatever our limiting historical horizon may happen to be. Indeed, they provide most of us with the only access we may obtain to the eternal horizon of human thought. As Strauss perceived, Maimonides was such a thinker, and hence our approach to him must differ from how we approach almost all other thinkers: we should want to know what he knew, as something of perhaps the greatest significance to man as man. While not denying any of those historical factors which might limit Maimonides' view on subordinate issues, Strauss perceived how Maimonides might help us to transcend our modern historical situation while yet also helping to reveal to us its true contours, i.e., he shows us our historical situation as seen in light of the true human situation. Strauss cannot guarantee that any of this may actually be the case, with respect to the possibility of transcending our historical situation as aided by the greatest thinkers, i.e., the great minds as they operate through the great books. But if we tentatively assume that this may be true about such thinkers as Maimonides (since, whatever may be argued, we do not *know* in advance that this is false), and if we live with their books as if they might teach us *the* truth, so we may both learn whether it is true as a premise and in the process at the very least (as a possibility) be taught a greater amount about our human situation from such minds as Maimonides than we could on the opposite assumption. Hence, Strauss's deeper premise seems to be as follows: historicism has brought us to the current pass (or impasse), which we cannot escape; but the achievements of historicism in scholarly recovery are dubious enough, and the state of modern thought on which historicism rests is precarious enough, that we should at least experiment with his opposite premise in order to discover whether this affords us a greater intellectual access to or scope of truth than is otherwise possible.

Thus, Strauss insisted that this entirely unconventional image of Maimonides, as a thinker who wrestled with the eternal questions of philosophy and religious thought, could only be judged accurately if the modern scholar was prepared to see the problems of medieval philosophy in the same light as Maimonides himself did. As this further suggests, the modern scholar must be prepared to consider the possibility that medieval philosophy at its highest was not captive to, or entirely limited by, its historical situation or ontological horizon; as this implies, he must consider the possibility that medieval philosophy taught *the* truth. For the claim of medieval philosophy in general, if not of "all philosophers of the past," is that they had discovered *the* truth. Must not the scholar take this claim seriously and give it its due, if he is even to make elementary sense of any thinker who thought so, and claimed as much about his teaching? Indeed, about Maimonides specifically Strauss is unambiguous: "The claim of Maimonides" is "to teach *the* truth," irrespective of his historical situation.[1] Strauss suggests (although this is not something he always makes as translucent as he might) that *the* truth which Maimonides claims to teach is not about natural science, which he knows man is limited by nature from ever fully knowing and hence can only speculate about, but about human nature, about political order or arrangements, and—in a certain measure only—about the relation of man to the divine.[2] The modern scholar must not close his mind in modern certainty to such a possibility, according to Strauss, but must at least be willing to doubt his modern convictions, of which principles the medieval philosopher did not know, i.e., "the principles of religious toleration, of the representative system, of the rights of man, of [liberal] democracy." Thus, he must open himself to an awareness of medieval philosophic thought as an attempt to wrestle with the *eternal* problems of Western philosophy and religious thought, as seen in light of the human situation, however different the solutions he may offer to them as contrasted with modern thinkers. He must also be willing to at least consider the possibility that on this basis, it had reached *the* truth about what is best for human beings. If we are not willing to do this at the very least as an experiment of thought, we shall lack the incentive to take medieval thought with full seriousness, and we will not give it its due as a thought that is potentially capable of teaching us things we might not otherwise know: what is best for man, and in what his uniqueness as a being consists. As this would seem to further imply, it is possible that the starting point of all philosophers and religious thinkers is the same, which we may call *the* unchanged human situation—unchanged with regard to its essential contours and contents. Similarly, this also entails the fundamental premise that no era is necessarily closer to the truth merely by its period in history, geographic location, linguistic usage, level of civilization, or cultural milieu—never mind by its religious tenets. If this approach is ultimately defensible, as Strauss maintains it is, even or rather especially for us with our modern historical premises about the status of modern thought as the primary standard in contrast with past thought and evolved beyond it, it is the demonstrated truth of the thinking alone that counts.

If this is the case about the great thinkers (i.e., they demonstrate the integrity of thinking by their ability to make the eternal accessible through the recurring human perplexities as these arise in history, but with a thinking never entirely determined by historical context, and yet often transforming history through their thinking), we should, according to Strauss, recognize that Maimonides was not only a great thinker, but also a revolutionary thinker. Indeed, Judaism was transformed by him, if only since it was immensely deepened by him: thinking through its truths, he shaped and redirected its fundamental character by allowing greater appreciation for their rational profundity, and for their capaciousness beyond what had thus far been imagined as their original compass.[3] To be sure, Strauss emphasized the radical character of all great thinkers, and he counted Maimonides among the great thinkers because of what he discovered in his books: the written record of the passion of a heroic mind, concentrated and channeled in a uniquely powerful search, to comprehend by thinking the great spiritual facts about humanity. He made evident, as had never yet been done by a single man, the significance of a noble tradition as one of the most impressive vehicles and aids ever devised for governing human beings, and for helping to guide them toward the achievement of their highest spiritual potential. For in the Torah of Moses and the tradition it produced, Maimonides had discovered a law aimed at surpassing intellectual excellence combined with eminent moral perfection—two things rarely achieved at such a high level and with such a wise dialectical balance by a single human tradition, at least as Maimonides presented it. Strauss was astounded and impressed by the powers of mind by which Maimonides made his search and discovery, and the literary and pedagogical art by which he taught, guided, molded, and passed it on to others, so as to inspire others to exceed its past achievements. What Judaism has been able to achieve since Maimonides, in the life of the mind and as a moral force, is in substantial measure due to him. He was thus not only a great but also a radical thinker, because by doing what he did, he made a gigantic effort to redirect its energy toward its deepest original impulses, as he was able to perceive them and recover them, and as he was also able to reactivate those sources of mind toward revived fruitfulness in the historical future.[4]

However much the medieval philosophers and their thinking critics like Maimonides may have wrestled with the spiritual perplexities and resolved the spiritual conflicts peculiar to their specific era, according to Strauss thinkers like Maimonides did so by honestly searching for *the* truth. And as Strauss discovered against expectations, Maimonides boldly stated in his books the views about the truth to which his search had led him, even if the truth he pronounced did not necessarily emerge entirely from Jewish sources, and even if it did not always accord with how those sources had been construed by previous generations.[5] However it may appear on the surface, Maimonides' intention was absolutely and always to educate those bolder souls who need unvarnished instruction and who can "handle the truth," and simultaneously to reassure those tamer souls who need a safe and pleasant message. Based on the experience of the critical study of Maimonides in which he had immersed himself for decades, Strauss seems to have been gradually persuaded by Maimonides that this pedagogical difference arises on the basis of a divide in human nature, representing a constant proportion of souls in human society distributed according to cognitive ability, which never seems to change essentially inasmuch as it never diminishes so substantially as to eradicate both the divide and the requirements which derive from it.[6] Strauss claimed to perceive the truth of Maimonides' argument, which he was willing to apply to human beings, irrespective of whether they were ancient, medieval, or modern: history, in whatever measure it may change significant things significantly, changes nothing with regard to the essential contours of human nature. This, curiously, is the basis for the radicalism of a thinker like Maimonides; it is also the case that his views about the truth, reached independently through his own thinking, shaped and determined how he conceived of the nature of the Jewish sources.[7]

As difficult as it is for modern man to admit this possibility (since he is disposed to believe that *the* truth was closed to all human beings prior to the modern era), the access of the medieval thinkers like Maimonides to the truth may not have been smaller than ours is. For them, the eternal was reflected by and glimpsed through those very perplexities and conflicts about the human things that we may paradoxically dismiss as "medieval." Yet even in thinking about those perplexities and conflicts, the human mind leaned toward and touched on the truth, as this is ever available to man as man—even if such awareness is difficult and rare in every era of history. Certainly what Strauss shows us is that we, as modern scholars or readers, must share with the medieval philosophers and thinkers a sufficient awareness of the eternal problems (and the limited range of solutions which accompanies them). We must do this tentatively or, as it were, heuristically, if we are to enter their minds, and if we are to accurately apprehend the depths of the premodern thinkers whom even we may still be able to acknowledge as great if we allow ourselves to perceive their thinking beyond, or even just hidden beneath, their "medievalisms": these cover them, but they do not need to define what they are. And if our further concern is with the explication of the texts written by a great thinker who is also a great writer such as Maimonides, most instructive to us is his way of comprehending himself and the task of thinking as conceived in his books: he constantly compels his readers to return to the original questions, and to rethink their necessity, as well as their benefit, to us. Hence, such rehabilitated awareness of the eternal problems—according to Strauss, in his unique approach to Maimonides—must be highlighted in our minds if the question of the possibility of philosophy is itself to remain an open question, even while it is confronted with the teachings of revelation in a holy book encountered as a fundamental challenge to it.

According to Strauss, the historical study of a medieval thinker like Maimonides can only be done conscientiously if the modern scholar approaches medieval thought with an awareness of medieval philosophy (and its competent medieval critics) as it conceived of itself: an attempt to wrestle with the eternal problems as coeval with the possibility of philosophy as a way of life. For the possibility of philosophy as a way of life implies the possibility of a life in search of the truth, and a life devoted to uncovering the truth and trying to genuinely know it.[8] It is animated by such love of truth as moves the searcher irrespective of the nature of the results at which he arrives. As this further implies, man can be happy in a life so devoted; the results do not count so much as the search itself. Or rather, to put it in terms which precede even the possibility of philosophy: Of which way of life is man most needful? Or then again, is there one way of life which is *the* "most needful"? Likewise, the moderns must recognize that they share such an awareness of eternal problems with the medievals, if this crucial question (i.e., of the very possibility of philosophy as a way of life) is itself to remain an open question for human beings, as Strauss believed it must. If philosophy as a way of life in search of truth is possible, and hence if it is what it claims to be according to medievals like Maimonides—which Strauss defines with greater precision as the life devoted to the "quest for the eternal order or for the eternal cause or causes of all things," with this quest based on the fundamental presupposition that "Being is essentially immutable in itself and eternally identical with itself"[9]—so it cannot change *essentially* with historical period. The eternal problems—such as the most obvious: Which is the right life for man? Is it the life which attempts to answer the eternal questions?—will compel us to address such questions, ever recurring to the human mind, as they are raised by Strauss's previous definition, whose fundamental presupposition he admits is itself not self-evident. Thus, an awareness of the eternal problems might almost be called, for Strauss, the true and proper definition of philosophy, since *what philosophy is*—awareness of the problems, with the questions themselves, as it were, the "piety of thinking,"[10] occurring to man again and again irrespective of historical circumstances—is, for Strauss, what is most fundamental as against any specifically formulated answer which philosophy addresses in detail. To be sure, there are a limited number of answers which accompany the eternal questions, and the philosopher must take attaining an answer seriously for himself, if he is to give the effort to reach the truth his most conscientious effort, which would then help him to avoid constructing philosophy as the mere playing of a game in the mind.[11]

Every modern scholarly approach to a medieval or an ancient thinker assumes a stance (wittingly or unwittingly) toward the problem of truth and in what form it may be known, as also of philosophy itself and its very possibility, which makes the modern scholarly approach itself (wittingly or unwittingly) a philosophic approach. In other words, the modern historical scholar, if he would study the thinkers of the past (who believed in the possibility of philosophy) with historical accuracy, must at least know what it implies or requires for philosophy to be possible.[12] For *what philosophy is*, besides being the eternal questions, is the way of life that meditates on them and attempts to answer them; this is the life of thinking as an act of love of thought. It is not merely the holding of a set of doctrines, in which philosophy is often conventionally believed to consist. And Strauss contended that Maimonides comprehended what this possibility implied or required with greater profundity than almost any other thinker, medieval or modern, who has chosen to wrestle with its specific difference as compared with its most serious and most worthy rival, i.e., morality and the moral life, which Strauss maintained depends on religion. This is especially the case as regards its difference from revealed religion, since that has often been conceived merely as the greatest defender of the moral life, and as the truest or deepest religious ground in which the roots of the moral life are planted. It will not suffice, but it will at least serve as a provocative point of departure, to suggest that, according to Strauss, Maimonides thought better of revealed religion than this: however noble such a title (highest defender of the moral life), it is also a mode of thought and hence it competes with philosophy on its own level, i.e., as knower. Their debate cannot only be about the defense of morality, since the philosophy to which he attended (Plato and Aristotle) did not much differ with revealed religion on the substance or the contents of morality.

Seen in light of the one issue which animates and drives Western spiritual history, Strauss believed that the question of the possibility of philosophy must remain an open question, if only in order to comprehend the medieval philosophers and their thinking critics. This is because, for the medieval thinkers, the question of philosophy itself is crucial for something else: it is the concern with *the* truth as the truth about the whole, and not just about those parts of the universe with which we are most familiar. Since this is a question that is only asked by human beings, it is related to the fundamental question What is a human being? Its variants are What is human life for? What is the best human life? And what is its highest perfection? This happens to be a complex of questions that was addressed directly and with utmost focus by Maimonides.[13] Conjoined with it is a doubt which cannot help but accompany philosophy as a mere type of thinking and not its inmost essence: Is philosophy capable of leading us to *the* truth, as the comprehensive truth about being? And is the way of life which leads to such truth also the best way of life for human beings in general? Or is man in need of a decisive supplement, specifically related to morality, which can only be located in revealed religion? To probe the meaning and value of philosophy as a challenge to religion and as a call on man from a different source, Strauss perceived how Maimonides also asked about the adequacy of its claim to properly guide man. Can the philosophic life, the life led in passionate search of the rational truth, provide a basis for human happiness (as both fulfillment and perfection)? It may be good for bringing us to awareness that the problems we face are eternal, but this still must be the right way of life for man per se. As much as medievals like Maimonides may have grappled just as passionately, and with just as much profundity, as did the ancients and the moderns who wrestled with the eternal questions, it is also essential to confront what the philosophic life *can* signify if it is not able to reach any ultimate answers, even though it may claim to be able to justify itself dialectically. If, as was previously suggested, philosophy is merely playing a game, if it is merely thinking in circles, however eternal, about questions unanswerable by reason, with no results adequate to guide us in what we must do, then it leaves the truly serious issues of life for something else to deal with. This effort of human reason, acting on its own ability, must offer us some sense of finality. Otherwise, if philosophy cannot guide human life to what is good for all human beings in their variety of types, it is not much better than a sport or amusement for clever idlers, as its critics have always been wont to charge, and cannot rise to the seriousness and elevated station which it claims for itself.

However wonderful it may be for us to grapple with the fundamental questions and to learn about all sides of the most significant issues as we strive to operate on an eternal plane, life does not admit and time does not allow our waiting to know the ultimate, definitive, and complete answers in order to live, but requires us to decide. Is it or is it not the case that man *can* grasp the truth by his own efforts and abilities alone? Or is he in need of assistance from beyond, perhaps in the form of revelation? And suppose, as religious tradition has assumed, that God is waiting for us to decide: Is this electing something we can postpone forever while we reflect? Or is the very effort of man to grasp the truth by his own rational powers, however effective his ability in the cause of knowledge, somehow a rebellion against God or the order of things?[14] In other words, is the life spent in pursuit of knowing the truth a genuine way to happiness, whether he attains the truth or not? Or will the search for knowledge, merely as a search that never attains *the* truth, bring man misery instead of happiness?[15] For philosophy, claiming itself as the one thing needful for human beings, it remains itself in question so long as full knowledge of the truth by our own powers is not genuinely certain for man. Knowing so little about what he is doing in the search for knowledge of the truth and even whether it is good, man seems frustrated and confused at the very start of his quest. Hence, this imposes on the philosopher the duty to always remain open to the alternative represented by revealed religion. Revealed religion has the advantage, as opposed to every alternative, that at least it has thought through this issue ("What is man?") with as much clarity, profundity, and thoroughness as philosophy—indeed, according to Strauss, in such a fashion as to offer a coherent and conscious alternative to philosophy, which is meanwhile aware of what philosophy claims and bases itself on.

Yet this is precisely the point, according to Maimonides as Strauss rediscovered him, at which Socratic philosophy and biblical religion join forces, however paradoxically it may seem: both believe in search for knowledge of *the* truth, and both believe that knowledge of *the* truth will guide man to the right way of life. Of course, "search" may signify very different things for the two discussants. However "formal" their mutual accord (since the "content" of the truth may also show a radical discord), it makes them different from other fundamental human alternatives, and brings them to a shared ground on which they stand together against most rivals in the realms of both philosophy and religion. As Strauss puts it in his comments on Genesis (which is formulated as a virtually Maimonidean thought), the "fundamental dualism" about the created world conceived by the Hebrew Bible is, as much as it was for the Greek philosophers, "intellectual" or "noetic." As a consequence, for both sources of the West, the world can only legitimately be seen in a cognitive light and must be explained "noetically."[16] Strauss recognized in this shared ground the reason why it was that Maimonides wished to defend philosophy at the court of the Hebrew Bible, which is certainly a stance different from anything known to modern thought. For, according to Strauss, Maimonides wished to show that these two alternatives to one another are not so opposed as both religious tradition and philosophic critics might have typically asserted: their common standard is truth. The tendency of philosophers to deny this convergence on the fundamental point is proof that "passions get the better of all sects, even of the philosophers."[17] If the religious tradition is not, in its very essence, opposed to the search for knowledge of the truth (whatever Genesis 1–3 might seem to imply on a superficial reading),[18] once established, this would allow the religious tradition to make legitimate use of philosophy for its own purposes, and in the limits set by the bold and pioneering thought of Maimonides.

Here Maimonides' advocacy in the court of religious tradition on behalf of philosophy was vindicated by an elementary scrutiny made by him from his youth: (premodern) philosophy and religion are in accord in the decisive respect, i.e., about both the oneness and the eternity of truth, which both name "God." And hence on the level of mind, they appear to at least start at or apply themselves to the same beginning point, and aim at or strive for the same end point, which is divine; they formally legitimate one another's pursuits in terms of a theology or metaphysics, even if the arcs they trace are not parallel. But it was especially the contrast with modern thought, aided by the focus on the medieval Maimonides, that had paradoxically allowed Strauss to perceive a uniquely shared commonality in the two sides of premodern Western thought. This unique perception held, whether the Western two-sidedness is viewed as a conversation between dialogue partners or as an argument between antagonists: they share a love of wisdom, which presupposes a shared love of truth, and their differences might be compared with the differences of jealous lovers who have to compete for the affections of the same woman.[19] I for one do not think that Strauss was fooling, or merely being rhetorical, in his saying that he wished us to consider the possibility of philosophy: he did not know, on his own standard of knowledge, whether this was a genuine possibility. But precisely because as human beings we want to know, and because our Western religious tradition also wants to know (or supports the desire for knowledge, so long as it is linked with God), their mutual dialogue and argument will be a fruitful one: they are both ways toward wisdom; and for us as the human beings we are, these and no other ways are possible.

The life in search of knowledge of the truth is, then, at least possible as either philosophy or revealed religion. Whether knowledge of the truth in any sense is impossible, which must be considered, seems to be grounded in the capacity to first dispose of both these persuasive claimants to know what is good for man. Strauss is of the opinion that every modern attempt to prove this ability to dispense with both, i.e., to refute both philosophy and revealed religion, has so far proved futile or vain. Both share the fundamental view that there cannot be access to the truth in its unity if it changes essentially with the changes of historical period or epoch: however variable its manifestation, and how much one must take account of history and give it its due as it makes a major impact on the form in which truth appears, even so *the* essential truth is unchangeable. This makes them jointly opposed to a certain side of modern thought that cherishes or elevates history as the only key to truth, compelling truth to remain subservient to history. But precisely with this fact stated as a definite tendency of modern thought, which allows a certain moment to history as a key to truth, it seems of even greater difficulty to justify Strauss's appeal to Maimonides, who put little stock in history as the source from which truth must be derived. Must not any worthwhile modern thought conceive of itself in historical, even if not historicist, terms? Yet with Strauss's aid in focusing on Maimonides' highlighting of the limits of history, which is still useful and which usefulness must be apprehended for its help with our modern beholdenness to history, it is possible for the modern scholar or reader to acknowledge that an adequate beginning point has now been located in the endeavor to discover a key to Maimonides' own thought, as a thought which provides us with an alternative to our current impasses: he doubts whether history is absolutely fundamental as the way toward man or being, even as he never doubts the usefulness, and in our era even imperative character, of history and its study in conducting the search. To be sure, Maimonides is certainly not as opposed to history as might at first appear from some of his statements, i.e., his notion of the origin of the biblical laws of sacrifice makes them depend on history and grounds them in its impermanent features and conditioned facts; and likewise he is fully aware of historical stages in the development of Judaism.[20] Yet even so, the truest nature of man as essentially ahistorical—i.e., as he who strives for virtue, and as he who is endowed with mind and who by nature has to use his mind—directs attention ultimately away from whatever ideas or forces may rule at the moment, however significant they may be, and toward those elements which seem to suggest a transcending of the historical flow in constant features of human beings as the beings who think. This is not just because of how Maimonides actually begins the *Guide* (1.1-2), i.e., with the notion that man is created in the image of God because he is endowed with intellect, which is also the key to human excellence. And likewise that is not only because he ends the *Guide* (3.54) with a concern with "wisdom," even if also with its equivocality. It is also because of that to which Maimonides points us as what we may always observe of human beings spontaneously and through history as the signs of their nature in its highest aspect (which defines it), and as not dependent on texts or reading,[21] i.e., their thinking or questioning, which directly results in their constant dealing with the problem of moral virtue. It is in and through this spontaneously generated "anthropological" evidence, by which human beings show themselves to be what they actually are, that we get a clue to Maimonides' most essential thought and how to approach it. This may also provide a clue to how to follow the logic of Strauss in unraveling the enigmas of Maimonides' often mystifying book, the *Guide*, since he regards its author as attempting to base himself on the evidence of what human beings are in every human and historical situation. Thus, Strauss seems to have proceeded on the following assumption: if Maimonides always respected and kept his mind closely focused on the particulars of human life in history, ultimately he searched beneath them for what is universal. And for Maimonides, this always reduced to the primary fact that human beings are thinking beings, which substantially determines what happens to them ("history"): do they choose to think or not to think?

FOUR

Untying the Literary Knots
Maimonides the Poet

THERE IS NO DOUBT THAT STRAUSS HIMSELF CHOSE A perplexing approach to the reading of Maimonides. Strauss judged Maimonides to be not just an unconventional thinker but also a teacher and writer who uses perplexity and concealment purposefully, and thus is not who he appears to be. But if this might have produced a condition of despair with regard to whether one can ever penetrate beneath the mask, then Strauss was not willing to declare the "true" Maimonides impenetrable. One must read him as if one is trying to crack a secret code, to decipher an ancient language, or to gather and put together clues so as to resolve a mystery. This is so much so, according to Strauss, that it imposes a duty to see Maimonides in an entirely different light, if his subtle purposes as a masterful author and skilled pedagogue are to be properly uncovered. But to make further sense of this assertion of radical difference, it is requisite that Strauss's own assumptions, which led him to his still-controversial approach, be considered. First things first: Strauss took an unprecedented "literary" approach to the *Guide* (as well as to some other of Maimonides' works). By doing so, he attempted to boldly disentangle himself from modern scholarly conventions and hermeneutical methods (which on one level can be reduced to "historicism"), as well as from any safely traditional or "orthodox" premises. Simultaneously he attempted to break through to the original intention of its author by an exploration of its peculiar composition, which was evident to any reader who had ever attempted even to peruse it, never mind to study it. Strauss also gave the benefit of the doubt to the author of the *Guide*, who had made the general compositional claim—spectacular and astounding on its own—that every single element in this book has been deliberately chosen, and assigned to its specific location for a conscious reason, with every element artfully related to every other element, even if they do not appear to be so related. In sum, everything in the book conforms to the complete, premeditated, and determined literary aims of its author. Maimonides definitively claimed, and Strauss tentatively accepted, that a book of this sort *can* be written, whatever it may require to probe such an author's work and the mind which composed it.

Thus, it is for Strauss no simple task to unravel the problematic character of Maimonides' thought, which was formulated so miscellaneously, which "scattered" its truths, and which concealed itself with trick knots. That elusive character is made worse rather than better by his abundantly complicated books, which deliberately render it difficult to unlock and enter this thought: his complex literary edifices and "ingenious devices"[1] are constructed so as to make it seem a mystery wrapped in a paradox concealed in a riddle. (Strauss was struck by the miscellaneous modes of his thinking in books: from the evidently supreme capacity for order which his *Mishneh Torah* manifests to the apparent literary deficiency and unavoidability of disorder in his *Guide*.) Note that this very insight about Maimonides' resourceful, versatile, and shrewd literary devices was almost at the very beginning of Strauss's comprehension: such artful construction (in whatever motives it might have been rooted) was deliberate, and it expresses a higher purpose on the level of human beings as they put in order their common life and moral-political affairs. In other words, the "motive" of Maimonides' craft as a writer operates on several related but differentiated and superimposed planes: the purpose of such seemingly disproportionate dissimulation is simultaneously political, pedagogical, artful, moral, and even theological. The key Strauss uncovered was aimed not to prejudge Maimonides in terms of modern thought, but rather to make him instead a potential guide to a premodern (if not ultimately ahistorical) wisdom. According to Strauss, our most fundamental question must remain What is truth?, and the effort to uncover Maimonides' obscure dialectic should never allow us to forget that he principally knew this: he aims, by building his books on such a locus of energy and motion in thinking, to keep us fully awake! But his dialectic is not so much a rejection of history (as our parenthetic comment on the ultimately ahistorical might seem to suggest) as it is an attempt to show the human pedagogy, the effort to elevate the soul, in which revealed religion as an organized teaching and law is primarily engaged and to which it is committed. Likewise, his books aim to educate and so to lead his reader gradually to the truth, once he has been made ready to receive it. Resort to history (as resembles the subtle dialectics employed by his books) only can justify itself as a relevant "method" in the pedagogy of truth, transcending immediate relevance: a timely mode needed to provide access to the timeless.

As also seems to have occurred to Strauss in his sudden perception of Maimonides' skill as an epic-dramatic teacher and poetical writer (in spite of his polemic against poetry), the need to remind ourselves of the fundamental issue compels us to often begin again and to constantly retrace our steps, since we are prone to forget what we are doing and why we are doing it.[2] Yet every modern scholar or reader who approaches a medieval thinker, or even an ancient thinker, must remember that he assumes (wittingly or unwittingly) a stance toward the possibility of philosophy in which his attitude toward knowing *the* truth as a human potentiality is encompassed. If remembered, this would force the modern scholarly approach to ground itself on an essentially philosophic approach, i.e., an approach in which eternal problems are acknowledged, and in which the question about the highest purpose of human life is raised, i.e., *Why* be a scholar? *Why* have the modern critical passion (and what is this saying about us that we entertain it)? *Why* pursue truth via historical scholarship?[3] Further, the modern scholarly approach, as philosophically grounded, would also need to make conscious (accepting or rejecting, explicitly or implicitly, with articulated and defensible reasons) its attitude toward the possibility of knowing *the* truth and conveying it poetically, as generally limited *solely* by what modern science or philosophy can know or claims to know. Strauss (to his surprise) uncovered in Maimonides a *medieval* scholar or scientist who did not neglect the study of history, although he may have muted his consideration of it, because only philosophy showed him the proper uses to which (in its critical capacity) it can be put, which was not entirely respectable among the medievals. He also fathomed that Maimonides, precisely as a scholar or scientist, had asked the fundamental question Why science? and had answered it in a compelling or coherent way. This was lacking, as he noted, even among most of those modern scholars who had made a study of Maimonides and yet who seemed to have a less adequate or more perplexed answer than Maimonides himself: once one reads him carefully enough and comprehends his thought in its original form, as Strauss further discovered, he paradoxically leads the one who is willing to be genuinely educated by him to ask "Maimonidean" questions of those contemporary scholars, as it were, turning the tables on them.

Strauss attempted to sustain an uncompromised autonomy of mind in the effort to drive as far as possible with criticism of the modern scholars of Maimonides, especially insofar as disallowing their premises had enabled him to discern what had not been noticed as it hid in plain view. Even if some might have faulted him for lapses in academic etiquette, he was never oblivious to the need to make his search consistent with scholarly propriety as regards rules of precise research and careful reading, which he always respected as an expression of intellectual honesty. For his most damning statement about his fellow scholars, which some might regard as a breach of academic etiquette, consider the following: "To recognize that a scholarly criticism of Maimonides is unreasonable is equivalent to progressing in the understanding of his thought."[4] The implication of this remark is that modern scholarly criticism tends to highlight almost the opposite of what is most significant in Maimonides' work. It would not be carrying this point too far to say that his advice to students is "whatever most modern scholars say, think the opposite about Maimonides." An example might perhaps be the tendency by most modern scholars to regard as literally intended Maimonides' criticism of certain arts or sciences, i.e., poetry on the one hand, history on the other. These scholars would next tend to proceed to criticize Maimonides (who is either exculpated or inculpated) for his medieval obtuseness (for which he is either blameworthy, or not to be blamed) to such elaborated modern forms as poetry and history, which have progressed so far since his era. Strauss also especially highlighted the modern scholarly tendency to put enormous emphasis on the doctrine of "negative theology" (in *Guide* 1.50–60) as the quintessence of the Maimonidean teaching, which led to the scholarly criticism that this is "unwittingly" contradicted (*Guide* 1.68, 72). But Strauss emphasized that if one reads the "negative theology" correctly, then one will not reach the views attributed to Maimonides by the modern scholars. Setting aside the exoteric-esoteric issue, Strauss noticed that this may not have been Maimonides' last theological word on speech about God, but only a primary position, even if permanently useful for some pedagogical purposes. Moreover, if whatever else in the *Guide* he may have subsequently explained about the divine is duly considered (i.e., the "positive" theology of God as divine mind), this may involve taking Maimonides at his word and giving him the benefit of the doubt that he may have actually deliberately contradicted himself. But as Strauss also stressed, if nothing else, Maimonides did this for plainly stated reasons which he expressed on the surface in order to make careful readers of his scholars, as well as to get them to think through the ultimate position toward which he was pointing.

To be sure, Strauss followed modern scholarly norms by laying emphasis on "exactness" and "intelligence" as the two main requirements for the proper reading of medieval philosophy, while he also was careful to define what he comprehended by those two key terms. In a passage of "The Literary Character of *The Guide of the Perplexed*," he made a statement in favor of precision and acumen that on this occasion speaks in praise of "micrology," i.e., the need to pay utmost attention, especially in a writer like Maimonides, to minute differences or slight variations in terminology, which one might otherwise dismiss as seemingly trivial: "There is, perhaps, no greater service that the historian can render to the philosopher of our time than to supply the latter with the materials necessary for the reconstruction of an adequate terminology. Consequently, the historian is likely to deprive himself of the greatest benefit which he can grant both to others and to himself, if he is ashamed to be a micrologist." Indeed, what impressed Strauss most in his first youthful encounter with Heidegger as a teacher about philosophy was his concentration on the precise and careful scholarly reading of a text. To be sure, in his subsequent encounters with Heidegger as a writer Strauss recognized that a sharp decline in the maintenance of this standard had occurred. His eventually "prophetic" reading of texts seemed to Strauss determined by a perverse and willful drive to prove predetermined results, such as the "forgetfulness of being," which allowed Heidegger to impose his view on an ancient writer like Plato. If philosophers (such as Heidegger) cannot or will not explicate a text with the proper historical approach that strives first to elucidate what an author actually intended, this being also to comprehend him as he comprehended himself, for Strauss there is an honorable duty which falls on the scholar to remind them how to do it.[5]

The additional point of this pressure on the modern scholars toward philosophic self-consciousness as mounted by Strauss is that the modern scholarly approach also assumes a (usually unstated) stance toward religion, one that might seem to make a decision in advance against its truth. But in point of fact, the modern scholarly approach of the future, once guided by Strauss in its reading of Maimonides, should at the very least have been persuaded to consider the claim of religion fairly and seriously, to assess its meaning conceptually as well as historically, and to value its adherence to the one truth. For the professed neutrality of the modern scholar, however critical, would not trouble religious tradition if it represented a genuine open-mindedness to all claims to truth—a "freedom of mind" which Strauss believes Maimonides cherished as a virtue, and which helps to account for his poetic virtuosity as a writer. For the poet is closest to the philosopher in his ability to freely express himself in such a way as to make his every word and its arrangement or station significant, which he requires his careful or serious readers to grasp in order to raise them to his often hidden insights about the way things are, so that this grasp can aid them to consider what might transcend their historical situation. Indeed, Strauss curiously maintained that he encountered this genuine freedom of mind or open-mindedness with greater force, conviction, and frequency in studying medievals like Maimonides than he did among most of his modern scholarly contemporaries, whose minds had all too often closed around the unacknowledged dogmas of historicism.[6]

Further, Strauss challenged the modern scholar who wished to understand Maimonides, if he would study the thought of the past (and especially the medieval past) with historical accuracy, that he must especially to be open to the possibility of knowing *the* truth himself, such that this would transform his relation not just to the past, but also to the present. And thus he must, at the very least, be willing to consider the possibility that the thinker whom, or whose work, he studies knew and taught this truth, which may somehow have an overarching relation to, rather than be determined by, historical periods—thus allowing this perception to make an impact on his historical thinking. This willingness to consider such a possibility is something that will help him to acquire a rudimentary awareness of what philosophy is, certainly as Maimonides viewed it. Considering it at least possible to know *the* truth, the state of genuine open-mindedness, and the rudimentary awareness of what philosophy is, are besides everything else required if any modern endeavor to know is have integrity and be honest. Strauss was convinced that the modern scholars—whether, on the one hand, with regard to the fundamental significance of political philosophy in Maimonides,[7] which he concluded had been thoroughly misconceived by the modern historical approach, or whether, on the other hand, with regard to theology, religion, and law, on which topics, as a result of the previously mentioned error, he perceived most serious misdirections and misperceptions to have occurred—had not thought through consistently and clearly their fundamental premises about who Maimonides was as a thinker and teacher, and what he was doing as a writer who wrote as carefully and with as much literary economy as a great poet. This often enough made their work not wrong in the simple sense, but certainly of a "superficial" character.[8]

It was eventually his own direct encounter with Maimonides and his books, unmediated by the modern scholarly approach and its prejudices, which seems somehow to have awakened Strauss from the dogmatic slumber of historicism, to the needs and conditions by which one is genuinely enabled to know. I would venture to suggest that this very awakening, especially to the need for a "freedom of mind" which strives to be as perfect as is humanly possible, also determined how Strauss viewed Maimonides as a thinker. It helped alert Strauss to a deeper level of self-awareness, originality, and radicalism in Maimonides, who constituted himself first as a self-directed and autonomous thinker not dependent on tradition (even if he was subsequently to be able to defend tradition, and to do so adequately), than he had previously been able to conceive of in most premodern thought. For only such "freedom of mind"—as freedom from "prejudice in favor of contemporary thought, even of modern philosophy, of modern civilization, of modern science itself"—will allow us to take a premodern thinker like Maimonides seriously and to give his thought "the full benefit of the doubt." "Freedom of mind," once it is perceived as the very condition of thought (characteristic of the poet as much as of the philosopher), makes it possible to comprehend thought as an endeavor not grounded in or determined by historical situation. Instead, this again raises the *possibility* that thought can be transhistorical: the thinker (free in his own mind to think *any* thought) can redirect history, rather than it directing his thought, which amounts to putting thinkers at the mercy of history. To pursue the thought of Maimonides by beginning with anything other than this premise, or so Strauss asserted, is to close one's mind from the start to surprises about Maimonides' originality and depth as a great thinker and even poet, especially concerning the boldness and unconventionality of a mind able to stand over and above his own era, viewing things transhistorically, and as a result also being able to end one era and to begin another for Judaism: "from Moses to Moses."

In his voyage of rediscovery, searching for the true but forgotten Maimonides, Strauss was compelled to launch several critiques of the dominant alternate modern scholarly views, namely, those of Julius Guttmann, Isaac Husik, and Harry A. Wolfson.[9] In the critique of Guttmann, who expounded his account of medieval Jewish philosophy in *The Philosophy of Judaism* (1933), Strauss articulated a fundamental dictum of his own scholarly work: "There is no inquiry into the history of philosophy that is not at the same time also a *philosophic* inquiry."[10] This is a key sentence that by itself offers a highly significant clue to unlocking Strauss's own perplexing explications of basic texts in medieval philosophy, for which he employed a quite unconventional scholarly historical approach. This eventually, but not only or at the first, manifested itself by perhaps the most eccentric or irregular feature of his approach to the great thinkers who wrote great books, i.e., bringing to light the literary consequences and conceptual issues that follow from the exoteric-esoteric divide, which makes itself evident among those select human beings who alone can obtain access to those most difficult truths. To Strauss, the great medieval philosophic books are not just archaeological relics appealing to the antiquarian impulses or romantic urges in the modern student of history, but are the best access we possess to the minds of great philosophic thinkers. In other words, these "old books" are our best access to the highest truths and the deepest thoughts of the greatest minds, irrespective of historical era. According to Strauss, the reason to explicate these medieval texts is to learn *from* them, and not just to learn *about* them—although to properly learn *from* them, we must first determine with historical exactness both what they actually said and what they actually intended by what they said.

However, perhaps most critical about this effort to rediscover such medievals as Maimonides (or Farabi) is that they may lead us toward a "new thinking," or at least a form of thinking which has been lost to us in our modern era. We must study medieval thought as it actually was, but in the process—if this is done correctly—we must consider the possibility, he curiously asserted, that we can also learn things we almost certainly are not likely to learn from any modern (i.e., post-Kantian) thought. Hence, our highest purpose in studying medieval philosophic books must be to engage in a living dialogue with their authors as some of the rare great minds (who did not share seemingly self-evident modern premises), which can be encountered by us through the good fortune of possessing their books. But we can only do so by allowing ourselves to become their students, by sitting at their feet, as it were, i.e., by learning to read their books again with fresh eyes, and so to hear the unfamiliar things they may teach us (whether or not we accept their arguments), in order to see again some of those truths whose light may have been made obscure to us precisely by the advance of modern thought, which cast them in the shade as supposedly works of scientifically obsolete, religiously dogmatic, and politically authoritarian thought. For modern thought arose and established itself precisely by its fight against medieval thought, however great it might have judged those premodern minds to be, which in its primarily polemical character tends to distort or even caricature the originality, freedom, and boldness of its opponents, who may not have been quite so obsolete, dogmatic, and authoritarian as we have been taught to believe they were.

Yet it may be asked: why is our modern or even our contemporary thought not sufficient, according to Strauss? Did it not encompass in a great historical sifting, in its accumulated wisdom of the past, the best (or the most worthwhile) of everything which has been transmitted to us from the past? Is it not based on a decisive progress beyond medieval thought (which progress is summarized in the form of modern science and modern politics),[11] so that whatever is needed has been preserved in our modern thought, and whatever is superfluous or obsolete has been jettisoned by the steady, if occasionally unpredictable, progress of modern thought? Even if we once wanted to conceive of modern thought as rightly superior in every respect to the thought of the past, it is not so clear that this can be done any longer: rare indeed is the contemporary thinker, philosopher, scientist, or even artist who assumes this sort of once-dominant attitude toward modern thought. For good or for ill, its problematic features have become too evident to ignore even by its friends (probably still many of the natural scientists, and a few remaining historical scholars), for whom it has become questionable. Of course, this unconditional defense of the modern, grounded in irreversible progress, can only be entertained to be the case if it has been demonstrated that the selection made by the moderns from the thought of the past was always lucid, judicious, unprejudiced, and proven. And likewise this can only be entertained to be the case if it has also been demonstrated that we have achieved such dramatic progress in the most essential matters pertaining to human beings and human life as to render medieval thought fully surpassed, and yet meanwhile truly and justly absorbed. If these things are no longer evidently the case, then there may also be eminently good reasons that make it clearer why we may need to reconsider the medievals. And the chief cause for this need of reconsidering the medievals, concealed beneath those obvious reasons, may not be so far removed from us precisely as moderns: it is quite likely to be rooted in the very excellence of modern thought, which was the clearing away of the prejudices of the mind. In a youthful review, Strauss already spoke about "*the* modern prejudice," which can be abandoned with no loss of intellectual honesty; indeed, it may have to be renounced just in order to free the mind for thinking even modern thoughts. This modern "prejudice" is, according to Strauss, the view that *the* truth was not already discovered and known in the past, but had to wait for modernity until it was at last brought to light.[12]

Thus, from the modern prejudice we are led directly to the subsidiary reasons for our continued need of the medievals in Strauss's mind, but one reason to be sure precedes every other: paradoxically to move further in the direction of the specifically modern mission or task, i.e., in order to free the mind from every prejudice, at the very least what we need is to free it also of even modern prejudices. Of course, if Strauss also wished as he put it to "awaken a prejudice in favor of . . . Maimonides," it would appear he was not as opposed to every "prejudice," as the moderns claimed to be. Indeed, once Strauss was putting together *Philosophy and Law* (1935), he seems to have recognized that this term is ambiguous, and yet is simultaneously mandatory. While according to modern thought, everyone who adheres to any notion which is "prescientific" is relying on "prejudice," Strauss instead seems to have equated the "prescientific" with opinion, an elementary form of genuine knowledge or quasi knowledge, used by the ancients and medievals so as to ground an unavoidable and also advantageous aspect resident in the searching mind. To be sure, from *Spinoza's Critique of Religion* (1928) on, Strauss was aware of the problematic nature of the modern notion of "prejudice" and wished to raise questions about its continued usefulness: prejudice is "the most appropriate expression for the dominant theme of the Enlightenment movement, for the will to free, open-minded investigation," and it is also "the unambiguous polemical correlate of the all too ambiguous term 'freedom.'" Yet the modern Enlightenment, as he perceived, attempted to substitute one set of prejudices for another. It also "never in fact completely freed itself from the very prejudices" which it embarked on its mission to eradicate. As a result, Strauss urged a gradual shift toward "opinion" as a truer, better, and fairer notion of what "prejudice" aims to represent (if it wishes to escape from being polemical). As such, opinion is the basic unifying element in what constitutes any human society, since it represents the grounding ideas (high and low) about which everyone shares the same view. In the "postmodern" era in which the thought of Nietzsche and Heidegger rules the Western mind, so that even science is doubted as true knowledge, *all* views, no matter how rational or seemingly self-evident, have been remade as "prejudices." This reconfigures even "truth" itself as whatever has been imposed by the greatest (spiritual) power, this being enforced through will, whether refined or crude. Consequently, it was enough for Strauss to get readers to consider that a favorable view of Maimonides is plausible again, which would at least make it one of the respectable or tolerated "prejudices." If Strauss entertained a higher hope, it was that this plausible view associated with Maimonides would help lead beyond the defective contemporary notion (i.e., of all views as being equal to one another) to the sounder notion of some views being truer, better, and fairer than other views, which it is in fact possible to know at least as a point of departure in the search for truth.[13]

However, it is possible to justify doing so because philosophy (as to its essential and original motive) is grounded in the love of truth rather than in the abolition of prejudice: Maimonides dedicated himself to the love of truth even in his conviction that this must occasionally be concealed insofar as it is presented "between the lines," abolishing prejudice only in a subtle fashion not of use to everyone. For if hearing the truth might harm some readers during any historical era, as a doctor of the soul Maimonides wrote so as not to cause harm in the unsuitable who might happen to read his books, become enraged, and make themselves an enemy at war against his enlightening project. Yet in spite of this conscious protection of the sort of reader who might wrongly get hold of his book, Strauss believed that Maimonides never compromised the truth as he comprehended it: he communicated it in its pure form to those who truly need it; he did not ever deny them what they need. It is at this point that it is helpful to recall the Maimonidean passage used as the central epigraph to the present book.

> I am the man who when the concern pressed him and his way was straitened and he could find no other device by which to teach a demonstrated truth other than by giving satisfaction to a single virtuous man while displeasing ten thousand ignoramuses—I am he who prefers to address that single man by himself, and I do not heed the blame of those many creatures. For I claim to liberate that virtuous one from that into which he has sunk, and I shall guide him in his perplexity until he becomes perfect and he finds rest.

True, his aim is to satisfy the "single virtuous man" irrespective of whether it "displeases ten thousand ignoramuses," and to "liberate" him from the spiritual misery of perplexity in which he is enmeshed, thus leading him toward "perfection" and a certain sort of rest. However, as is also made unambiguously plain, Maimonides can only so guide the perplexed by teaching him a "demonstrated truth," signifying that this "truth" has been put to the test through the most rigorous standards maintained by philosophy and science. Thus, an inextricable link binds together the medical or therapeutic aim of healing the doubt-sick soul with knowledge of the truth in mind and heart.[14] And thus Maimonides also assumed, as Strauss began to perceive, that these same "single virtuous ones" for whom he wrote should be able to penetrate his substantial literary defenses, should be able to handle the truth once he has prepared them to receive it, and should be able to help society to absorb the truth (in part, even if never in whole) and to advance ever closer to it. He educated the educators, himself instructing them by example how to digest the truth properly, how to accept the radical moderately, how the intellectually excellent should convey it imaginatively, and how those few should conduct themselves in a seemly fashion among those many who do not possess the cultivated need for knowledge of the truth. But he made them work for it: they must become diligent students or careful readers. This eventually was a strategy Strauss himself adopted, especially in his last essays, which seem to imitate much of the circuitousness and even evasiveness characteristic of what Strauss discerned in Maimonides.

~ FIVE ~

Why the Moderns Need the Medievals

ONE OF THE PRIMARY CONTRIBUTIONS MADE BY LEO Strauss to the study of philosophy is his keen observation that modern thought, in its rush to distance itself from the past, lost sight of a definite wisdom, and certain essential human lessons connected with this wisdom, that it can only reacquire by careful, critical study of medieval philosophic thought. His scholarly work reflects an effort to act on this observation and on the imperative that it seemed to imply, i.e., to recover what has been lost. It was also his view that this lost wisdom received its most brilliant expression in Maimonides' *The Guide of the Perplexed*, and that it is possible to recover this wisdom by both careful explication of the text and by intelligent effort of thought. This venture in recovery may at least ultimately, even if not immediately, make it possible to reappropriate those truths still present in medieval philosophic thought that, in their absence, may have led modern thought to certain perilous impasses, if not almost fatal crises, which it cannot seem to resolve or do away with from its own philosophic resources. In addition to this preliminary premise calling for fresh interpretation, Strauss provides three subsidiary reasons for the continued need to recur to the medievals, and especially to Maimonides. With respect to Strauss's far-reaching argument about recovering a lost wisdom, to be sure, this is *never* advice that we swallow the medievals complete or try to make everything of what is in their books our own, and so much of it must undoubtedly be cast aside. Rather, it is only a suggestion for us to search in the works of the greatest medieval thinkers so as to appropriate principally a lasting but lost human wisdom, once it has been isolated. Thus, the first reason to consider the medievals again: there may be things they knew which we should know for theoretical reasons and still need to know for practical reasons, especially pertaining to man, but which we cannot get from any other available modern or even contemporary source. As it would then seem, our modern or even contemporary thought has forgotten or obscured certain needful things, especially about the human situation or human nature. The sort of things to which Strauss pointed was (again) especially concerned with aspects of the nature of man as a thinking being in his connection with society. Society will naturally not focus as much on how significant thought is for man, other than on how it may be useful for society.

However, Maimonides, precisely because he mastered the literary art so as to better communicate his thought, taught Strauss to think about the responsibility of the thinker in his capacity as teacher, especially as it unfolds with respect to the following issues: What are the requirements of the life of the mind which define the impact it makes on the sphere of the individual human being, such as to know why it is pursued and whether a thinker can also be a good citizen, on the one hand, or a man of resolute faith, on the other? Is it possible to justify the life of thought in terms of how it serves the collective good, and can it account for itself by a self-awareness conveying properly what it consists in and showing its harmony with vital religious law or faith as well as with orderly political life? What are the ways and contours of the human soul in its search for the mindful life: is the life of the mind such as to transform the situation of man in a single, definite direction, with this further suggesting that the thinking man is of one type aiming at his own specific end, which may at least in certain cases even oppose what is significant and ultimate in the life of other human beings? How must one view oneself as a thinking human being in terms of one's personal or moral relations with other human beings: is one to establish relations primarily with those who think, or is one to disregard thinking as a moral criterion because a comprehensive or higher moral law rules everyone? What specific requirements are imposed by the moral life, what are the divergent claims of the life of thought, and what in general are the unresolved tensions between them: is man as thinker compelled to act, speak, or write in a different manner from how he otherwise might (and how far is one to carry it) if he remains unaware of these tensions, so as to avoid fatal conflicts with the moral and religious life and with those who are limited to it?

Certainly one of the themes that runs like a leitmotif through Strauss's mature thought is a recognition of a consistent deficiency in modern philosophy: it is unable to justify and account for itself on the basis of modern thought alone with regard to what it is to be a human being. This is because it refuses to employ the intellectual life (in its love of wisdom) as a standard of human excellence in man, if not as man's preeminent natural perfection. From the very beginning to the most contemporary manifestations of modern thought, Strauss points to the fact that the modern thinkers repeatedly get themselves entangled in the same fundamental self-contradiction: they cannot account for themselves on the basis of their own principles, which are grounded in a constricted or reduced view of man. It seems that the modern thinkers, the children of Machiavelli, obscured this factor because they were driven by a certain "necessity." This was the need to separate man from revealed religion, which was viewed as a force that diminishes the potential for human greatness in the realm of action. However, as Strauss observed, this no longer holds, because their thought "no longer possesses the evidence which it possessed while their adversary was powerful." Judged on its extrinsic merits, i.e., by its need to combat an enemy of reason, modern thought seemed sound in the past; but in the present, it must "be judged entirely on its intrinsic merits." This requires that we highlight the forgotten but leading factor in human nature which modern thought deliberately obscured, because to remember it or to bring it to light would once have been viewed as lending aid and comfort to the enemy, i.e., to medieval political theology. Since that fortress held by their enemy was always judged by the modern thinkers to have been constructed on a ground cleared by Plato and Aristotle, and subsequently built on by their "students" Farabi and Maimonides (however critically the latter may have followed the former), they were all judged in their common philosophic thought as helping to support medieval political theology, if not being directly beholden to it. But this is a strategy that can no longer be maintained, since, according to Strauss, one can no longer afford to ignore the deficiency of modern thought about man (consistently and repeatedly manifesting itself) to which such a strategy led, however justly driven by "necessity" it once may have been. For not only has it led to the collapse of confidence in modern thought and even reason, but also through its efforts the possibility of philosophic thought itself has been made a matter of fundamental doubt through its last heir, radical historicism. The "powerful adversary" that had once produced the necessity impelling modern thought was of course Christianity as a dominant political force. To be sure, this might justly be generalized to embrace all orthodox revealed religion, although saying so is not aimed to obscure the specific features of Christianity as they aggravated the predicament in which the modern philosophers were caught, and hence occasioned the necessity constraining them. By seeming to favor "Jerusalem," it is not that Strauss even remotely counsels a return to medieval Christianity, or to any orthodox revealed religion, as a political force.

Instead, this speaking so noticeably in favor of orthodoxy was done by him so as to make the true nature of philosophy visible or distinguishable again, separate from the distorting visage that it was lent by its need to deal with the specifically medieval circumstances as this consequently led to the modern situation. Doing so may also allow the true face of revelation, at least as it presents itself in thinkers like Maimonides, to also show through again. Strauss was also struck forcefully by the numerous "modern" features he was able to discern in the thought of Maimonides (which provided a safeguard against medieval errors), even though Maimonides curiously did not commit the modern error of trying to obscure the rightly leading role played by mind in human nature. Indeed, Strauss was also impressed that Maimonides made sure to offer an explanation of man in this fashion which was sure-handedly grounded in what he maintained was sound biblical interpretation.[1]

Rethinking these aspects of the nature of man is something that modern thought tends to deny, because it believes it has a superior grasp of this, as it does of every other aspect of nature, and hence of human nature as one simple thing (which it can in any case remake at will), and because it tends not to think of the mind as in any permanent conflict or unadjustable tension with other aspects of man or of society, since no fixed hierarchy of the faculties in the soul prevails by nature. Thinking and society (or the moral life) are for modern thought in an ultimate harmony, at the very least tending toward the same goal. But something additional may be needed for a distinct overview, or at least a clearer understanding, of the larger human situation inasmuch as it pertains to the free mind, which must know how much freedom it needs in order to become what it is aimed to be: might human society be much smaller than it seems, once thinkers permit themselves (as they need to do if they are to think) to render dubious those things held dearest and holiest by most fellow citizens? Thus, the study of a medieval like Maimonides—who is acutely aware of the impact his words and thoughts can make on those he can reach and whom he wants to teach, *and* on those he cannot reach and who will never apprehend his purposes, although he might temper their passions and imagination—might awaken the need for a rethinking of what limits those who think, and who speak or write their thoughts, might want to freely impose on themselves as reasonable precautions. This is especially the case if we relate such considerations to our modern historical experience: it is the case that modern thinkers have not always been very attentive to the political impact made by the free expression of their intellect; as a result, they must bear responsibility (in certain cases, very great: Heidegger vis-à-vis Hitler and Nazi Germany) for the spread of confused minds, the social chaos which ensues, and the destructiveness which issues from harmful movements animated by their ideas. This suggests that we might be able to use instruction from some such older source (like Maimonides' *Guide*) beyond ourselves which represents a deeper thinking about these issues still besetting us and on which we are not much accustomed to reflect. A source like the *Guide* stands at an ample distance from us, insofar as it might allow us to view ourselves and our newer ideas with greater balance, offering us perspective on and disengagement from our current passions, so as perhaps to avoid the grave errors all too frequently made and sadly often repeated by our modern politics, religion, and morality. This is to further suggest about Maimonides what Strauss in the name of Lessing suggested about the ancients: it is neither unreasonable nor perverse to consider it possible that he, looking with his eagle eyes, may have seen better, further, even deeper than us, however voluminous our modern eyes.[2]

The second reason to consider why we might have continued need of the medievals in our modern condition is the imperative to achieve independence of mind, one of the crucial elements of the philosophic life, or even of the life of those who love to think. Indeed, even in modern thought it has been cultivated since the start as a specifically modern virtue (set in stark contrast with the supposed vices of medieval thought).[3] But looking at the course of modern thought, Strauss thought it more than merely a likely drift—at least as he sees it, it is close to a simple fact, based on what had to be established in the wake of its victory—that with the "progress" and eventual victory of modern thought, this virtue has been gradually less emphasized and eventually dropped, if one refuses to treat the phrase "independence of mind" as merely appearing on the surface different from others. Curiously, it might seem to stand at the opposite pole to the point emphasized in the first reason previously discussed, i.e., the need of intellect to accept limits on its absolute freedom. However, that limit on freedom was most emphatically put in terms of expression, and not of thought; this stresses the need to preserve, as an absolute right, thinking in the privacy of one's own mind, whether one ever makes the thought fully public. (Strauss emphasizes even the astonishingly bold Spinoza's "caution.") In order to free oneself from the prejudices of one's own time and to strive for a timeless—or at least not so time-bound—perspective, one needs a solid ground and a high prospect which allows one to stand free of the most sacrosanct current dogmas and their blinders. The best medieval thought (in contrast with our modern image of it) can actually help one to think for oneself about all substantial matters because (with thinkers like Maimonides) it ventured to condense things thoughtfully to their essences. Or to pursue the same point in a slightly different direction, the best medieval thinkers ventured to consider *all* significant things, because they strove to contain in the realm of their thought a deep and encompassing knowledge, on the model of Aristotle, even if they were only able to reach such comprehensive knowledge by their effort at "correcting" Aristotle.[4] While our studying medieval thinkers like Maimonides is not in order to be bound to accept everything they teach, they not only provide us with a certain distance on ourselves which offers a potential to attain an autonomy from the present, but they also teach us how to fully use the freedom of our minds to interest ourselves in the most expansive focus, and they also serve as a model for thinking through the issues with the greatest possible clarity, thoroughness, and completeness.

To be sure, Strauss maintained that the ancients afford the same advantage to us, and especially but not only the teachings of Plato and Aristotle, which we also need to reappropriate or begin again to apprehend with a fresh view. ("Not only" because he unconventionally counted among the most worthy ancients such thinkers as the moderns prior to him tended to dismiss: Thucydides, Aristophanes, and Xenophon.) If it is not the proper moment to append anything additional about this aspect of his thought, because it is not the focus of the present discussion, it is still at least to be noted that this shows the astounding breadth and ambition of Strauss's own mind, which did not call to revive study of the medievals because it was merely rooted in romanticism, reaction, or nostalgia, and which refused to limit itself by any category defined by the moderns and established as a convention as to who it is worthwhile or relevant to study. Strauss's unremittingly curious mind lived to discover any worthy thinker of the past from whom we might learn things to help us deal with the crisis of thought in the present. Thus, what is most crucial is what medieval thought strives for, not what it achieves, since the end for which it strives may illuminate something truer about human thinking and human life, which may well not otherwise be available to us from any of our modern conceptions of how scientifically encompassing or historically determined the human mind is. Studying the medievals can help us rectify the former thing, i.e., defined by what it strove for and not what it achieved; it may help us to free ourselves from the prejudices of our own time; and it may also properly do the latter thing, i.e., it may help us to better think for ourselves about all essential matters, and so rise to a freer mode (as in an ampler and farther vision) in the life of thinking. In other words, contrary to everything we have been taught to accept by modern thought about medieval thought at least since Spinoza (who made it his mission to deconstruct medievals like Maimonides, whom he convicted as guilty of limiting our vision and getting us mired in dogmatism), it better epitomizes the life of thought, the impulse and the imperative to thinking freely and courageously in the most trying of historical circumstances, which often stood directly against such freedom of thought. There is no sufficient reason, then, according to Strauss, provided by modern thought to reject out of hand, necessarily, and in principle, either the possibility of thinking which is not primarily historical or time bound (as the medievals were not, although they may have been sensitive to history) or the possibility of thinking about all things, as the great medieval thinkers teach us how to do (although their ambition of comprehensiveness need not have led them to claims of attaining it, as is best shown in a thinker like Maimonides who remained skeptical about what is genuine science in medieval physics and astronomy). The greatest medievals, as genuinely free minds, assumed both of these things were possible, but they (unlike the ancients) also shared with us our biblical tradition, even while their thinking may not (contrary to our modern prejudices) have been rooted in mere simple-minded belief, blind legal authority, or deaf dogmatic theology. For Strauss, they began their thinking with certain fundamental questions or unavoidable problems, which recur to the human mind irrespective of historical period, enlightened beliefs, or cognitive limits.

And then there is a third reason to consider for reflecting seriously on the medievals as our potential teachers, which is also certainly not irrelevant in the context of Strauss's resort to the study of Maimonides: Jewish concerns are also critical, substantial, and legitimate. To begin with and as is well known, Strauss concerned himself with what he regarded as the unresolved argument between reason and revelation, "Jerusalem and Athens," which unsettled tension he even judged the secret of the survival of Western civilization. He uncovered in Jerusalem (i.e., ancient Judaism as contained in or represented by the Hebrew Bible) the "most original" form of revelation, as did his predecessor Hermann Cohen. But even with his rejection of Cohen's moralistic quasi historicism, his consciousness of the need for history to recover its true teaching (disencumbered of tradition insofar as it might tend to view the true teaching through a distorting lens) did not permit him to slight originality as a prime determinant. Indeed, the original shape ("ancient Judaism") is also regarded by him as still the most fundamental form in which revelation continues to present itself, endowing it with perhaps the greatest profundity because fully self-conscious (while not apologetic toward "Athens," i.e., Greek philosophy), which is why subsequent revelations still had to be based on it.

Yet however much we might try to "return to the sources" and recover their original essence as fundamental form, in order to provide resources as aids to the present, the challenges faced by modern Judaism and Jews (as connected with previous tradition) remain recalcitrant, and this unabated recalcitrance reveals something significant, even fundamental, about the nature of modern reality. Jewish history suggests that formulas generated by modern, post-Kantian idealism with respect to "solutions" to the "Jewish problem," however noble and charitable their aims, may not be as sound, as plausible, or as simple as they at first appear, so as to allow modern Jews to rest their deepest hopes on these formulas and to make the building of future Jewish life dependent on those hopes. Perhaps the noblest and most charitable formulas are, for Strauss, still post-Kantian, i.e., liberal democracy and Zionism (insofar as these two formulas began with Spinoza but were "perfected" by neo-Kantian morality); as such, they have certainly enabled the Jews to achieve decent and self-respecting settlements which, however, are only fragmentary as well as often highly flawed solutions to the Jewish problem. Strauss maintained this unrelieved doubt about these two modern formulas, which were composed to help the Jews alleviate their suffering, even if he also recognized that they represent in their best aspects a definite sort of progress on a certain level with respect to elementary justice.

Indeed, following these flawed though still praiseworthy solutions to what Strauss named a seemingly "infinite" problem (represented by the hatred for Jews euphemistically named "anti-Semitism"), our modern or even contemporary Jewish thought may not be equal to meeting adequately the challenges of the 21st century. Is it possible that our medieval (especially Maimonidean) legacy may astonishingly approach some key theological and political matters, which still challenge us, with greater power, profundity, and comprehensiveness than our modern legacy has been able to do? Are at least some crucial modern Jewish questions occasionally better answered by this medieval Maimonidean tradition (such as the proper balance among noble participation in the life of politics, esteem for science or philosophy, and fidelity to a venerable religious tradition)? If this is the case, are we barred by loyalty to modernity itself, and by the undoubted and recognized blessings that this era has brought with it (albeit also while fraught with dilemmas), from the effort to probe for continued use the medieval depths of a thinker like Maimonides, who may offer us access to a forgotten wisdom of greater balance and deeper penetration, which we jettisoned or neglected because of those modern hopes? Had those modern hopes not projected a future for the Jews and Judaism as they were to be reconstituted on a diminished level, no longer to be determined by the eminent and majestic human considerations (as to aiming for the highest things) which a thinker like Maimonides still made the focus in his reflections on the Jewish situation in history and hence also on the political and theological situation for all human beings? Has not modern history proven those hopes in their most confident form—that this reduced Jewish type was to be somehow no longer susceptible or vulnerable to powerful, even if "irrational," hatred by keeping a low profile, and being made to resemble everyone else—to be unfeasible? If even a great modern philosopher, like the neo-Kantian Jewish thinker Hermann Cohen, recognized the claim that tradition makes about how wise Maimonides was (and Cohen even claimed to prefer the medieval Maimonides to the modern Spinoza, in terms of the depth of their thought), this got Strauss wondering. Might we not potentially derive from Maimonides lessons useful to our troubled situation, and better for dealing with the recurring and recalcitrant challenges which bedevil us as modern Jews, and indeed even plague us merely as modern men and women?

Thus, it should be clear that Strauss did not turn to Maimonides for traditional reasons. Indeed, he paradoxically turned to Maimonides because almost every aspect of tradition—Jewish, Christian, and modern Western—had been challenged if not rejected in the post-Nietzschean era. If the shattering of tradition meant that nothing previously valued could any longer be taken for granted, then this certainly embraced Maimonides' worth as a thinker, and he obviously could not be highly estimated merely because tradition exalted him. However, this also did not mean that Strauss was interested in Maimonides only because he was out of fashion with current thinking. To be sure, the question of tradition presented a unique challenge in Strauss's discernment of Maimonides. As has been previously stated, Strauss at first just happened to give consideration to Maimonides for reasons unrelated to tradition: he merely needed to assess the role a medieval predecessor played in the modern thought of Spinoza and Cohen. Yet what became evident to Strauss, very much to his surprise, was Maimonides' almost completely untraditional manner of reasoning for someone who embedded himself in the heart of tradition, which even if it struck most tradition-based readers, somehow did not impress itself forcefully on them. He was assumed to be a traditional thinker; Strauss perceived that this was not so.[5]

Reading Maimonides in an era of predominantly antitraditional (if not posttraditional) thought, Strauss uncovered this unorthodox reasoning in someone who almost everyone had assumed could not have been a truly open-minded thinker, since he was a defender of tradition, if not also an architect of "orthodoxy." Yet Strauss noticed just how free Maimonides was of the prevailing opinions (often called "prejudices") which tradition had furnished him with, and which paradoxically he often enough seemed to pronounce himself in favor of, but for unorthodox reasons. Indeed, Strauss was astounded to acknowledge how much Maimonides judged the opinions of tradition (both religious and philosophic) for himself: he confirmed them if he judged them true or useful, and he changed, ignored, or neutralized them if he judged them false or harmful. Reverence, though an attitude of mind characteristic of tradition that Maimonides was certainly able to appreciate as necessary for religious life and perhaps also for preliminary students in the search for truth, was not a sufficient basis on which to decide what was true and false. About this, one had to think entirely for oneself, and as Strauss discovered, Maimonides thought for himself with a vengeance. This point was made best by Gershom Scholem, a contemporary scholar who was a good friend of Strauss's, even though their stances toward Maimonides were almost diametrically opposed to each other. Consider the following unembellished statement by Scholem that might have been uttered by Strauss if he were in a rare mood of unguarded disclosure:

> I do not know whether in previous generations there were those who were impressed with the tremendous daring of this genius. In any event, Maimonides' daring in *Mishneh Torah* arouses astonishment from every possible angle. We all know that there is none as great as Maimonides, yet no one has explained in a satisfactory manner how Maimonides dared to establish as halakhic norms, in the name of Halakhah, things which have no basis whatsoever in any tradition of the fathers of the nation—neither in the Bible, nor in the Mishnah, not in the two Talmuds, nor in the Midrashim! Maimonides summarized the laws of the Fundaments of the Torah, regarding much of which one is astonished. The man had the gumption to write down certain things which seemed to him to be correct, on the basis of his study of the Gentile sages—Aristotle, Alfarabi, and there is no need to enumerate here all of his other sources—and converted them into halakhot. From whence did he draw this great courage, this tremendous daring, the like of which was unknown in the history of the Halakhah prior to himself? It was only in his generation that others began to follow in his footsteps and to say: if Maimonides was able to establish as law for future generations things for which there is no source in the Jewish tradition, so can we! And they began to preface their books

with chapters of halakhot, which likewise aroused infinite astonishment. Just as Maimonides had the daring to establish halakhot which had no basis in the tradition, he was no less daring when he came to reject those things with which he did not agree. Maimonides censored many things; moreover, he was successful in doing so, as many generations, including our own, have been raised upon the Maimonidean doctrine.[6]

Moreover, Strauss began to become aware of the fact that the way in which the Jewish tradition had viewed or valued Maimonides contained a hint, whether witting or unwitting, as to his fundamental unconventionality. For example, the tradition indicated its reverence for Maimonides by endowing him with the honorific title of "the great eagle," implying a view of him as one who achieved a higher view and could see further and with greater acuity than almost any other Jewish thinker. As such, he was brought close not only to Plato's ancient model of the philosopher-king but also to Nietzsche's modern model of the "superman": only a man of eagle-like capacity, who can fly completely over and above the tradition and hence can view it freely and so judge it in its totality, can properly set it in order. Further, the tradition boldly compared Maimonides to the biblical Moses with the use of the popular adage "From Moses to Moses, there is none like Moses." As Strauss recognized, tradition itself acknowledges that it is possible to conceive of an untraditional authority who is almost equal to Moses, and who by his unmatched attainments beyond tradition makes a continued life in tradition possible. This might also suggest that tradition needs a superlative thinker of entirely free mind like Maimonides in order to sustain itself, even though Maimonides unlike the biblical Moses was avowedly not "prophetically" sent by God. This might consequently even imply that the formation of a higher class of men like him is fully warranted.

To be sure, Strauss was scarcely trying to contend that Maimonides was opposed to tradition as it was constituted. Instead, he was interested in grasping what kept a tradition (Western and Jewish) vital, through reflecting on a figure like Maimonides. Yet what was Strauss aiming to achieve by his fairly blunt exposure of Maimonides as an untraditional thinker, since did this not at the very least seem to run against Maimonides' own tendency toward discretion? Although Maimonides was courageous, autonomous, and even eccentric with respect to traditional *ideas*, at the same time he was always careful to unfailingly appear conservative about traditional *actions*. But as Strauss wished to clarify, Maimonides never made the characteristic error of the conservative (for which Strauss paradoxically faults the liberal Cohen): though he was always careful to seem only to place himself in the line of tradition, he hinted at the need for change—even radical change—in order to preserve the tradition by the bold actions that he so often performed at the deeper level, which was missed by those who noticed only what was happening on the surface. Maimonides' conservative demeanor was a key to his success as a revolutionary. In other words, Strauss seems to claim by this revealing of secrets (which he emulated) that Maimonides knew what he himself was doing with his boldness and ultimately wanted its significance to be recognized as establishing a model to be imitated: "The typical mistake of the conservative . . . consists in concealing the fact that the continuous and changing tradition which he cherishes so greatly would never have come into being through conservatism, or without discontinuities, revolutions, and sacrileges committed at the beginning of the cherished tradition and at least silently repeated in its course."[7] Although Maimonides is not denying the need for occasional "discontinuities, revolutions, and sacrileges," he himself leaves the door open for someone like Spinoza, if he is not actually concerned to prognosticate and prepare him. To be sure, he may not have envisioned quite the actual Spinoza, the disciple of Machiavelli, but he knew that vital traditions require periodic disruptions, if not revolutions like the one he himself had brought about (however quiet and nonviolent it was), for the sake of their well-being. As Jefferson ventured about the American republic, "periodic revolution" is "a medicine necessary for the sound health of government." Discontinuity is needed for the sake of continuity; a wise tradition, like a wisely ordered state, will be so organized as to accommodate such "periodic revolutions." In other words, the political, philosophical, and pedagogical lesson which Strauss was trying to teach by his not-so-roundabout emphasis on Maimonides' radical freedom of mind, and which he was also careful to show as dialectically combined with fidelity or reverence toward tradition, is that tradition itself only remains vital if it allows for those who can think about tradition in an untraditional way, and hence who are capable of freeing themselves from tradition in their minds. This simultaneously allows them to determine what tradition needs in order to survive and how it must change in order to do so.

This dialectic undoubtedly caused Strauss to wonder what it might signify that by a "mighty hand"[8] Maimonides assumed the challenge of Plato and Farabi and made himself a sort of philosopher-king who untraditionally shapes a tradition. As Strauss seems to have concluded, a figure like Maimonides shows what is possible for the mind of man to achieve, who can both philosophize and legislate, and who can combine the two in a feat of literary artistry. It is likewise significant, Strauss seems to highlight, that this attainment occurred not only in the realm of thought (whether in the form imagined by Plato, Farabi, or Nietzsche), but also in historical actuality, which authenticates a genuine possibility about human nature. Indeed, for Strauss Maimonides shows something about human possibility not entirely dependent on direct divine action, which may well transcend historical eras: if this is what man may be and become in the realms of thought and action, Maimonides' achievement also provided Strauss with the impetus to rethink man, who may have to be considered beyond the limiting categories of modern thought on human nature. Indeed, this may well have been the achievement that Machiavelli tried to imitate and surpass.

To be sure, if Strauss considered Maimonides "a deeper thinker than Spinoza" even while he also seemed to concede that Maimonides may have granted a quasi or half blessing in anticipation to the Machiavellian revolution which Spinoza humanely if cynically helped to advance for the West and for Judaism, what is this saying about Strauss's ultimate judgment on the two men and their two modes of thought? To be the deeper thinker need not make one the wiser thinker about what is to be done at the moment and in the circumstances of history. And if both were wise, who was the wiser? Strauss grasped that they obtained a different result from thinking through how to most auspiciously harmonize political order and theological-moral teaching with philosophical wisdom. His appreciation of this difference suggested a proportionally greater practical wisdom relative to historical condition awarded to Spinoza—even if Maimonides curiously and perhaps paradoxically retains a greater theoretical depth as a thinker. Nevertheless, Strauss seemed to wonder in the spirit of Maimonides if the modern revolution was as thoughtful or fully judicious in its conception of human nature, even if in certain essential political respects it may represent a progress. Yet even if this wondering about these issues by Strauss was the case, it is not to deny that he also seemed to treat Maimonides and Spinoza as if they remain, on a certain level, somehow brothers-in-arms (even if often antagonistic ones): they were both committed unconditionally to the life of intellect as the specific excellence of man, and they both acted according to a shared philosophical policy toward nonthinkers (in the most comprehensive sense of the term) as in need of some concealment. These two general principles for both of them somehow transcend the modern and medieval—and even ancient—divide. They seem to have been, for both of them, permanent truths about human nature.

Strauss arrived on his own, and for curiously modern reasons, at this view of the still-vital thinking of the medievals. And once he had achieved it, he held to it tenaciously, even though some deemed it misguided in its key perception and claim, i.e., of Maimonides as somehow a wiser or deeper thinker than Spinoza. This view did aim to imply that Spinoza was not as great a thinker as Maimonides; however, it did not aim to imply that Spinoza was not a great thinker in his own way, even if as a judgment this ranked him beneath Maimonides, by reason of their respective *philosophic* thinking evident in their books. To be sure, Strauss's view was neither an idealized prospect on the medieval thinkers nor a romanticism about the medieval historical era, but rather was based on a sense precisely that some of the great minds who appeared in this phase of human thought had had a better grip on reality than some leading thinkers who appeared in the modern era and presently dominate it, whether through their own thought or their direct heirs. Strauss's tenaciously held, favorable view of selected medieval thinkers presupposes that the scholarly search for historical truth subserves the search of the free mind for the philosophic truth, and so the former must also remain subordinate, or "ministerial," as Strauss puts it, to the latter.[9] And yet in order to be properly "ministerial" to these thinkers and to the great books that they composed, the first duty of the truly free mind in a modern context is, according to Strauss, to be a disciplined historical scholar.

Strauss, speaking only of his *experience* as a reader, and not of any system or method, says it is marked by what he calls the "irretrievably 'occasional' character" of every good interpretation. But Strauss also speaks of what one might call the responsibility of the reader, which is to assume the right attitude or stance toward a great book by a great thinker, and (as already noted) he defines this attitude or stance as that of being "ministerial to the text": the proper function of the interpreter in the reading of great books is to become the vehicle for expressing "the thought of someone else as he meant it," and so to help readers to judge for themselves. It assumes that it is possible to fully grasp and to accurately articulate what an author of the past essentially intended to express in his book. As this also seems to imply, it is not an unavoidable thing for a reader in the present to distort the significance of a book from the past: if one's mind is free, one is not compelled by history or by any other extraneous force to make the book conform with one's own views as determined by one's historical period or philosophic situation. To have such a reverent attitude toward the composed text and its writer, which is almost a moral stance, is not to impose on the reader any duty to suspend or deny his critical faculties. Rather, it requires the reader to presuppose, at the deepest level, that the author and his book may be wiser than the reader, even if this wisdom is not evident to him immediately on the surface: the reader's highest responsibility is to bring to light the wisdom, the thought, or the teaching which may not be evident, but of which the reader may possess the greatest need, especially if the author is one of the great minds. This capacity to precisely know and say what a past thinker thought is only attainable if one's own mind is at least open to the possibility that the author as a great mind through his great book may potentially teach *the* truth. For by such ministerial reading, it must at least be considered possible by the reader that this author possesses what Strauss calls *the* "adequate or complete" view, i.e., *the* true view, of the most essential things, although not necessarily of everything. Hence, such a ministerial stance or attitude will help the reader to reach a comprehension of what the author himself actually thought, even if he may not have articulated this in such a way that the reader is able to immediately grasp it. What makes a ministerial reading excellent is if it brings to light most intelligently the substantial contents of the original teaching, however hidden. Strauss seems only to assume truths of the mind about man and the world, which, however difficult of access and of recovery, are constant and permanent and hence at least potentially on the deepest level beyond being limited to any specific time and place. Consider also a different working set of rules for reading with which Strauss contrasts his own approach, i.e., the purely historical hermeneutic principle of Spinoza in the *Theologico-Political Treatise*. This critical hermeneutic principle may be juxtaposed with Strauss's own historical principle, according to which one strives to recover and to accurately restate as exactly and intelligently as possible what a past author originally meant. In the approach of Spinoza, the meaning of a historical book, and especially of *the* book, i.e., the Bible, is determined solely by what it teaches consistently on its surface, in the context of its historical era (at least for every book which is not geometrically demonstrated); if the surface is not consistent, it is safe to assume that this book teaches nothing at all on the topic that is so variously discussed. Although Strauss recognizes a certain similarity between "the two principles," and especially their common seriousness about the surface, for him "the difference between [them] is fundamental." Applying in action his different principle of reading in a study of the Book of Genesis, Strauss shows how it is possible to likewise historically read the same book which is the focus of Spinoza, i.e., the Hebrew Bible, and to similarly dwell on the surface. But then he reaches entirely different results about the "mind" which produced it, about the consistent teaching in it, and about its teaching as *not* so much limited as to the possibility of thought by the historical era in which it was formed and the context from which it emerged.

Thus, the previously mentioned contradiction between the ministerial duty toward the text and proper historical discipline, as a charge which Spinoza and his biblical-critical heirs might level against Strauss's approach, is only an apparent contradiction. This paradoxical aspect seems to arise because the first duty of the modern scholar is to understand these books and their authors as accurately and correctly as possible, trying to explicate those texts and writers by interpreting their teaching with historical exactness. However, Strauss also wished us to apprehend that the essentially transhistorical teaching to which such authors aspired may have been lost due to modern polemics against its medieval character (while, as great thinkers, their self-conscious "historical situatedness" may actually constitute a surface phenomenon only), as if this relegated them to an imperative desuetude. Merely by uncovering and grasping what their authors intended, seen in light of what they expressed, the properly oriented historical scholar helps to recover the full challenge of these books to the modern perspective. The historical scholar thus performs his highest service to the life of thought and of the human mind by his interpreting the past thinker and what he actually thought as exactly as possible, i.e., free also of contemporary prejudice, however sacrosanct. But as Strauss also adds most provocatively, the historical scholar may need to become a philosopher in order to do so properly. However, even if the scholar is unable to become a philosopher himself, in most cases the philosopher will be the beneficiary of these scholarly efforts, i.e., he will be helped to know and to approach closer through them what past thinkers actually thought, and he will employ those results for his own purposes. These purposes will be determined by the requirements of independent thought, which (to state it again) is at least potentially "transcendent" of history for anyone who has not surrendered his mind to a dogmatic historicism. In other words, however much the thinker and the form of his thought whether medieval or modern are, as Strauss never forgets, fully situated in history, as great thinkers or great minds they need not be *assumed* to be fully products of history.

The historical approach is essential for us because of the obstacles to comprehending the medievals properly, obstacles of mind which have been set up precisely by our predecessors who established the modern perspective. They needed to obscure the true teaching and thought of the medievals in order to lay down the law by which the modern perspective was to be made authoritative, which is not a task to be too readily dismissed as unworthy.[10] What Strauss's historical approach compels us to do, however, is to try to get beyond these obstacles of mind, to make the requisite effort to comprehend the medievals again as they comprehended themselves, not as the modern perspective comprehended them, which tends to still obscure them for us, ever keeping in mind the continued need for the reiteration of the modern perspective (if only so as to make sense of its "prejudice" about the medievals), even if it is seemingly passé, since its purposes have been achieved and its standpoint is triumphant. Similarly, even these medieval books and their authors, according to Strauss, did not achieve what they did in the realm of thought by disregarding their own historical context, or their "hermeneutic situation," which contemporary historicist thought (both radical and moderate) would prefer to lay as its major charge against the medievals. Rather, he believes (in contrast with modern "prejudice" against them) that they comprehended their "hermeneutic situation" deeply, clearly, and thoroughly, and it was precisely this comprehension of their historical situation which enabled them to respond properly to it, and to move through it and beyond it, to a view that is higher than this historical situation. In other words, precisely because and only because they could comprehend the essential contours of their own situation (both hermeneutical and historical) deeply, clearly, and thoroughly, could they as "free minds" move beyond it properly in the realm of thought. Hence, what makes our modern view dubious is the claim that we can comprehend their historical context, or "hermeneutic situation," better than the great writers of the past comprehended it themselves. This claim is grounded in one hidden but precarious premise, i.e., of historical progress as decisive in the realm of thought (although progress may, Strauss admits, be true in other aspects of human life), while tacitly denying the transhistorical truth on which progress would have to be made dependent, since it has to be measured against a truth which is firmer than mere historical movement.

In order to comprehend how Strauss came to regard the work of Machiavelli and his successors and how this work laid the groundwork for modern thought, one must compare and contrast Strauss's ideas with those of Francis Bacon, whose "idols of the mind" encompass four classes of "idols" that, according to Bacon, needed to be rejected at the beginning of modernity. As this suggests, modernity is an all-encompassing philosophic effort to go against every standing conception of man, political order, systematic theology, and nature, done in the spirit of a religious reform (cleaning away the "idols"). Jean Bodin, Bacon's predecessor, also attempted to "humanize" Machiavellianism in order to adapt and modify his thought and criticism of the biblical worldview (and even to purge it of "demons") so as to make it somehow compatible with the biblical ethos. Is this sudden currency of this "idol" (or "demon") metaphor an indication of a change of mind, in which a tendency of philosophers to view nature as potentially directed or stage-managed by man receives expression? As Bacon admits, what moved him to delineate the idols in their four classes was not unrelated to the need to substitute a newer (better) set of idols for an older (worse) set of idols. Thus, consider the following (aphorism 35): "It was said by Borgia of the expedition of the French into Italy, that they came with chalk in their hands to mark out their lodgings, not with arms to force their way in. I in like manner would have my doctrine enter quietly into the minds that are fit and capable of receiving it; for confutations cannot be employed when the difference is upon first principles and very notions, and even upon forms of demonstration."[11] This appears to imply that, for Bacon, a certain sort of "idol" seems to be required in human life and by the human mind, since "first principles and very notions," as well as "forms of demonstration," cannot be decided finally by fully scientific proof (as Aristotle previously admitted).[12] As it would seem, it is merely a choice of better or worse "idols" about the highest things, which as it happens is not so different from Aristophanean gods as "clouds" to which the poets assign a defined character. These Baconian "idols" are something between Platonic-Aristotelian "opinions" and Cartesian-Spinozistic "prejudices," but much closer to the latter than to the former. Since he apparently lends as much weight to empirical method as to mathematics, he is not in full accord with Descartes and Spinoza, who subsequent to Bacon assigned a more or less complete priority to geometry as the principal key which can best unlock the mysteries of nature through philosophy and science. In a centuries-later attempt to correct the earlier thinker, Hans-Georg Gadamer claimed, proceeding from radical historicism in *Truth and Method*, that a "fusion of horizons" between the ancient (or medieval) view and the modern view is accomplished through his hermeneutic. These are not new "idols" to confute the old, as Bacon postulated, but this "fusion of horizons" is a sort of philosophic syncretism, which is as Gadamer further claims unwittingly accepted even by Strauss in the form of the necessity for an ancient-medieval-modern "fusion of historical and philosophical questions" in contemporary thought. Rejecting as the proper escape from our modern dilemmas this "fusion" and what it seems to imply for the conception of and approach to past thought that he elaborated, Strauss responded to Gadamer on two fronts. On the one hand, according to Strauss, Gadamer's "fusion of horizons" relativizes the truth; on the other, the "fusion" amounts to redirecting (wittingly or unwittingly) the premoderns toward modern truth, which Gadamer unwittingly assumes has progressed beyond its predecessor.

Strauss criticized the tendency of Gadamer (as he likewise criticized Franz Rosenzweig) to charge medievals like Maimonides with deficient "subjectivity," which is to imply a fatal lack of self-consciousness about the historical situation in which they lived. Such historicist criticism (whether moderate or radical) of Maimonides and the medievals sees and judges them in light of the most modern thought, rather than trying to grasp them on their own nonhistoricist terms, such as to allow them to offer a teaching from which modern thought might learn something, and which indeed it might benefit it to consider. If in this historicist criticism Maimonides and his fellow medieval thinkers are faulted for being deficiently aware of history, that deficiency is coordinated or parallel with their lack of genuine science: they are faulted because they cannot perceive truth in its *pure* objectivity, as modern science claims to know it. But such claims for modern science, which historicism in any case tends to reject, have to be limited even by thinkers who estimate human reason highly; Strauss notes that this is a so far unattainable (although a thoroughly commendable) goal. In fact, it has never been achieved by the moderns, never mind by the medievals. In other words, science and history as the two mainstays of modern philosophy are not so completely or so certainly grounded in knowledge as we once believed they were. As a result, Strauss recommends studying the medievals for a wisdom which they can teach us, and which we cannot so readily obtain from modern thought.[13]

Once the mere *possibility* of obtaining access to the transhistorical truth as something potentially knowable has been lost, forgotten, or obscured, the search of the free mind for philosophic truth begins to wither and disappear. He believed that the solution offered by Nietzsche as well as his postmodern philosophic and scholarly heirs to the radical historicist problem is self-defeating. They endeavor to deny truth as possessing any eternal aspect, because it seems to support revealed religion *and* modern Enlightenment. As a result, they assert historicity as victorious, through either a prophetic envisioning of a future fulfillment or letting great if fantastic hopes rest in the myth of the eternal return. They thus attempt to revive philosophy as truth beyond modernity by subverting it as ultimately a search for truth, and allow it instead to remain primarily an ultramodern effort to change the world or remake human nature. This, according to Strauss, is the case in the present, the sign of which is that the scholarly search for historical truth of the actual facts (never to be slighted as "mere" facts) has been elevated in significance to an even greater height than the possible transhistorical truth contained in those facts. But the modern scholarly search on its own, if appropriately conducted and pursued in the contemporary historical situation, far from being merely subordinate to the search of the free mind, is indeed the fundamental prerequisite of obtaining access to the lost, forgotten, or obscured philosophic truth which has everything to do with what is constituted by the actual historical facts. The modern scholarly search alone can prepare the mind to consider how the transhistorical truth is plausible, what it might signify, and why it is valuable, by helping to recover the memory and hence the thought of what it meant in the past. The modern scholar, if properly "ministerial" to the search for truth, is the archaeologist of philosophy. But unlike the archaeology which recovers lost civilizations that are truly past and hence are mere curiosities or of historical interest only, this type of modern scholar may rediscover or bring to light a genuine truth which has somehow been neglected or overlooked, or which (because buried) has been unseeable.[14] In so doing, he who makes the unseen visible may alter the contours and change the entire future horizon of human thought. If *the* truth does not change, then the modern scholar who is properly "ministerial" to the premodern texts may help to show us that there is such a thing as transhistorical truth. By doing this, i.e., by modestly but accurately shedding light on what the great thinkers of the past truly thought, through devoted historical research which carefully and precisely explicates their thinking through their texts, he prepares the ground for future great thinkers. In other words, he enables us to see something about God, man, and the world, which we had hitherto been unable to see. Or rather, he enables us to see clearly those things, especially human things, which we had been taught to look away from but which were always present, almost in plain view, as it were, and he raises the quotient of truth visible to those human beings who can make good use of his results.

Consequently, Strauss pursues a quite radical approach to the modern scholarly search for historical truth, if it is to make possible an adequate approach to an unconventional medieval thinker like Maimonides. He first requires it to maintain itself as a rigorous scientific discipline in the general historical and philological sense. But he so requires it precisely in order that it should provide, as it alone can, an accurate and complete account of the thought of the past as that thought actually was, and not as filtered through the thought of the present. Of course, for the modern scholar to properly comprehend past thinkers and their texts as they were obviously requires the modern scholar himself to be a serious thinker who at least aspires to be as serious as those great thinkers of the past were. And thus there must be present in the modern scholar a definite awareness of what is beyond the thought of the present. Over and above its character as science, then, Strauss raises in dignity the scholarly study of medieval philosophy to the next to highest level, and this for two most imperative reasons. First, the scholarly study of the thought of the past should bring us to the actual historical truth, i.e., what the thought of the past actually was. And second, the historical truth may be the best help available to us in recovering our access to the lost or obscured philosophic truth, or at least the one eternal truth which philosophy and revealed religion otherwise continue to converse and to argue about. It is this "philosophic" truth available among selected medieval thinkers that, beyond what the modern scholar can achieve entirely on his own yet evidently dependent on him, may help us to ascend and glimpse, or to point to, or to "divine," the one eternal truth which will be as relevant here and now in the present as it was then and there in the historical past. Strauss's reflections on Socrates certainly illuminate an aspect of the position of Maimonides, who roots his theological position in a Socratic philosophic ground. Indeed, the cause of "Socratism" is advanced just as much by those like Maimonides who might be conceived to have diverged from it on several fundamental issues, such as in the affirmation of prophecy or revelation. Yet Strauss speaks about a needed historical effort to recapture opinions (even theological opinions) as "soiled fragments of the pure truth." And if one allows Karl Barth (alongside Franz Rosenzweig), whose "postcritical" theological study of the Bible made such a great impact on the youthful Strauss, to enter the discussion, one perceives that for Strauss Barth discovered a way by which one need not disavow modern critical history but may still attempt to utilize this while also transcending history. In other words, history is not necessarily the last word on truth—although it is substantial enough that one cannot get to truth if one neglects or attempts to deny this modern approach to what human beings can know. In this regard, it is instructive for Strauss's thought to note the lines that appear in a poem by Goethe to which Barth himself paid homage, and which I believe are also sufficiently expressive of Strauss's conviction:

> Long, long ago the Truth was found,
> A company of men it bound.
> Grasp firmly then—that ancient Truth![15]

In other words, as paradoxical as it sounds in Strauss's view of things, only the precise ascertaining of the historical truth allows for the possibility of transcending the historical truth.

It is for this reason specifically that it is essential to recognize Leo Strauss as, if nothing else, a most competent historical scholar. Strauss, of course, refuses to entirely separate the modern historical scholar and the thinker or philosopher, since he regards modern historical scholarship as itself resting on philosophic thought, and especially on *modern* philosophic thought. Indeed, the truly serious modern historical scholar will have to be aware of the thought or philosophy on which his own work or actions rest (as themselves historical actions), if only due to the conscientious need as a serious historian to trace his own historical origins. Whether the serious historian, driven by a passion for knowledge to which history is subordinate, will be able to think through the philosophic premises of his own historical thought will, according to Strauss, depend on just how serious his passion is.[16] To be sure, prior to the concern with the historical origins of history, among scholars of the history of philosophy, Strauss has been duly recognized as one who made a major contribution to the academic study of medieval philosophy. As a historical scholar, Strauss helped to make a decisive advance in the accurate understanding of the texts and thought of some of the great though often neglected medieval philosophers (besides Maimonides), such as Alfarabi, Judah Halevi, and Marsilius of Padua. Moreover, he also helped to overturn what he perceived as erroneous scholarly approaches based on modern rationalist and historicist premises that distort the proper study of the medievals in their original thought form. All of this seems to assume, however, that Strauss's work must be comprehended in the main as an achievement of historical scholarship. This assumption, as I would like to suggest, judges wrongly the true contribution of Leo Strauss. In fact, following much reflection on Strauss's scholarly achievement, i.e., on his subtle, vibrant, and complex historical works, which seem to promise a deeper wisdom concealed beneath their quiet and unspectacular surface (although he usually also tells his readers an exciting story and issues them an intriguing challenge), I have been led to reach the following surmise. I suggest that Leo Strauss was, primarily and perhaps most significantly, a thinker (i.e., about the nature of philosophy, and about the Hebrew Bible), and he was only secondarily a historical scholar, albeit a masterly one. Yet he concluded that he needed careful historical study, which has to be accurate and precise, in order to pursue transhistorical thought as he construed it in the present era. Thus, his scrupulous and meticulous historical research efforts have always subserved his grander philosophic purposes as a project, but these purposes as a project require complete scholarly honesty and rigor, which he strove to achieve. Whether or not he always attained it is a different matter entirely; this is something that only his fellow historical scholars can judge; but so far they have, in the main, conceived of his work especially on Maimonides as most competent and so judged him as a student of medieval thought in the scale of utmost merit.

As a thinker in his own right, Strauss's scholarly studies were produced with contemporary issues, philosophic as well as theological-political, never far from his mind, although these concerns never determined his results, nor did they impede his ability to see things in a clear, honest, and historically accurate light. Indeed, the principles of historical exactness and of technically accurate scholarly interpretation were established, perhaps paradoxically, as fundamental principles of his *philosophic* enterprise. In other words, he made a study of selected works by medieval (and, of course, ancient) thinkers with the utmost precision, but he did not ever engage in such study either as an antiquarian or as a romantic.[17] He insisted on, and believed in the possibility of, comprehending past thinkers just as these thinkers comprehended themselves: "to understand the thinkers of the past *exactly as* they understood themselves, or to revitalize their thought according to their own interpretation."[18] If we believe ourselves to know that, prior to studying past thinkers, "the present is in the most important respect superior to the past," this will tend to produce a belief in the possibility of understanding past thinkers only *better than* they understood themselves.[19] "Historical truth" requires "historical exactness," but it is only possible on the condition of being "passionately . . . [and] seriously interested in the past" as the *potential* basis for greater access to *the* truth than anything available of equal worth in the present. He considered this to be the only equitable and honest approach consistent with the modern scholarly tradition of historical exactness. Indeed, he believed that "one must approach [earlier thought] in a philosophic spirit, with philosophic questions. . . . But if one approaches an earlier thinker with a question which is not *his* central question, one is bound to misinterpret, to distort, his thought. . . . It can be no other question than the question of *the* truth about the whole."[20] As a result, Strauss the philosopher never forgot *the* fundamental question about the modern scholarly life and modern scholarly activity: What is historical scholarship for? Or to put it otherwise: What good does it serve? Why does one do it? The answer to these questions is one and the same: the scholarly search subserves the search for *the* truth, which (at least in part) is equivalent to what the philosophic search is in the highest sense. To raise the question of the good of science (encompassing what is done by the historical scholar) is, of course, closely linked to the thought of Nietzsche, who made it a key element in his assessment of modern man. This assessment showed that modern criticism of all past thought usually forgets to ask about the critic and in what he bases his criticism and whether what his criticism is for can justify itself. To be sure, Strauss did not wish to identify with some of the antimodern or postmodern thinkers who (for mostly disreputable reasons) oppose the very principle of science. He certainly always shared the aims of modern science insofar as they are grounded in genuine reason. Instead, he attempted to return the problem of science to its philosophic origins, i.e., to its Platonic roots, which meant to ask about the purpose and hence the good of philosophy itself in human life and in the human soul.[21]

Thus, to study a past thinker "in a [truly] philosophic spirit," it is imperative that a scholarly approach be pursued that strives to comprehend the thinkers of the past as they originally comprehended themselves: this requires us to think of them as searchers for *the* truth in the most complete and deepest sense of the term, and not as captive minds beholden to medieval prejudices which it was impossible for them to think beyond. But likewise we must not succumb to the temptation to approach them as the repository of everything good and wise; we must consider with open-mindedness and critically what they can teach us. Such a scholarly approach provisionally assumes only that it is, in principle, possible to attain this original comprehension of what those thinkers had in their minds inasmuch as they were able to communicate the essential contours of their thought in their books, and (as it moves from possibility to actuality) that this original comprehension will confirm the concern of past thinkers with the attainment of *the* truth. Hence, this scholarly approach better approximates "a philosophic spirit," because only by means of it is a past thinker treated as if he may be able to answer "the question of *the* truth about the whole" for us as well. We need to consider their answers because *the* truth is our philosophic question as much as it was theirs; it is the end of our philosophic search as much as it was of theirs. If there is *the* truth which is eternal (something open-mindedness requires us to consider possible), then it was (in principle) as accessible to past thinkers as it is (in principle) accessible to us, however much the thread connecting us to it may have gotten tangled by certain modern trends of thought, which we are called to untangle through historical study. Thus, it may be of the utmost helpfulness to us to truly know what they knew, and how they arrived at thinking it as well as teaching it. However colored their knowledge may have been by accidental aspects associated with a past era most of whose features are antiquated, knowing what thinkers of the past knew—and *rethinking* what their thought was—may also be vitally helpful to us in the present, in our search to know what truly is. Indeed, this knowledge is especially vital for us if they knew things that we have forgotten or have allowed to be obscured by modern preconceptions often amounting to prejudices, which debilitate our thinking and limit our capacity for thought.

At the same time (as has already been noted), Strauss was not a romantic: he did not want to uncover an imaginative escape from the present, nor was he tempted to conjure up an idealized past to which we might return. He acknowledged those accidental aspects which colored the thought of past thinkers, and which associated their thought with a past era most of whose features are antiquated. But he did not believe that those accidental aspects or antiquated features allowed us to pass final judgment on the relevance of past thinkers, i.e., on the possible truth of their deepest thought and teaching, as if this ephemeral historical surface made their thought dismissable as thoroughly obsolete products of a past historical era. This is not to ignore Strauss's curiously opposed contention that some historical situations or settings may be peculiarly "favorable to the discovery of *the* truth." Indeed, Strauss refuses to shirk from the correlated implication: "all other historical situations" or "historical settings" may be "more or less unfavorable" to "the discovery of *the* truth." In other words, even if, for him, *the* truth transcends the historical situation or setting in which it was discovered, the historical situation may act as a decisive aid in the discovery of such truth. The historical circumstances of the discovery need not determine what is laid bare; the situation or setting merely reflects or even produces the historical conditions that conduce to this discovery, but they are not its actual source. If one proceeds "on the basis of the classical presupposition," one will have to make "a radical distinction" between the "conditions" and the "sources" of knowing the truth. In fact, it seems to resemble Maimonides' understanding of divine revelation: revelation occurs in or emerges from a historical situation, but the truth revealed is not dependent on the historical situation. Hence, although Judaism conceives that Moses revealed the Ten Commandments to Israel while they were assembled at Mount Sinai directly following their being liberated from Egyptian slavery, and so the historical situation may well be significant (i.e., since this made them especially receptive to God's message), even so this is a teaching that is not limited to or determined by these circumstances: it intends to express fundamental and unchangeable truths. Or as Karl Barth's remarks, "The differences between then and now, there and here, no doubt require careful investigation and consideration. But the purpose of such investigation can only be to demonstrate that these differences are, in fact, purely trivial. . . .

My whole energy of interpreting has been expended in an effort to see through and beyond history into the spirit of the Bible, which is the Eternal Spirit." As is worth stressing, Strauss twice emphasized precisely these and related remarks of Barth's on the new way that he devised to read the Bible as absolutely crucial for setting his thought in the direction in which it moved. However, perhaps what is most crucial about this statement for Strauss is not how it issued in Barth's new way of reading the Bible, but rather its assertion of the possibility of discovering or rediscovering truth in history that transcends history. Strauss did not study the historical past because he had any wish to return to it or to live in it; what he wanted was merely to learn from it. What he wished to derive from historical study was lessons which one can potentially apply to any similar historical situation.[22]

To the contrary, Strauss was searching for a still-relevant rational philosophic thought for modern man, the same aim by which the modern Enlightenment had been once motivated and guided. But Strauss neither assumed the unqualified rational superiority of modern thought to all past thought, whether medieval or ancient, nor corrected this error by asserting the countererror that past thought (whether medieval or ancient) is unqualifiedly rationally superior to all modern thought. He stressed the need to look with fresh, even "naive" eyes, as free as possible from modern prejudices or blinders, so as to learn things from the medievals to deal with the "peculiar character" of the modern situation—its fundamental dilemmas, its unyielding challenges, and even its unique virtues or advantages—with which we must live, especially if we are beset by a grave theological-political crisis of the modern West which puts our very civilization at risk, due to events and thinkers which make doubtful everything which we used to assume as self-evidently worthwhile and good.[23] It is this radical doubt of ourselves, and the purposes in which we ground ourselves, that he usually calls by the name of "nihilism." He especially approached the medieval thinkers as potentially a vital source of thought for the present, and even as offering a uniquely unmodern critical perspective on present-day thought, because they were not thinking in the grip of nihilism, even it is true that this very nihilism shatters all traditions and uniquely enables us to open our minds and to see everything in a fresh light again.[24] This is because he regarded the only historically serious approach as one which "is willing to consider the possibility that medieval philosophy is simply true, or [rather] ... that it is superior, in the most important respect, to all that we can learn from any of the contemporary philosophers."[25] If this sounds like a wildly improbable premise to some even to consider the possibility of medieval philosophy as "simply true, or ... superior," it would be wrong to assume that this refers to every detail of the thought of the medieval philosophers. Instead, Strauss is referring to essential truths which they knew, which we have forgotten, and which perhaps we can recover from them—even as to the possibility of recurring to "Jerusalem" as a potential source of truth alongside "Athens."

Thus, Strauss pursued scholarly work in a concentrated and passionate effort of mind dedicated to discovering the "merely" historical truth, but precisely for philosophic reasons which are greater than historical reasons. This further means that even if Strauss was a philosophic thinker first, he was also (to repeat) a very serious historical scholar. The philosophic reason for his "seriousness" as a scholar, and the reason for their inextricable connection in his thought, may be discerned in his belief that only by means of historical or archaeological research can we actually recover the true and original sense of what it signifies to be a philosopher—insofar as the original sense of this has been lost or obscured by the modern way of looking at the most significant things. According to Strauss, the premise of the modern search for truth is that this search is possible only once progress has been presupposed; this premise is actually the precondition of that search in the present era. Viewing the results of modern thought at least as it culminated in radical historicism, Strauss was doubtful that this premise about progress is very helpful in the present moment; in fact, it may well impede the genuine search for truth. To be sure, Strauss never aimed to deny the entire truth of progress in numerous aspects of human history which manifest advancement toward the good and the true, e.g., medical science and technology, astrophysics, moral notions abolishing slavery, principles of political order and law as well as the principle of natural human equality in liberal democracy, etc. But he did not believe that these improvements in human affairs, which he was glad to admit and to appreciate, compel the acceptance of progress as revealing *the* truth about being, and especially as this manifests itself in human nature. For to accept this far-reaching truth about progress is to conclude that the essential nature of man and the good has been changed by human history and will, as well as by the world as it has evolved. Yet for several aspects of modern political progress, and especially as a Jew, Strauss was in every sense willing to gratefully acknowledge these as undoubted changes for the better. However, based on what history had taught him, and on his doubts about progress as fixed and permanent, he manifests much greater uncertainty as to whether these changes for the good will endure forever. And even aspects of modern scholarly method, products of progress in human study, should be properly maintained and, if so, can be great aids in the uncovering of truth, both historical and transhistorical. Yet none of these advances guarantee either a superior access to the truth in the single human mind, or a deeper and broader absorption of it by an ever-greater number of people.[26] And they do not surpass or progress beyond the notion of human moral and intellectual excellence, and hence of superlative human achievement (or what Maimonides calls human "perfection"), which was fully known to both the ancients and the medievals.

To be sure, in his academic work Strauss insisted on most rigorous standards of scholarly exactness, i.e., on linguistic precision, careful textual reading, and the critical-historical method in the study of medieval philosophical thought, or philosophical thought of any period. This also means that, contrary to the already conventional view of Strauss (and even against his admirers who wish to obscure what was for Maimonides the needed grounding—not just of medieval thought—in the Hebrew Bible), he was a very keen and devoted philosophic student of the medievals, and not *just* of the ancients and the moderns. Indeed, his three model philosophic thinkers, I would further venture to suggest, were one ancient (Plato), one medieval (Maimonides), and one modern (Lessing). From these three thinkers he believed we may learn the highest possible meaning of our Western philosophy, inasmuch as it shares a common intention, although in each the themes and the modes of expression reflect three distinguishable historical manifestations. He was also impressed with how each of these thinkers wrestled comprehensively yet freely with the human situation, drawing on and confronting political issues as well as religious concerns as much as "purely" philosophical matters. As should also be noted, Strauss was a scholar of medieval philosophy of unusual breadth and range: unlike most scholars, he studied equally Jews, Christians, and Muslims. Also, he studied the most diverse types in each tradition, and so he produced significant and even groundbreaking studies of some of the most widely divergent medieval philosophers: Judah Halevi, Moses Maimonides, Levi Gersonides, and Isaac Abravanel among the Jews; Thomas Aquinas and Marsilius of Padua among the Christians; Alfarabi, Avicenna, and Averroes among the Muslims.[27] Whatever it may imply about the depth of his thought, it certainly shows the breadth of his mind. Just as in his considerations of the ancient Plato and the modern Lessing, Strauss did not limit the relevance of the medievals to their "purely" philosophical orientation. For Strauss, the great thinkers in every era wrestled with the same fundamental and comprehensive issues: God, man, and the world. He never diminished the significance of theology and politics alongside, and even in criticism of, philosophy. As he was able to maintain in his study of the medieval philosophic and antiphilosophic thinkers of the three Western religious traditions—and not just because they were specifically *medieval* thinkers—philosophy need not own the truth, or even the search for it; all it claims for itself in its orientation toward truth is the love of wisdom.

From what has been suggested thus far, it should readily be recognized that Strauss's approach to the medievals was almost unprecedented, certainly peculiar, and surely singular for a modern scholar, and especially one who was not romantic or antiquarian or orthodox, but some other species of scholar not yet defined because not available in any contemporary category. As much as thinkers who lived in any era, he regarded them all as searchers for *the* truth, from each of which in their diversity or variety we may be able to learn contemporary lessons for our own quest for wisdom. They had open, free, critical, and capacious minds and were as able as any of the great ancient or modern thinkers to think for themselves as "free minds" about all issues—even about those on which modern science claims to have alone made decisive progress.[28] The greatest among them were not, in their minds and even in their books, ever merely bound by dogma, even if they were often compelled to pay formal obeisance to it and to bow literally and theologically in its direction, on the one hand assessing it as prudent or advantageous to affirm it, but on the other hand also on numerous occasions thinking to judge it wise and hence defending it willingly, while able to level subtle and even damning criticism of their own traditions in cases which required it. Strauss did claim to recognize political issues and conceptions as the most fundamental, comprehensive, and orienting, indeed as the master science, in the quest for philosophic wisdom of every era, and as the aid of theology in its support for decent human life. Thus, in this quite untypical approach to the great thinkers of the medieval period, Strauss did not embrace historicist antiquarianism or theological dogmatism or existentialist decisionism as adequate to characterize what a complex thinker like Maimonides achieved. Was there, then, anyone else among his contemporaries who followed an approach even similar to it? Perhaps the closest comparison to Strauss's own position on the medievals (especially on Maimonides, but also on Farabi) is how modern Thomists approach the medieval thought of Thomas Aquinas: these scholars and thinkers regard it as urgent for us to know what he thought and taught for our own cognitive needs. Thus, they regard their medieval model as both a teacher and a thinker of eminent relevance and acute profundity for contemporary concerns, even while they also do not betray scholarly honesty about the peculiarly medieval aspects of his thought.[29] However, major differences remain between Strauss and the modern Thomists, three of which I believe to be key differences in whose light numerous others are illuminated.[30]

First, as Emil L. Fackenheim has observed, Strauss took with much greater seriousness the full course of modern philosophy than did the modern Thomists. Strauss clearly perceived the need to study the modern philosophers on their own terms, and not just in the light of their differences from the medievals, in order to apprehend properly what Hans-Georg Gadamer calls "the hermeneutic situation,"[31] as has been previously discussed. However, this is connected to something else, which emphatically differentiates Strauss from the modern Thomists. He was somewhat *less* critical of the moderns, because he acknowledged that modern philosophy arose for at least one good and sufficient cause: it rejected in principle the distortions which had been allowed to occur to ancient philosophy among some of the medievals (especially, but not solely, among the Christians), just as it rejected the ground in which these distortions were rooted—the forgetfulness about what philosophy itself presupposes, which is the doubting of every unevident and unargued authority, even if it is divinely revealed authority. Strauss accepted the modern revolution in philosophy as justified, and hence as still imperative or binding, insofar as it aimed and energetically endeavored to recover the ancient, prebiblical roots of philosophy. But because of "the hermeneutic situation" brought about by radical historicism (or what Strauss also prefers to call "the theological-political crisis"), he was also in certain respects far *more* critical of the moderns than the modern Thomists, insofar as the crisis of modern rationalism (which prompts us to reconsider the medievals) also leads us necessarily to at least reconsider even modern science (though never denying its genuine advances), which has been led astray by the same forces which mislead modern rationalism.[32] And while Strauss offered an overview of the history of philosophy and science which fully acknowledged the meaning and value of modern science, insofar as it has been able to make great and even irreversible discoveries about nature as well as even about its proper method or manner of study, still he was willing to doubt it insofar as it itself can no longer claim, or is no longer willing to claim, to be *the* perfection of man's natural understanding of the world or of the nature of the whole. Abandoning this claim (in the wake of radical historicism) is to forsake that which was its original promise, and which at least in part made it "science," i.e., the claim to yield finished and encompassing knowledge. In other words, the modern Thomists were rather too sanguine in accepting the authority of the modern scientific worldview insofar as it might still seem to possess the rationally binding power (absolute and unconditional) peculiar to the known and the necessary. In spite of what they might seem to share, Strauss thus makes a sharp criticism of modern Thomism as it relates to its distance from Aristotle:

> This means that people were forced to accept a fundamental, typically modern, dualism of a nonteleological natural science and a teleological science of man. This is the position which the modern followers of Thomas Aquinas, among others, are forced to take, a position which presupposes a break with the comprehensive view of Aristotle as well as that of Thomas Aquinas himself. The fundamental dilemma, in whose grip we are, is caused by the victory of modern natural science. An adequate solution to the problem of natural right cannot be found before this basic problem has been solved.

In other words, this is not a "fundamental dilemma" that he claims to have handily resolved or readily escaped by a "return" to the ancients or the medievals. Rather, the un-Aristotelian "dualism" faced by such modern attempts to recover Aristotle's moral doctrine is something he claims merely to maintain a higher awareness of than those who accept proceeding on the basis of current conditions. This is especially the case in terms of modern science (in the form of historical study), which has been regarded as sufficient for knowing what is authentically contained in medieval thought. It presents a challenge and a difficulty to the entire enterprise of defending, or even just reconsidering, natural right in a modern context, which cannot but make the investigation somewhat experimental or tentative. Strauss makes no compromise with intellectual honesty as a vital component in the search for truth and maintains that (though he was an advocate of natural right) this impediment must be brought to light for proper examination. This is an obstacle that is truly fundamental for those who support natural right, although the modern Thomists merely try to ignore it, or at best venture to maintain an untenable compromise. Similarly, recent efforts to reconfigure Thomism so as to avoid Strauss's criticism suffer from a different, but equally fundamental, dilemma: the attempt to make natural law or right rest on nonteleological nature as rooted in Kantian—or to be precise, neo-Kantian—grounds, while not accepting the implications in terms of Kantian—or rather, neo-Kantian—moral teaching (in the sense of a radicalized human moral autonomy).[33]

Second, also as a result of "the hermeneutic situation," Strauss's view was that as moderns we are not given direct and unmediated access to any previous great thinker—especially to ancient and medieval thinkers—but rather we must make tremendous efforts to recover their thought. This is not only because of the difficulties with their thought, of which even the moderns have made us aware, but also because of the prejudices against them created by the moderns, which we cannot escape by mere rejection. Of greater impact as a result of the decisive break with tradition in which the radical historicism of Nietzsche and Heidegger has issued, we stand at a vast distance from the medievals, separated by a historical chasm, which is not bridgeable merely by proceeding to comprehend them. Their recovery requires immense spiritual struggle, and hard cognitive effort, and we cannot proceed as if they were our unmediated contemporaries, or rather, as if we were theirs—which is not in any sense obvious, or easily accessible, or of ready conceptualization, with the consequence that we must begin by trying to appreciate and assess our distance from them. As we must recognize, we stand in the breach, and the ground moves beneath us. In point of fact, we already wear blinders fitted by modern thought (and seemingly confirmed by modern history), which prevent us from fully seeing things, at least if they do not conform to our preconceived modern assumptions about the nature of things and the history of man. The thought and teachings, as well as the view of things, of past thinkers, have actually been almost fatally obscured for us. This is because we tend to assume that the modern premises are self-evident. Consequently, we can neither readily retrieve our clear-sightedness in a simple move or by an act of will, nor should we slight the obscurity which has deeply reshaped our ability to perceive things as they are, especially as concerns what Strauss calls the "human things." This is the case even if it is also true that we would have to acknowledge the skewing of perspective as something we imposed on ourselves, as something first done for an apparently good purpose: to awaken our minds from their dogmatic (theological and political) slumbers. We must, as it were, recover our natural eyes and our ability to, as it were, see again. Thus, we must begin by radically thinking through these prejudices as blinders imposed on us, and we must make ourselves as fully aware of them as possible in order to consider what it would imply to liberate our thinking from them. This must be done in our theory but not in our practice, according to Strauss, since we should not forget not only the tentativeness and the dilemmas which accompany the task that we must set ourselves and contemporary thought, but also the good purpose for which much of modern thought did what it did and which may still bind us in a moral sense: the freeing of the mind. Yet we must be able to recognize the difference between the two: to free the mind from dogma is one thing, and to do so by supplanting it with a substitute dogma is another thing, which we must constantly beware of and keep in view as a threat.[34] Hence, we must do this rethinking precisely by awakening ourselves to the fact that even our study of past thought is determined by modern thought and unwittingly leads us to assume its superior value.[35] And so we must also study the ancient philosophers on their own terms, and not just in the light of their differences from or similarities to the medievals or the moderns, since the ancients too have often been distorted by the Western tradition in general, not even to mention by being filtered through the specific character of modern thought on its own.

In other words, the dislocations, confusions, and missteps produced by the current "hermeneutic situation" that we face—and for Strauss this means the philosophy which dominates our horizon and detaches us from the tradition—allows us an unusually free moment for the reconsideration of everything merely taken for granted as given in the thought of the modern era, if not also in the thought of the medieval era.[36] The modern Thomists do not seem fully awake to the crisis produced by the "hermeneutic situation." They do not seem to appreciate the silent dangers to an accurate comprehension of the thought of the past, as it was actually grounded, which is posed by the contamination of our study with the beliefs of modern thought as well as with those of the radical historicism which (though a creature of modern thought) still strives to subvert it. But they also do not seem to grasp the unique (if paradoxical) opportunity that is provided to us, and represented precisely by the essential doubt about modern thought which radical historicism raises. For insofar as this essential doubt is effective and attempts to functionally demolish piece by piece (or "deconstruct") the standing structure of modern thought and its premises, or even just makes them dubious again, it is the cause of a possible beginning again, which can return us (admittedly by a different route from the one through radical historicism) to the human origins of philosophic thought and its great counterpoint, biblical thought. In other words, it may clear the ground and expose the roots to the light again, showing their health, even as it makes a fresh inquiry possible. At the very least, it allows for an unencumbered digging for the roots, i.e., a recovery of an original awareness of the thought of the past and its grounds, *potentially* freed of modern prejudices. The decentered condition of the present that is our "hermeneutic situation," i.e., the contemporary crisis in Western thought as to how we are to comprehend ourselves, is rarely appreciated for what it is or how far-reaching it is by the modern Thomists.

According to Strauss, a full awareness of this contemporary crisis is the requisite and only adequate beginning point for contemporary thought and study of the medievals or any premodern thought, however much such awareness makes further advances toward enlightenment difficult, since we do not know for certain how to begin again. If Strauss takes the side of a full-blooded Heidegger against his somewhat anemic disciple Gadamer, whom he presents as offering an academicized Heideggerianism suitable for modern scholarly uses, and if Strauss admits that this reversal in their stances toward Heidegger is "strange," since on most fundamental issues Strauss deeply opposed Heidegger, it is because Gadamer gives priority to hermeneutics almost because he wishes to avoid the implications of Heidegger's assertion of the "world-night" in which we dwell. Although Gadamer must assume this Heideggerian state of affairs (why else would he make hermeneutics such a crucial concern?), he promptly ignores its radical implications, since Gadamer writes as if the question of interpretation answers a merely academic concern, rather than being our attempt to climb out of a hole into which we have fallen as modern human beings and in which we currently dwell. For Strauss, it is only if we face the full implications of Heidegger's analysis of our problem that we can we begin to feel the need which might lead us to be willing to consider what has been lost of ancient and medieval thought, in which a certain true wisdom may have been preserved. For if Heidegger's diagnostic analysis of the contemporary dilemma is not entirely erroneous (although even if that is true, for Strauss, it does not imply that he also thinks we need to accept Heidegger's solution to our dilemma), this may well be due to modern thought, which has been radicalized by Heidegger by fully thinking through its tacit historicist logic. Thus, Strauss is not willing to accede to Gadamer's approach, which he seems to regard as at best a sort of a "dodge." Viewing the course of their brisk though brief exchange of letters, what we see in them is Strauss withdrawing himself fairly quickly: he terminates the discussion once his main points have been made, and he allows Gadamer to think through the issues and to put the rest together for himself, perhaps swaying him to look again at his own premises, and certainly eschewing any attempt to instruct Gadamer in the fundamental issue which he has rejected. As this seems to imply for Strauss, both the modern Thomists and the modern (academic) Heideggerians share a certain fixed unwillingness to apprehend the gravity of our "hermeneutic situation" with regard to the obstacles to our grasping or even approaching the thought of the past.

And third, almost opposite to the last point, Strauss promulgated his own unique perspective on the matter of our complex relation to premodern thought, which moved him beyond Hans-Georg Gadamer's strictures against any attempt at a return to prehistoricist thought.[37] For Gadamer believed that any attempted return to the origins of Western thought in its prehistoricist form, especially as this is done by the modern study of history, will have to be entangled in historicist premises, and hence will unconsciously carry with it the unavoidable encumbrances of modern thought. In contrast, Strauss made this simple observation: he believed that we could not perceive this legacy of history or tradition (or of the historicist premises by which we comprehend it)—of modern thought imposed on the thought of the past—if we could not also simultaneously dimly perceive *the original form* of those past things which historicism imposes its view on. However much our perception of the original form of past things has also been affected in our vision by the modern distortions or colorations, and whether or not we wish to accept and work with the original form as we would seem to be able to dimly perceive it, it must still be essentially visible to us, *if we are able to observe the changes which historicism has wrought*.[38] Even so, he was also not able to embrace Etienne Gilson's sympathetic and yet apparently simple reappropriation of the medievals, which might seem to be the logical alternative to Gadamer. Thus, if the eyes of our minds can still see the original form as it was, why not just make our own again "the wisdom of the ancients," just as medieval tradition judged such ancient thinkers as Plato and Aristotle to have been wiser or better than any alternative?[39] What prevents us from proceeding to reappropriate past thinkers by a simple move, once we espy their essential and original thought? If there are ahistorical standards according to which the medievals or the ancients may be judged and these were good enough for tradition, then why not also for us? Why not rest satisfied with the traditional judgment of the tradition? Or why not make their thought ours by merely leaping across the gap between us and the medievals (or the ancients)?

In this regard, Strauss assumed an entirely original (and undoubtedly still controversial stance) toward the study of the medievals: he boldly asserted that as a heuristic device, i.e., as an essential scholarly aid to our learning, we must assume that our medieval models may teach us *the* truth, and are potentially superior to the moderns. The contemporary crisis cannot prevent us from searching for the ahistorical truth, but it should lead us to cease relying on judgments derived from the tradition of Western thought, or from the traditional view of the tradition, for two reasons. First, the tradition is itself enmeshed in the crisis and cannot provide us with a simple antidote, an Archimedean fulcrum, or an absolute standpoint by which to cure what ails us, to remove every obstacle, and hence to resolve the crisis by a simple uncovering or tearing away of what has been hidden in a modern gauze. We can glimpse the original form; we cannot so readily grasp it or reappropriate it (and even if we could do this, it is not clear that any use to which we might put it would not still be determined by our modern premises); the distance between us and them remains, produced by centuries of thought and historical change. Second, we do not know from the start whether or how much the tradition might have been responsible for what brought about the crisis. The rethinking of the tradition requires an effort in which it is still not clear whether the contemporary crisis is not a product of the tradition itself. (Thus, we must be willing to consider the Nietzschean argument, although this does not seem to have been accepted by Strauss, that modern nihilism is itself rooted in the biblical tradition.) Together with this, however, Strauss also never forgot that this notion of the possible helpfulness of recurring to the medievals (or ancients) does not free us of the *philosophic* duty to prove such an assumption to be true, which we who are ruled by modern premises may discover to be of greater difficulty than anticipated. Strauss neither offered the medievals as a dogmatic *practical* standard, i.e., as unconditionally superior to the modern in terms of what is to be done, nor defined the ancients as possessed of a ready-made *theoretical* doctrine (*philosophia perennis*) which we can entirely reappropriate pure and simple. The "return" to the medievals, as much as to the ancients, has to be primarily in the nature of a tentative search: it is an intellectual experiment of an admittedly high order (since it aims, but only aims, to help us escape our contemporary crisis), and most essentially it remains a *search* for the truth—which may not ultimately yield what we want. He merely called for an opening of the modern mind: to consider the medievals to have perhaps taught something of the truth and to be able to perhaps teach us something of the truth is a heuristic device only until we know whether it is true.

As a fourth point, which likewise bridges the modern Thomists and the academic Heideggerians, Strauss put much greater emphasis on the "political" than did Gadamer, who, not following Heidegger, forsook the German language and the concrete national spirit as his guide to Being and turned instead to "our (i.e., the Western) tradition" as normative—which, however, tended to let him further abstract from the political. Similarly, Strauss emphasized the "political" much more than did Gilson, who relied in much greater measure on his Catholicism than Strauss did on his Judaism for the direction of all such human matters. This was especially the case since the Jewish theologian who was "authoritative" for Strauss, i.e., Maimonides, laid great stress on the need for an *autonomous* political philosophy prior to theology, while for Gilson his authoritative theologian i.e., Thomas, was never quite as deeply moved and was certainly less guided by political philosophy in his theology. Certainly this difference in approach to the political is also true of Strauss's closest friend, Jacob Klein, who seems to have retained a virtually Kantian sense of morality as primary. Of course, the question of just what it is that Strauss meant by the political, and how it relates to the philosophical, are matters for careful reflection. No doubt Strauss's ancient-medieval leanings imply that what this term ("the political") came to signify for him is much closer to what would commonly be called the moral or the ethical and goes to the heart of this matter: what is the right way of life, and what is it that it encompasses? Hence, the notion of the amoral (never mind immoral) philosopher, or one who willingly collaborates with political evil, at least as it was manifested in Heidegger's life and doctrine, is a most revealing case of the problem of the thinker who has not been educated by political philosophy: this teaches us why we must learn the proper political lessons as well as why it is imperative to live with moral decency if the life of philosophy itself is to be defensible.[40]

To be sure, Strauss's "return" to the ancients and the medievals was always very tentative. While it was much more than a mere thought experiment, it was also much less than a simple act of faith in the possibility of the pure and unmediated intellectual reclamation of their thought.[41] Even if Strauss assumed the possibility of properly recovering and knowing comprehensively certain key aspects of ancient and medieval thought in its thrust and ambit, he never believed it was possible to apply or adapt even these immediately to the modern situation, if only because so much is still unknown, and so much has changed from then to now. Thus, Strauss was never able to make the sort of unconditional statement which Gilson made toward the end of his *The Unity of Philosophical Experience*: "*Perennis philosophia* is not an honorary title for any particular form of philosophical thinking, but a necessary designation for philosophy itself, almost a tautology. That which is philosophical is also perennial in its own right. *It is so because all philosophical knowledge ultimately depends on metaphysics*" (the emphasis has been added). If Strauss did in fact share a certain premise with Gilson (i.e., the necessary connection between politics and metaphysics), even so he would have articulated any such similar statement with much, much greater hesitation and doubt about what we can actually *know* metaphysically. Similarly, the statement made by Jacques Maritain could not have been made by Strauss: "The tragedy of the philosophers who call themselves existentialists . . . lies in their having the feeling or apperception of the primacy of being, or existence, while at the same time denying . . . that the notion of being has any value: so that they see in it only an empty word. If I, on the other hand, am a Thomist, it is in the last analysis because *I have understood that the intellect sees, and that it is cut out to conquer being*" (the emphasis has been added). Granted, Strauss was accused of maintaining a similar position by Isaiah Berlin. I believe, however, that Berlin certainly misapprehended and hence misrepresented what Strauss claimed for his position, which did not assume a direct and unmediated metaphysical access to the truth. Strauss shows a full awareness of the serious problems with any attempt to "return" to the ancients, or, mutatis mutandis, to the medievals, and for him no ready-made solution to this is available. As I have been trying to emphasize, Strauss was as sharply critical of any asserted claims to an unmediated return to the ancients—as somehow absolutely superior in every respect, or as somehow offering formulas or prescriptions ready-made for modern use—as he was of similarly asserted notions about the medievals. As has been noted, this was an ailment that he tended to diagnose as occurring all too commonly among the modern Thomists. What usually happens, instead of a genuinely unmediated return, is that all sorts of modern ideas get smuggled in—consciously or unconsciously—to the comprehension and "reappropriation" of the ancients or medievals. But this is a peril which, for Strauss, we must constantly be on our guard against, at least if we are to achieve full self-awareness of what we are doing. As one observes in Strauss's criticism of John Wild, it is erroneous if not perilous to treat the ancients, especially but not only Plato and Aristotle, in the same fashion as the modern Thomists tend to treat Thomas Aquinas, because their recourse is in a certain measure based on a common faith, while a reconsideration of Plato and Aristotle cannot honestly proceed on the same basis. Although Wild was not a modern Thomist, but rather a type of existentialist, he had recognized the contemporary crisis of modernity in modern thought and had attempted to resolve it by recommending a (seemingly) unmediated return to the ancients. Strauss was not impressed. Though Wild was never a colleague, friend, student, or affiliate of Strauss, in Nathan Tarcov's analysis Strauss is presented as employing the happy accident of Wild's book counseling such a direct return to the ancient philosophers as the fitting occasion on which to offer a cogent and unyielding critique-in-anticipation of certain defined potential abuses of his own view or position which, based on his reading of Wild, he imagined might well arise in the future, and which he wished to correct in advance.⁴² In other words, however much Strauss may have considered the healing potential of the great books in the Western tradition for the contemporary historical situation, his counsel was always of a decided caution in trying to make use of any past thinker in modern circumstances: whatever may be true must still be adapted carefully, judiciously, selectively, and with appropriate changes to quite different conditions from those in which a past thinker wrote. It must never be forgotten what has happened between then and now. And this warning entails that it is imprudent, ill advised, and indeed impossible to try to apply any past thinker's thought directly to the present.⁴³

But perhaps the one most crucial difference between Strauss and all of his contemporaries is the thinker he chose to focus his scholarly attention on—an unlikely choice that one could say determined not a little his view of medieval philosophy. This was his passionate interest in, and devoted exploration of, the writings of the medieval Jewish thinker Moses Maimonides. True, Strauss also dedicated much study to other medieval thinkers, and especially the pivotal philosophic figure of the Muslim Alfarabi,⁴⁴ but also the curiously antiphilosophical Jew Halevi, as well as the untypically republican Christian Marsilius. In spite of this, I believe it is accurate to suggest that Strauss was or became a true modern "Maimonidean" through an untiring effort to recover the long-buried original thought of Maimonides, and indeed much of what he discovered in the wake of his work on Maimonides (i.e., "esotericism") was shaped by it.⁴⁵ Although the two leading contemporary historians of medieval Jewish philosophy, Julius Guttmann and Isaac Husik, also lavished the highest praise on Maimonides, who was hailed by both of them as the greatest medieval Jewish philosophic thinker, if not the greatest Jewish thinker ever (whether "medieval" or "modern"), Strauss did not regard their approaches to Maimonides' Jewish philosophic thought as adequate, and he mounted elaborate critiques of both of them.⁴⁶ Consequently, Strauss rejected the two leading "methods" in the study of medieval philosophy as distorting the true meaning of the original, which "methods" we may call critical-romantic historicism on the one hand, and neo-Kantian phenomenology on the other hand. He wrote instead in favor of what he would call "classical Platonic rationalism," which he regarded as more authentically Maimonidean, and also less beset by grave modern dilemmas than the two leading alternative approaches.

SIX

Absorbing and Surpassing the Alternatives

IT WAS STRAUSS'S VIEW THAT THE VARIOUS MODERN scholarly approaches to Maimonides' work were essentially representative of the spectrum of modern philosophic thought and were unacknowledged exponents of its positions: Enlightenment rationalism, historical romanticism, neo-Kantianism, or existentialism (whether in its Nietzschean, Kierkegaardian, or Heideggerian variety). As he conceived of it, both the strengths and the weaknesses of each specific scholarly approach were indicative of the elementary virtues and fundamental defects in the original philosophic position. This is especially the case as compared with the dialectical balance of Maimonides' own "original" position, which Strauss claimed to have uncovered. Of the leading scholars in the study of medieval Jewish philosophic thought whose approaches Strauss judged defective—besides the true philosophers' own polemics or apologetics, as in Spinoza's virtual caricature of Maimonides as house ideologist for the medieval priestly regime, or Cohen's glamorized and retouched portrait of Maimonides as advocate for modern autonomous morality *avant la letter*—certainly the dominant figures from whom he diverged were Salomon Munk, Julius Guttmann, Isaac Husik, and Harry A. Wolfson. Strauss made only passing critical comments on Munk and Wolfson, but he elaborated detailed critiques of Guttmann and Husik. Perhaps the most deficient scholarly position encountered by Strauss was that of Guttmann, and his youthful criticism of this position helped to clarify and advance his own contrasting view as it emerged in the wake of his critique. Strauss faulted Guttmann for putting the thought of Maimonides in the context of modern "philosophy of religion," which is an entirely unmedieval conception, badly distorting the essential purpose and character of the Maimonidean enterprise.

According to Strauss, Maimonides was impelled to write in order to justify the philosophic life in the face of the revealed law, so as to acknowledge its authority while showing the legitimacy of such a life. In consequence, if one must use a modern term, the Maimonidean enterprise is closer to "philosophy of law."[1] Strauss also believed that Guttmann missed the priority of the political in Maimonides' approach to philosophy and religion, which approach (as he had been schooled in it by Farabi) he employed in order to carry through his "philosophy of law," and to warrant the life of freely thinking in a revelation-governed era. This priority of the political was generated by the conflict between revelation and reason, "Jerusalem and Athens," which cannot be (or at least has never yet been) resolved on theoretical grounds but can only be harmonized on practical grounds. This requires an acute consciousness of the political basis in which that conflict most often manifests itself, and by which it is best mediated. Guttmann neglected all of these factors in favor of a Maimonides who was driven by purely theological concerns, which issued at the highest level in his negative theology as a response to dogmatic desiderata.

Guttmann also put most weight on the debate between Judaism and other rival monotheistic religions in Maimonides' thought, which Strauss thought was subordinate to the debate between revealed religion—the most essential and original form of which was for Maimonides ancient Judaism represented by the Hebrew Bible—and philosophy. In other words, for Guttmann Maimonides merely used philosophy (as an apparently uncontroversial tool) to aid in the proper reflection on and articulation of those urgent theological concerns specific to his faith and its historical-existential situation. Besides Guttmann's effort to impose a modern dilemma and "method" on a medieval thinker, Strauss detected a further fatal flaw in his unwillingess to consider how difficult it would have been for a thinker like Maimonides to use philosophy as a mere tool. As a result, Guttmann also refused to consider how much of a challenge to revealed religion would actually have been implied in such a "use." In the case of a thinker like Maimonides, such use brought with it the duty of unlimited intellectual honesty as a condition of the highest spiritual perfection, which duty arises if one is one is bound to think through everything: this "tool" requires an effort at absolute knowledge *and* absolute self-awareness that, for Maimonides, henceforth sets the standard of excellence in human life. But such a standard cannot limit itself by circumscribed theological dogmas of any sort, however much it is possible to phenomenologically amplify or morally magnify them: fidelity to the truth alone is its measure. This makes clear how this tool (which is always something other than a mere tool) is, by needs, a great, fundamental, and irreducible challenge to revealed religion, one that Guttmann seems to have either missed or dismissed too lightly. Subsequent to his youthful critique of Guttmann, Strauss would add, as it were, an addendum, that the challenge of philosophy is as a way of life, and this way of life may conflict with what the revealed law seems to require of a human being in electing what he should spend his life doing.

In the wake of *Spinoza's Critique of Religion*, this very criticism led Strauss to begin to seriously reflect on the issue raised by a seemingly competent scholar like Guttmann, and why he may have missed the motives of Maimonides that entirely transcended any dogmatic theology. To be sure, Strauss may seem to have been prone to a similar approach during his earlier study of Maimonides, but this was especially the case during his work on *Spinoza's Critique of Religion*. However, this is because it was written and appeared in print severely constrained by certain conceptions of Maimonides that Guttmann imposed on Strauss; indeed, Strauss regarded these impositions of Guttmann's as virtual censorship, according to what he would later contend in letters to friends. Strauss was certainly cognizant of the frequent use and even defense of traditional language used by Maimonides in *The Guide of the Perplexed*. However, by the period during which he wrote *Philosophy and Law*, Strauss had started to perceive a strategic method directing Maimonides' use of such language, which did not constitute a blind embrace or endorsement: it is quite legitimate to primarily use it just so long as one leaves hints for the wise that this language is not the final arbiter or highest standard of what is ultimately true and false. In other words, what is called both the esoteric and the exoteric "method," or the decision "to write between the lines," makes greater sense of how Maimonides resolved the conflict in his soul between tradition and truth, or how he allowed philosophy to teach him to carefully distinguish in his use of rhetorical, dialectical, poetic, and scientific language. The conflict was resolved by Maimonides' decision to maintain a consistent thought beneath the surface concealed by coded language, and to use traditional thought in deliberately contradictory language on the surface. This was done while pointing to the hidden depths beneath it for those who were able to pursue it, guided by what Strauss calls "an entire system of secret words" (ein ganzes System von Geheimworten). Or as Rémi Brague put it, "While this first book [by Strauss on Maimonides] still refused to see in Maimonides the free thinker that he was often considered to be before the nineteenth century, the later texts rejoined this traditional conception." While I neither share the view that the correct term for this stage in the development of Strauss's thinking about Maimonides is a "refusal" to perceive nor am convinced that this book's "image of Maimonides" departs very little from "current opinion," I do share Brague's view of *Philosophy and Law* that the last essay in this book, i.e., "Maimonides' Doctrine of Prophecy," composed originally in 1931, decisively facilitated the breakthrough which would bring in its wake a series of even greater discoveries. It is in the context of this issue that Strauss's statement to Jacob Klein, made in the enthusiasm of discovery, which has shocked some, makes perfect sense: "Maimonides in his beliefs absolutely was no Jew." It is obvious from everything we know about Maimonides that he was evidently a Jew in the beliefs which, enacted as law, he definitely himself followed, and indeed which he "legislated," or rather reiterated and organized, as law code. But he chose to follow them because he had reasons to so choose. Those reasons relate to the fact that the truth did not always reside *in* the beliefs; instead, this truth may rather reside in the function which those beliefs performed. This is to say, they serve a true or necessary purpose of sustaining Jewish life and its specific teachings, just as one may apply those same moral and religious truths to human life or traditions in general. Hence, it is no surprise that although Maimonides defended Jewish law and even Jewish dogma, reason is always to be followed first, as Strauss reminds his readers, if reason teaches a truth that is genuinely known, whatever may appear to have been commanded by law, and even while what has been commanded is still binding. Strauss undoubtedly already knew about this unconditional priority of reason for Maimonides in his first work, *Spinoza's Critique of Religion*, which was even then not the conventional view; it was only that he did not yet perceive what it might fully seem to imply, or what radical consequences there might be concealed beneath that unconditional priority.

Strauss continued to pursue this theme in *Hobbes' Critique of Religion* (1933–34). In a letter to Gershom Scholem (of 2 October 1935), he gives expression to the intention to write a book on the *Guide* "in the course of about the next ten years." Moreover, in the same letter he curiously characterized his about-to-be-issued book, *The Political Philosophy of Hobbes: Its Basis and Its Genesis*, as "an introduction to the *Moreh* [*Guide*]"! In this comment he might have been implying that *Hobbes' Critique of Religion* and *The Political Philosophy of Hobbes* are both connected with his study of certain permanent political-philosophical as well as theological themes which were evident to him in Maimonides (such as, What is the status of revelation in a projected rational society? and How is the irrational element of revelation to be dealt with?). But he was only able to bring these critical Maimonidean themes to the awareness of philosophic scholars by dealing with them obliquely, i.e., via Hobbes, since almost no one was yet willing to recognize them as present in Maimonides and so take him seriously as a still-significant thinker. Strauss had not been able to deal with any of these themes other than by hints in the writings he produced during his period as a researcher standing in the shadow of Julius Guttmann (in the late 1920s and early 1930s). Yet strangely it seems that doing scholarly work at the behest of Guttmann had circuitously taught him—although this was only to become fully clear to him subsequently—about the art of writing between the lines. And it was to emerge that Guttmann himself perhaps first began to recognize this and as a result changed his view of Strauss and the standpoint in which his perspective on Maimonides was rooted, as Guttmann began to notice what Strauss himself characterized (in a letter to Gershom Scholem of 17 November 1972) as the greater "flexibility," or "slipperiness," of his own thought. Some maintain that Strauss was to ultimately abandon the ground, which they call "existentialist," on which he had supposedly stood in *Philosophy and Law* in order to criticize Guttmann (and in this they follow Guttmann himself). This is a view on Strauss which I happen to regard as deficient, but however that may be, the main point of all this maneuvering about how Strauss stood and how he changed at a certain point is that he believed he had begun to grasp the original meaning and value of philosophy, in terms that he recognized to be closer to the position of Maimonides himself. Thus, Strauss's Maimonidean position became *essentially* the same as that which Maimonides himself delineated, and by which Strauss perceived it still possible to guide one's life and thought, irrespective of one's historical period.

This position is based on the fundamental and eternal questions that have occurred to man in all times and places, and that as a result it seems he must pursue. And this is the basis that, in its original significance, enabled Maimonides to make his peace with revelation. According to Strauss's Maimonides, all that philosophy as philosophy (which precedes Socrates) needs to justify itself is the fundamental and eternal questions. If philosophy dies in certain civilizations (such as post-Averroean Islam), it is always reborn once those questions as fundamental and eternal are remembered. True, all it can offer as a "proof" or "defense" of its own way of life is the compelling nature of those questions. And because of their being compelling, revelation is not able to dispose of them as an irrelevancy or worse. Revelation cannot get rid of those questions and, indeed, it does not want to do so, because it too depends on them to differentiate itself from myth or the gods. And so long as it cannot and does not want to get rid of them, the attempt to answer them (whether or not by means of a specific philosophic approach as the most adequate way) cannot be simply dismissed by revelation so long as it too depends for its own self-defense on the same questions, the search for which ends in a certain set of answers. Thus, it seems that man as man is always in need of these questions, and cannot help but spontaneously rediscover them in their unchanged character. This is, for Strauss, not to decide whether once man becomes aware of the Socratic philosophic approach to dealing with them, it is possible to *know* whether it is more adequate than any alternative. But this uncertainty about how best to approach and how best to resolve them is also what "leaves room" (to use Kant's terms) for reason or philosophy to legitimately continue on its way, even in the face of revelation. Yet it too never gets rid of revelation as a genuine and substantial challenge, precisely because it does not know the ultimate answers to the most significant questions: it only knows the need to pursue the questions and to try to get such answers. Any attempt to get rid of or suppress the questions depends on answers about what man needs which, other than the questions themselves, are not self-evident or demonstrated. This is what Strauss uncovered in Maimonides, but he discerned that this teaching in Maimonides is less than satisfactorily dealt with by modern scholars who followed in the philosophic school of Hermann Cohen, such as Guttmann. According to Strauss, this philosophic school and the scholars who embrace it have forgotten the true basis of philosophy in favor of a certain set of modern answers as most primary (its virtual "faith"), but awareness of the true basis was still very much alive in Maimonides.[2]

In the case of Husik, Strauss was much impressed by how accurately his historical-critical approach allowed him to penetrate to some layers in the hidden depths of Maimonides' thought, not previously appreciated by most modern scholars. But Husik, even by avoiding the "philosophy of religion" as a modern framework imposed on a medieval thinker, almost succumbed to an opposite error. In point of fact, Strauss highlights three errors or "limits" which he discovered in Husik: the issue of objectivity, the status of historical evolution, and the idea of Jewish philosophy. On the first point, Husik rightly promoted historical "objectivity" insofar as it is (just as for Strauss) the proper standard of approach in historical research. This was in contrast with what Husik regarded as the flawed approach of Hermann Cohen and his "idealistic" method, which measures a doctrine of the past in terms of its "highest possibility," i.e., what is (subjectively) highest for us, or in terms of our contemporary thought. But once Husik was called on, e.g., to delimit the field of "what is Jewish philosophy?" and "who is a Jewish philosopher?" he did so on a basis which manifests sheer "subjectivity," justifying it only by his own preferences. Even though Husik asserted that Maimonides distorted or forced the Jewish sources in one way (which remade them as Aristotelian), and Hermann Cohen did the same in another way (which remade them as Kantian), this did not prevent Husik from reading Maimonides in, and Hermann Cohen out, as a legitimate Jewish philosopher, with no apparent reason for his preference other than perhaps the artfulness of the former in doing what he did, and the relative artlessness of the latter compared with his venerated predecessor in doing the same thing. On the second point, Husik believed that Judaism itself had passed through a significant historical evolution toward modernity, which had rendered the "orthodox" thesis obsolete. In other words, he raises progressive history to the authority of supreme judge of what is still true in Judaism. But, for Strauss, this granting of authority to progressive history obscures how Judaism rests on a truth that claims to transcend history even as it marches through it, and likewise consequently how the continued evolution of Judaism cannot, other than dogmatically, disallow the possibility of a restored "orthodox" thesis in the future, which has been merely eclipsed by contemporary trends. If orthodoxy is admittedly in a state of intellectual crisis for the present, its unrefuted fundamental premise has the potential to help extricate it from its current crisis.

On the third point, Husik designated the very idea of a "Jewish philosophy" a product of a certain period in history, i.e., the medieval period. This manufactured entity was made possible by the illusion (or to put it with greater politeness: the climate of opinion) that the said period was itself based on: this is the illusion that one can "interpret" the past so as to explicate from those texts "true" doctrine supposedly in them. It is an invention grounded in a fictional manner of exegesis. But we moderns, with our superior historical knowledge, know that what this way of reading fabricates has nothing to do with what the revealed text itself originally taught and what is contained in it. If there was not sophisticated "thinking" actually available to the ancient historical authors of the revealed text in any form, then especially as to cognitive contents it is not of the same essence as what is comprised by philosophy. Whatever may have been the merits of Husik's contrasting the Hebrew Bible with Greek philosophy, this argument amounted to a historical reductionism, encompassing as it did even the thought of Maimonides that he admired and held in the highest regard. Even though Husik regarded Maimonides' thought as deep, clear, powerful, and thorough, it was for him also the impressive fruit of what might be called this magnificent illusion that is rooted in a historical accident. He certainly could not imagine Maimonides grasping the chief contours of such a conception for himself and employing it in his own conceptual scheme and for his own purposes. In any case, the very idea of a Jewish philosophy, even according to Maimonides, depended on the belief in the possibility of a synthesis between the completed science of Aristotle (i.e., as equal to philosophy itself) and the once-only, historical revelation of the Torah (i.e., as equal to Judaism itself). But as Strauss noted, with seeming (but not actual) simple-mindedness, these definitions of what philosophy is, and of what Judaism is, are almost completely arbitrary, rooted in Husik's personal preferences as to which beliefs had once happened to make a higher or superior Jewish thought possible, i.e., the thought of Maimonides as he comprehended it. Yet, as Strauss also observed, even Husik considered the need for a Jewish philosophy, elaborated in response to contemporary thought, to be a desideratum and even an imperative for modern Judaism. However, it is difficult to know how such a thing as a modern Jewish philosophy could have still arisen, according to Husik's view, if he confined its possibility to the beliefs of a certain historical period in and by which—as he seemed to maintain unambiguously—it had been preconditioned.[3] In other words, the possibility represented by Maimonides, i.e., of a Jewish thought animated by the encounter between philosophy and the Hebrew Bible, is not a mere figment of the past, which renders Maimonides' own thought still worthy of keeping in view as a living thing.

To be sure, prior to both Husik and Guttmann, Maimonides was long dismissed by most modern philosophic Jews, not to mention by most modern philosophic non-Jews, as irrelevant and obsolete, although he was perhaps noticed as a noteworthy historical curiosity. An instructive example of this is evident in the account that is provided by Hegel in his *History of Philosophy* (part 2, section 1), which in a mere half-page paragraph on Maimonides characterizes his philosophy as possessed of "a strong kabbalistic element, on the one hand, [which] makes itself felt throughout, in astrology, geomancy, etc.; [while] on the other hand, . . . the foundation is laid in history." With such a confused system (although Hegel was able to astutely recognize his seriousness about history), it is no wonder little interest was expressed in Maimonides, in spite of the enormous efforts in the 18th century of Solomon Maimon, whose commentary on part 1 of the *Guide* was grounded in a critical version of Kantianism. It was not until Salomon Munk in the middle of the 19th century that there was an attempt made to write a definitive modern philosophico-historical commentary on the *Guide* for Jewish romantic-antiquarian reasons, this being based on the best historical knowledge then available.[4] Even beyond him, in the late 19th and early 20th centuries, Hermann Cohen attempted to recover Maimonidean thought in the name of neo-Kantianism (as has already been discussed in some detail), but only as a medieval precursor of Cohen himself or at least of neo-Kantianism, not as a still vital "modern" thinker on his own terms.[5] To be sure, Cohen took Maimonides with the utmost seriousness and gave an account of his moral thought which accorded it a greatness not diminished by modernity—reflecting not just the authority of "the great eagle," but also a veritable compulsion among modern Jewish thinkers to rediscover themselves in Maimonides.[6]

However, to return to Hegel for a moment, even if he regards Maimonides as a thoroughly medieval thinker, Hegel is curiously perceptive in claiming to discover the basis of Maimonides' thought to be grounded in history, which is modern enough—and which everyone following him regarded as a fantastic projection by Hegel! Strauss would have been impressed by how Hegel unconventionally perceived an orientation toward history in the thought of Maimonides (to be sure, Hegel and Maimonides each for his own reasons), which most modern scholars dismissed. To his credit, Hegel more or less admits that this brief account may do less than full justice to Maimonides. For about the writings of this medieval thinker Hegel acknowledges that "much more of a literary character might be said": he almost admits to espying hidden depths pertaining to the literary art which had so far been mostly undiscerned. Curiously, this cryptic remark is somewhat in anticipation of Strauss—even if probably to a very different purpose—in the sense that Hegel seems to notice or embryonically detect some key to the thought of Maimonides in something unique in the "literary character" of his *Guide* specifically, or of his works in general.[7] Indeed, it is likely that even the "kabbalistic element" which Hegel detects in Maimonides pertains to the element of deliberate concealment or "esotericism," or of what Strauss will also call the "method of contradiction" (although, as we know, this is a lesson that the Kabbalah drew from Maimonides, rather than vice versa).[8] This was as much as Hegel was willing to concede: history and the literary. It did not seem worth the effort to pursue his thought further. Indeed, very rare was the modern thinker or scholar who even vaguely conceived of the possibility that the principles of Maimonides might be separable from their medieval context and might somehow be relevant to modern thought. This rare next step seems to emerge from the fact that, as most modern thinkers assumed, Spinoza had either selected, absorbed, carried on, and completed (in the Hegelian sense of *aufgehoben*, as Hegel himself maintained) whatever was of value in Maimonides or had laid to rest everything else. Maimonidean thought had therefore been pretty much declared obsolete and defunct for modern philosophy.[9]

It should also be emphasized that Spinoza in the 17th century had been sufficiently cognizant of the abiding power of Maimonides' thought, and of what he regarded as the negative influence that it might continue to exercise. To be sure, Spinoza recognized Maimonides as some sort of a philosopher, though one who imposed the teachings of reason on those of revelation in a scheme which Spinoza calls "dogmatism." To fulfill his scheme, Maimonides concocted a method—"harmful, useless, and absurd"—which put philosophers seemingly beyond error as readers of scripture, and which aims to establish a new church with philosophers as "priests or pontiffs." (Even so, Spinoza must have had a keener awareness than he shows that, for Maimonides, this scheme would have to be achieved by the philosophers' concealing themselves and appearing in the guise of traditional piety. He notes that if the people were made aware of this scheme as something advanced by philosophers, they would "ridicule rather than venerate" them.) Spinoza seems to tacitly acknowledge about this scheme that Maimonides devised it in order to ensure the freedom of philosophy in a revealed religion. As Spinoza judged it, however, he pronounced the cure worse than the disease: the scheme of Maimonides is the greatest threat to freedom of thought yet devised. It compels the philosopher to conceal his life of thinking in the basement (or at best the attic) of society but leaves him room for free thought just so long as he keeps his thinking to himself and pretends to support the fiction of scripture as an agent of enlightenment. Meanwhile, it puts a lethal weapon (vis-à-vis thought) in the hands of unscrupulous but ambitious priests who, only required to have some modicum of knowledge, or to be semieducated at the very least, suppress the free mind if it threatens their rule and privilege, i.e., if it emerges from the basement (or the attic) of human society in any segment. The pride of a modern philosopher kept Spinoza from any endorsement of the continuation of the Maimonidean scheme as he construed it, and obligated him to "deconstruct" it as a moral sham and an intellectual pretense, as well as to expose it as a grave social menace.

Almost from his youth, Strauss wondered whether this reduction of Maimonides to the rationalizer of the priestly or theocratic regime was sufficient to do justice to the truly free mind that he manifested so often in his writings, showing him not only free of obedience to authority albeit often in a subtle manner, but also suspicious of authority in its asserting a prerogative to stifle freedom of thought.[10] Maimonides assured a realm of freedom in the law for thought, which already put him beyond the caricature projected on him by Spinoza. Yet precisely by doing this Maimonides was also the necessary condition that prepared the emergence of figures like Spinoza himself (not to mention numerous figures who preceded him) in any Jewish community which guided itself and educated its youth by Maimonidean principles. But the freedom for thought assured by Maimonides was not enough for Spinoza, and so he "deconstructed" the Maimonidean scheme as a halfway house and a school for theological-political authoritarianism. In other words, Spinoza wished to primarily neutralize in the short term, and ultimately abolish in the long term, the well-calculated political usefulness of the Maimonidean scheme to long-established religious authority, since Maimonides still embraced the legitimacy of *any* limits on freedom of thought and freedom of speech, which freedoms had to be confined to subordinate status on the surface. As a result, Spinoza decided in his *Theological-Political Treatise* to mount a massive attack on Maimonides; this critical attack was of lasting significance, and had perhaps the most devastating impact on his reputation compared with every previous attack on the Maimonidean position. Mainly as a result of this critique, Maimonides' philosophic thought was declared dead, buried, and all but forgotten for several hundred years. This is with the exception of orthodox Jews, who faithfully preserved his legacy at least as a great codifier of the law, although they remained deeply suspicious of him insofar as he engaged in autonomous philosophic or nonmystical Jewish thought unrelated with legal matters.

If one considers Spinoza's *Theological-Political Treatise*, especially chapter 7, while keeping in mind just how much the argument with Maimonides runs through the entire *Treatise*, the attentive reader will notice almost constant Maimonidean resonances and counterpoints. It is possible to conclude from this that it is not misconceived to speak about "Spinoza as a Maimonidean"—a label rightly affixed by Warren Zev Harvey—even if it is often a Maimonideanism turned upside down.[11] Hence, in certain decisive respects, perhaps first suggested by Strauss, the *Treatise* represents a thoroughly modern revision of "Maimonideanism" which, even with the revisions, is still built on the model—or at the very least, the ground—of the medieval original. Both thinkers put the greatest emphasis on comprehending biblical religion through prophetology and the political realm (in the most comprehensive sense), and both emphasized paying careful attention to the deliberate and precise use of language in grasping the Bible's message (or lack thereof). Strauss stressed that Spinoza mounted this criticism of Maimonides' thought not because he happened to study the *Guide* in his youth, but rather because he regarded it as the best case that has ever been made by a philosopher speaking in favor of a more or less religion-dominated polity, albeit religion of an enlightened sort, as even Spinoza might have acknowledged about Maimonides. However, it is questionable whether Maimonides himself was actually in favor of a religion-dominated polity, especially if one scrutinizes his views on the role played by the king in society. For Maimonides, the best type of ruler uses entirely "secular" reasoning in the matter of most advantageously or wisely governing the polity. Spinoza claimed to recognize that Maimonides argued in this fashion not because he acted as a dogmatist of revelation, but rather because he acted as a dogmatist of reason—which, as brought to light by Strauss, was indeed for Spinoza the most regrettable error to which Maimonides fell prey. For religion will not long be ruled by philosophers (whom the pious at best consider ridiculous figures), but will result in the ascent of semienlightened "priests" who are only aided in their tyrannical impulses by the philosophical reform of religion. Such priests can advance in surreptitious fashion their power drive and unseemly ambition to rule by concealing them beneath the superficially rationalized political functions of religion, as philosophers sanctify them. Scripture and tradition, according to Spinoza's Maimonides, must conform with reason, because it is this that animates their innermost spirit—even if in his use of scripture and tradition he who makes them conform with reason is also made to recognize the limits of reason alone as the basis for the life of most human beings. According to how Spinoza characterized Maimonides, the effort to impose (dogmatic) reason on most (irrational) people must be concealed as much as possible from most people, while it leaves the reason of him who imposes it free in his own mind. In other words, Maimonides leaves room for absolute freedom of thought in the attic of the polity or the community guided by the law of God, insofar as it follows a Maimonidean approach to such law. Spinoza regarded such an attempt to make for a limited and concealed freedom of thought in the attic of the house of state as being grotesquely misguided, if not essentially futile. It is certainly corrupting to rulers in the political order, and definitely destructive to reason, which philosophers and scientists are supposed to cultivate. But it is also demeaning to the dignity of human beings, which is exemplified in their freedom and which the state is intended to guarantee, since any attempt by the state to limit freedom of thought diminishes human beings in their power and hence also in their dignity. As this leads Spinoza to conclude, reason needs the absolute freedom that only a complete separation between philosophy and religion can provide. Philosophy (or science) and religion will each get their own rooms in the house of the state on the main floor, each performing an assigned but separate task. Moreover, each will be subordinate to the secular reasoning of statesmen who will govern primarily for the good of the entire people, but ultimately for the good of reason in human beings as their most powerful affect. This is because the expectation is that freely constituted rule by enlightened statesmen will serve their own power drive precisely as it is simultaneously coordinated with reason, which calculates for human good. Seen in light of this scheme, it follows that Spinoza would view Maimonides' way to be contrary to the human goods which he desired to advance.

However, on closer inspection Spinoza's plan of action, while based on a seeming rejection of the scheme of Maimonides, was actually a mere modification, or rather modern adaptation, of it. This is because he believed that the Maimonidean scheme, even if acting in the cause of reason, still lent too much power to the irrational to limit and impose itself on the rational. Spinoza contended that the rational as a political force only works properly if it is relatively free in public, endowed with formally authorized status (as "Science"), protected by the secular law, and not limited to the privacy of the mind. Properly comprehended, this difference between Maimonides and Spinoza turns not on whether "revelation" of some sort is necessary, i.e., in scripture (which both think is the case), but on whether ancient reason is sufficient. Or to put it otherwise, Spinoza was concerned with whether ancient or medieval reason's deficient control of the unavoidable immoderation of revealed religion was not in need of correction by modern reason. This would allow reason (as "Science") to be elevated to a free force of secular character that is dedicated to doing civic good and to obliquely governing the course of human actions in the political sphere. Spinoza rejected the political scheme of Maimonides on behalf of reason because he believed that this scheme, at least as Spinoza construed it, makes the rational too much directly responsible for the governance of the irrational through rationalized religious law, which it cannot efficaciously achieve. According to how Spinoza read Maimonides, the political duty of the rational (philosophy and science) is to protect the irrational sphere (superstition and religion) from too much rationality, for it is against the needs of most human beings to be too immersed in rationality. But, for Spinoza, this protecting of the irrational sphere through comprehensive law distorts human life, since human beings are better served by a religion that is guided in a rationalized moral direction and limited to it, which reduces the sphere of the irrational. Philosophers do not need to provide a rational defense of the irrational in religion in order to elevate it; it is better to leave religion as candidly grounded in the irrational and meanwhile reduce its sphere, while also compelling it to moralize itself. For the rational to defend the irrational as if it were somehow quasi-rational, in the sense of potentially rational, allows too much tolerance and legitimacy for the need of irrational rituals and dogmas in ordinary human life. The irrational passions of most human beings (nurtured by the imagination) are best discharged by redirecting them as much as possible to such cathartic vents as patriotism and commerce. Yet as Spinoza conceived of the political purposes communicated in Maimonides' thought, the political duty of the rational is to be tolerant of the irrational as religion, insofar as this gives credence to the needs and rights of such irreducible irrationality; what must instead be taken seriously, according to Spinoza, is the capacity of ordinary people to rule themselves quasi-rationally (i.e., to calculate their own interests and to lend accurate expression to them). This can only be achieved once religion has been limited to the moral and purged of the blatantly superstitious, for in such circumstances the people can be trusted to free themselves from priestly rule. According to Spinoza, Maimonides too much makes the rational supervisors responsible for acts and words which will help to rationalize the irrational (while letting irrational dogma and ritual remain what they are), which tends to corrupt with power those who think and act rationally, animated as they are by the belief that the force which guides them can also shape at a distance the minds and life of those who think and act irrationally. Strauss did not so much judge Spinoza's strictures wrong as instead wonder whether he had fairly comprehended and criticized Maimonides. Indeed, he seems to suggest that (while historical circumstances were undoubtedly different) Spinoza had in fact offered a program quite close to Maimonides'. This raises the issue of their genuine difference, which for Strauss is concentrated on the intention to promote surpassing human excellence, which he attributes only to Maimonides.

Spinoza relegated Maimonides' scheme to a megalomaniac fantasy of the medieval (if not also ancient) dogmatic rationalist, attempting to entwine the rational with the irrational and so also control or temper it, though definitely on different levels, i.e., rational few above, irrational many below. Curiously he considered his own modern scheme humbler, because the arrangement is apparently parallel, although actually hierarchical in a different sense: let the rational govern from one side, which is fully lawful and covered by the curtain of science, while it relegates the irrational to the other side, which is safely separate, subordinate, and hence neutralized. So long as the rationalists are allowed to define the limits in which the irrational may operate (i.e., superstition and religion are reduced mainly to morality), they may leave the irrational many free to operate in their own sphere and so permit the rationalist few to dedicate themselves unhampered to the pursuit of reason (philosophy and science), warranted as legitimate by their commitment to advance the social good. And yet in the end Spinoza's project, however altered, was still a revised version of Maimonides' scheme. Maimonides remained the teacher by whom Spinoza was originally schooled and from whom he diverged; he adhered to his teacher's fundamental passion for the life of the mind as it defines the human individual and, though delimited differently, also the human collective. For Strauss it was not clear that Spinoza was not merely carrying through certain aspects of Maimonides' logic in a modern context, which to be sure certainly laid greater stress on the rights of the demos and trusted it to regulate itself by quasi reason, i.e., by a right to the rationally calculated expression of its own interests. But, as Strauss perceived, this was not so far from Maimonides as Spinoza claimed, since Spinoza followed Maimonides in thinking that a badly educated or ignorant "priestly" elite is one of the worst forms of human governance. This needs to be corrected through a pedagogy which rationalizes the religious sources on which such an elite claims to govern, and which also helps to free the people from subservience to (religious) ignorance. But as Strauss also discerned, Maimonides thought this through with greater depth than Spinoza by suggesting that another political form is worse than rule by badly educated or ignorant "priests," i.e., tyranny (whether religious or secular), and it needs constantly to be guarded against. On this point, namely, the question of the nature of better and worse regimes, Maimonides' "ancient" wisdom was sounder than its modern correction as enunciated by Spinoza, because he better recognized that corrupt religion is only one of the bad regimes by which human beings govern themselves and which can threaten the rational life of human beings in which their nature is supposed to fulfill itself: Spinoza too readily got around human misrule by artificially limiting the problem to certain causes only. In this respect, Strauss seems to have regarded Maimonides as "more modern" than Spinoza. To be sure, it was for Strauss not unreasonable for most modern scholars to give their allegiance to the latter rather than the former in political persuasion, rightly favoring the modern liberal democracy of Spinoza. Yet in the face of 20th-century "totalitarianism," Strauss was impressed with Maimonides' wise teaching and took to heart his reminder that bad regimes such as rule by badly educated or ignorant "priests," while abhorrent and in need of being corrected or even opposed, are still less evil than tyranny. The ever-present potential and grave threat of tyranny must always be properly comprehended in its true dimensions so as to guard against it, as Spinoza, not to mention Cohen, and their scholarly descendants in the study of Maimonides did not always do.[12] In this context, one may wonder whether Strauss regarded Maimonides' intention to promote surpassing human excellence in exceptional individuals (like himself) as not only in the cause of the true human telos, and because they benefit their fellow beings through the "overflow" of their virtue (or "perfection"), but also because they are a bulwark against, and potential leaders in the resistance of humanity against, tyranny.

One should also not forget to mention and acknowledge modern researchers like Salomon Munk, among whose apologetic aims were to provide Maimonides and those like him with a decent and proper scholarly interment. The purpose of that was to plant a scholarly gravestone by which to preserve his memory, among modern Jews specifically and modern people in general, and so to recall and establish what the Jews and their medieval thinkers had once contributed to the emergence of the modern West. Perhaps the most notorious statement to this effect was made by Moritz Steinschneider (1816–1907), one of the great scholars of "*Wissenschaft des Judentums*" (i.e, "science of Judaism," or "modern Jewish studies") in 19th-century Germany, whom even Gershom Scholem while leveling damning criticism at him had once also praised as "one of the most significant scholars the Jewish people has ever produced." He was regarded by most 19th and 20th-century scholars as a heroic figure in his pure dedication to the cause of building a critical, textually accurate, and historically sound basis for modern Jewish knowledge. But this notorious statement by Steinschneider to which I refer contains a much deeper significance. It was an *obiter dictum* spoken to a student, Gotthold Weil, who reported it as follows: "We have only one task remaining: to provide the remains of Judaism with a decent burial." Note, however, that the "remains of Judaism" tended to encompass even towering figures like Maimonides, who was judged to have retained little to teach modern man, other than perhaps his negative theology; the rest, like most elements in past Judaism, is only of antiquarian relevance and is not in any sense even potentially superior to modern thought. This attitude can be detected in the works of most modern scholars prior to Strauss, even though most of them had made the effort to apply themselves assiduously to studying Maimonides' writings for his thought (and did not just critically edit his texts). Although they should undoubtedly be recognized for their serious scholarly endeavors to comprehend Maimonides' contributions as a worthwhile historical legacy, they almost never believed that his writings contain directly useful knowledge and are of utmost relevance to contemporary philosophic thought. As one can tell from Strauss's remarks on Salomon Munk and other scholars like him, he was markedly skeptical of the ultimate achievement of the late 19th- and early 20th-century Jewish scholars who had been researching Maimonides and other great medieval Jewish philosophers like Judah Halevi. In his view, they had only made the tiniest first steps in the effort to penetrate a labyrinth-like edifice of thought of much greater profundity than had been hitherto acknowledged. In other words, they had neglected to "enter the king's court" (to use Maimonides' own parable), and hence did not even consider the possibility that Maimonides is a perennial thinker who still has an enormous amount to teach. Indeed, it seemed almost absurd to suggest to these modern scholars of medieval Jewish philosophy that modern man might have need for Maimonides' thought in order to contend with contemporary dilemmas (theological, philosophical, ethical, and political).

As Strauss emphatically makes this point against his leading predecessors, albeit with respect for their achievement, however limited, "Everyone working in this field is deeply indebted to the great achievements of Salomon Munk, David Kaufmann, and Harry A. Wolfson in particular. But I am sure that these great scholars would be the first to admit that modern scholarship has not yet crossed the threshold of such works as Halevi's *Kuzari* and Maimonides' *Guide*: '*Ben Zoma 'adayin baḥuẓ*.' We are still in a truly preliminary stage." Strauss's Hebrew phrase (which one may translate as "Ben Zoma is still outside") alludes to a passage of the *Guide* in which Maimonides mentions his own skepticism about an ancient scholar who supposedly entered the secret garden of the truths in the Torah but who actually did not get very far. In similar fashion, Strauss paralleled these modern scholars to Ben Zoma, who was judged "still outside" the garden (*pardes*) of the secret teachings concealed in the Torah, considering them "still outside" the king's court of Maimonides' own innermost teaching. Strauss was even moved to apply this judgment to the views of his friend Gershom Scholem with regard to how he perceived the aims of the genuine Jewish philosopher. For Strauss, Maimonides' approach to popular religion (for which Scholem faulted him as compared with the Jewish mystics) was grounded not just in what is needed for the survival of the Jewish people, faith, and tradition in history, but also in what is required for the unhampered pursuit of truth as essential to a fulfilled human life. This was central for Strauss's defense of Maimonides in spite of the fact that he was in accord with his friend Scholem on several fundamental issues pertaining to modern Judaism, such as the need for a modern, liberal-democratic Jewish state, and the obligation to maintain modern Jewish studies that are free of both orthodox dogmatic constraints and censorship, as well as of assimilationist tendentiousness, liberal apologetics, and modern rationalistic prejudices. As Strauss was determined to highlight, even Scholem, the greatest Jewish scholar of his generation, seemed unable to appreciate the true depths and genuine radicalism of Maimonides' thought. Indeed, based on what had to be admitted even about Scholem, Strauss doubted that most scholars of this era even knew how to assess the true character of Maimonides' greatness as a thinker, especially insofar as this was an achievement not limited to his time and place. To be sure, this criticism of Scholem, the friend whom he so admired, did not signify that Strauss was claiming that he had alone fully probed the depths, but only that he wondered whether these depths might not be even deeper than anyone had previously imagined. To even entertain this possibility required the daring of an imaginative leap, in which Strauss reconfigured Maimonides, allowing him to escape from the historical-conceptual straitjacket in which he had been permitted to languish as a thinker. Perhaps the political crisis of the West in the 1930s and 1940s had compelled Strauss to break free of conventions, and to try to establish a new basis on which to preserve the old order of the West.[13]

However, Strauss seems to have begun his journey toward Maimonides by wondering something simple—yet linked with an astonishing boldness, and with a true radicalness of thought—in contrast to both traditional scholarly defenders of Maimonides' piety as the paragon of religious lawfulness, i.e., the anti-Spinoza party, and to modern scholarly enshriners of Maimonides' burial site as hallowed Western ground, i.e., the pro-Spinoza party, one which was able and willing to admit Maimonides' achievement, albeit only once Spinoza's project had completely triumphed, and in a context of not yet doubting the legitimacy of such a triumph as counting in favor of Maimonides. The simple thought that moved Strauss as a not yet fully mature thinker may be stated as follows: he wondered whether Spinoza, whatever good his thought may have done, had properly comprehended what Maimonides was doing. Thus, he eventually wondered whether the deeper scheme of Maimonides, which Spinoza attempted to undo, had truly been undone. Indeed, he discovered a Spinoza who was compelled to imitate Maimonides (by also appearing in the guise of an esoteric writer), even if he was determined to qualify and limit Maimonides' "method" decisively by putting it to a different use. And he proceeded to study Maimonides in a fortuitous manner that, by good fortune, brought him to rediscover deeper strata in this scheme, although all believed they already knew it through and through. As a result, Strauss uncovered an unknown, deeper, hitherto concealed Maimonides, whose thought had never been conceived among either the medievals or the moderns to have had the contours Strauss attributed to it, yet who thought with a profundity not acknowledged by Spinoza even while he benefited from it and remained beholden to it. As this led Strauss to conclude, Maimonides claimed as essential—and Spinoza conceded the point de facto (i.e., by how he wrote), even if perhaps not de jure—that both concealed and revealed levels are needed, and must deliberately be so constructed, for anyone who wishes to write a great book.

This deeper scheme as Strauss discerned it may be characterized as a project to preserve religious tradition while reforming it in the direction of reason. Maimonides could only do so by rethinking radically what tradition is, which also required him to think through—deeply, clearly, and thoroughly—what religion is, i.e., with a completely free mind, not determined by either the passions of the partisan or the prejudices of the adherent. Then, acting as a philosophic statesman in the highest sense, he had to enunciate politically (or in terms of human nature) why there might be, in our Western religious tradition, something better than any available—or maybe even conceivable—alternative. Thus, contrary to the shades in which Spinoza painted his portrait of Maimonides and by which Spinoza characterized the tendency of Maimonides as an unmitigated "dogmatist" in thought, Strauss used a different style and technique in his depiction of Maimonides, showing the fully colored light on which the dark shadows depended. Or to change the metaphor from art to architecture, Strauss perceived how Maimonides, contrary to the presentation of Spinoza, permitted the greatest freedom, and even radicalism, of thought at a level much closer to the surface, and not just in the basement (or the attic), of the house he built. Maimonides may seem to have only rearranged the old furniture on the main floor of the house of religious tradition, while perhaps adding a couple of new pieces. But he also simultaneously, if with subtle art, showed that this house (i.e., the house built by Moses) makes, *if dwelled in according to the proper rules*, for a most habitable and decent civilization, while also being hospitable to the most free possible life of thought, and hence is an enlightening tradition which is in favor of rational enlightenment.

According to Strauss, the possibility that biblical tradition is consistent with the life of free thought was something greater than Spinoza had been able to imagine or willing to admit, even if he did think the original prophet-lawgiver Moses, unlike the Christian church and the rabbinic reform of Judaism in the wake of defeat by Rome, focused mainly on actions, and rarely regulated thought, which might seem to show he, too, appreciated the *authentic* or *original* biblical tradition as allowing for the freedom of thought. This is because Spinoza was convinced that the decrepit house—most evident and powerful in medieval Christianity, but even worse in the aggressive empire of Islam, which he was acquainted with as ruled by the Ottoman Turks—could not be renovated or salvaged by however brilliant an architect might be drafted to rescue it, never mind a clever designer merely shifting around the furniture. He believed it was so because it could not accommodate someone like him, i.e., one who was bound by no religion, but only by science. Or rather, if he believed it was possible, this was so only if it was refashioned in the configuration that he designed for it: the fundamentals of the religious tradition had to be reshaped in a secular "manly" spirit, which allowed for full human freedom, both of action and of thought, unconstrained by revealed imperatives. He was not willing to acknowledge how much someone like Maimonides had made provision to accommodate him, just so long as he maintained a basic loyalty, while Spinoza regarded religious tradition (for someone like him) as a hindrance to free thought and nothing much else besides. If, as Spinoza did recognize, religious tradition could continue to serve a good purpose in the teaching and the maintaining of morality, he regarded reason as a sufficient moral guide for him and those like him. As Strauss, based on Maimonidean reasoning, seemed to suggest about Spinoza, he did not think through whether on the basis of his defense of religious tradition (which we may summarize as "false but necessary"), it could survive and perform the function that he still assigned to it, as this is still needed (once reformed) to regulate the ignorant. For Spinoza, the house built by Maimonides had to be demolished and reconstructed from the ground up, because everything on which it rested was decayed, if not utterly corrupting. Strauss indeed did not reject Spinoza's assessment of the facts, or even his redesign and rebuilding effort. He merely wondered whether the new house, rebuilt on old ground and employing key elements or materials of the original (i.e., God, scripture, ancient Jewish history, biblical morality, churches and synagogues, Jews and Christians, theological notions like just retribution, repentance, and the future life, etc.), did not preserve—and hence continue to depend on—some of the most essential features of the original.

And besides this, Strauss had also witnessed the falling down of the secular house in Weimar Germany, which brought him to wonder whether it had made adequate provisions for its own preservation and self-defense.

As a last word on the forces of mind from which Strauss had to liberate himself in his youth, it is also likely that Strauss owed a substantial debt, in his ability to see this precise limit on Spinoza's project, to Nietzsche, who had offered a fresh pair of eyes with which to view biblical tradition. In Nietzsche's seemingly most radical rejection of everything biblical, he attempted to shine an x-ray on what is tacitly contained in the scriptural tradition and what low drives or high hopes motivated it and kept it in motion. As a result, he was also able to show how it has continued to shape surreptitiously the modern Western mind on just those points which were claimed as produced solely by autonomous reason (especially as pertained to morality, but also even to science). In consequence, he offered a fresh view of Western thought to those who were willing to adjust their sights to it, which Strauss endeavored to do by absorbing Nietzsche's lessons critically, rather than by being swept away by them and by his powerful rhetoric. But Strauss also noticed how Nietzsche himself, in his supposedly radical rejection of everything biblical, had not escaped being enmeshed in biblical thought and its categories—and because of that needed to justify, better than he did, his own, not fully acknowledged, retention of the Hebrew Bible, or at least of certain essential aspects of its spirit even in his projected future for redesigned human beings. In the end, Strauss wondered whether Maimonides had not actually provided a better model for how to combine rational criticism with retaining what is still of greatest power and profundity in the biblical tradition.

SEVEN

The Maimonidean Revolution
Western Tradition as Reason and Revelation

OUR EFFORT TO MAKE EVIDENT THE CIVILIZATIONAL thrust of Strauss's revolutionary project (scholarly-philosophic-political-theological) as it bears on Maimonides may be helped if we recur for a moment to the architectural metaphor. The new house built by Spinoza—i.e., modern Western liberal democracy, and the liberal forms of biblical religion which are rooted in the politics of Spinoza—continues to be threatened with a collapse of its own. Meanwhile, it is not always the shelter for reason that it promised to be, since this house invites the exaggerated or irrational faith in reason which he tended to foster on the tactical level, i.e., to abolish the old religion, even if he was not so convinced of its possible use to most people on the strategic level, i.e., since most people will still have need of faith, revelation, and scripture, even if only in the form of the new religion. So far as Strauss was concerned, the effort to save Spinoza's construction project—whose habitable quality, so long as it did not collapse, Strauss readily acknowledged—required an unprejudiced study of the plans of the unadmitted architect of the old house in the original, unrenovated form (i.e., Maimonides) on which it was built, and whose materials, structure, and design it reused. Similarly, he thought that this same effort would benefit from a study of the surrounding grounds (i.e., ancient and medieval philosophy) on whose solidity it depended for support. Precisely in the effort—as Strauss conceived of it—to preserve the new house, this also required attaining a fresh grasp of the deeper history of the thought about human need, dwelling, and habitation that contributed to the design of the old house: what about its groundwork endured and what required correction. By doing just this, Strauss also discovered that the aim of Spinoza was to rebuild—albeit on the same essential ground used previously by the religious tradition, at least in its enlightened form, as conceived of by Maimonides—the political order whose moral framework was provided by scripture and by the God who "revealed" or, better, authorized it by acting as its supreme authority. And it was on just this ground that Maimonides had taken his stand, and on which he still gives us perhaps the most compelling account of how to preserve in a healthy state the two roots of our Western tradition, "Jerusalem and Athens."

Indeed, Maimonides is, as Strauss can be recognized to have suggested, almost the unacknowledged legislator of the modern Western tradition, especially for Jews, but also just as much for Western Christians derived from Thomas Aquinas, by whose "method" we believe it is possible to "synthesize"—however, only in the sense of "harmonize" or "synchronize"—reason and revelation at the highest level. Spinoza's approach may have been a merited "correction" of Maimonides, but his criticism of Maimonides to the contrary notwithstanding, it remained in a certain, very definite measure grounded in Maimonides, since Spinoza did not accept the full program of Machiavelli, as completed by Bacon, Descartes, and Hobbes. Spinoza accepted one of Maimonides' most crucial distinctions, even though he put it to uses other than how best to clarify scripture. Thus, José Faur writes about Maimonides' position on how reason (in the form of science) and revelation (in the form of scripture) are to be harmonized: "Essential to this belief [i.e., in the harmony of scripture and science] was the thesis that there are two levels to Scripture: an exoteric level accessible to the vulgar, and an esoteric level accessible only to the elite. Without this distinction, all attempts to reconcile the Scripture with science are impossible." Faur's succinct summary of this religious issue is a fine expression of what makes Maimonides still so interesting, and why he can still be viewed as a revolutionary figure in Jewish and Western thought. Maimonides perceived that there is a crucial divide in human nature which cannot be avoided and which cannot help but bear great consequences, whether these manifest themselves in the way Maimonides conceived them or the divergent way Spinoza apprehended them. Although Faur then pursues quite a different line of approach from that of Strauss to Maimonides, he has been taught by this contrasting line of approach to appreciate the esoteric-exoteric distinction as fundamental to comprehending Maimonides' thought, especially in the manner it elucidates human nature and its unavoidable divide. Faur was able to discern that Maimonides had achieved the highest understanding of what it entails to attempt to reconcile scripture with science or philosophy. In this sense, Faur perceived that such an attempt has to be based on the overarching distinction between the exoteric level (i.e., written for the intellectually vulgar many) and the esoteric level (i.e., written for the cognitively excellent few). However, Faur deviated from Strauss in that he claimed to alone recognize how this distinction remains problematic for us in our modern, politically egalitarian liberal democratic order, and in our modern scientific worldview, structured as it is by a methodological egalitarianism, which always begins with matter and so equalizes everything. Faur may be correct that there is a difficulty, but then this is in great measure because of Spinoza, who established both orders, i.e., the political and the scientific. And yet, though Spinoza sharply questioned the approach of Maimonides and made most modern thinkers radically doubt it, he never actually abandoned its essential features or contours. He retained the idea of the many and the few as a relevant and even essential distinction, even though it may not bear the same direct "medieval" political consequences as it did for Maimonides. Spinoza just moved the issue from one plane to another: he transposed it from speculative truth to moral truth. In other words, he moved it from a political metaphysics of souls to an economy of souls, the disproportion produced from below (rather than from above) by the needs of the body-soul complex. The scripture that he read—supposedly "literally" rather than "allegorically"—as yielding one clear and consistent moral teaching, also required him to make some (nonliteral) textual "adjustment," by which he may be said—against himself—to "allegorize," so as to make this reading of scripture fit with what he derives as its clear and consistent moral teaching. Meanwhile, he also called for the acceptance by everyone of a moral teaching which is supposed to be good in actuality for most people, although as it happens it is not, according to Spinoza's philosophy, in literal accord with the philosophic truth.

Thus, the notion of two levels in the text persists as reflecting the two types of souls in any human society—although in truncated form as a copy of its Maimonidean original, since in Spinoza's modern version the "concealed" level points beyond scripture (because of its contradictions) rather than toward its hidden depths. Spinoza moved the duality from something in scripture alone to scripture correlated with society. The exoteric level remains (i.e., its valid moral teaching) as useful for politics and religion; but the esoteric level lies, as it were, "on top of" scripture, i.e., in the separate domain of science or philosophy, for those who can appreciate it. Biblical criticism points the capable students toward the higher historical level by the very contradictions in scriptural theology that this science highlights for them, pointing toward its ultimate deficiency. This is not to suggest that biblical criticism is necessarily able to do greater justice to scripture than the lexicographic method used by Maimonides, since its science of terms in their multilevel significance leaves it with a potential cognitive depth, while this is a possibility that had to be disallowed by Spinoza. But in any case, as Maimonides was the first to perceive—and as Spinoza did not advance beyond—the two human poles of scripture and science will always be needed, and a single level will never be sufficient for the complexity of human nature in political order, and they will forever be bound to one another by an inextricable connection. Indeed, they will require some form of the exoteric-esoteric distinction to preserve their connection. For the exoteric-esoteric distinction is correlated, as even Spinoza was compelled to accept, with Judaism (and thus with scripture), insofar as this tradition based on a book preserves both the "subterranean" or irrational level and the surface or rationalistic level. The latter is evident in the law, but the former is evident both in its theology and in the people that, through its survival precisely as aided by scripture, shows itself mysteriously possessed of the power to regenerate itself, to be "chosen again." Strauss makes plain how Spinoza adapted Maimonideanism for his own uses, based on a prudent assessment of how it can be adapted to the modern situation: "At first glance [Spinoza] might well appear to be much more medieval than Descartes, to say nothing of Bacon and Hobbes. . . . Spinoza, however, attempts to restore the traditional conception of contemplation. . . . He was thus the first great thinker who attempted a synthesis of premodern (classical-medieval) and of modern philosophy." In other words, Strauss observed that Spinoza did not escape the basic idea of Maimonides, which rooted that which is most essential in human beings in the life of theoretical thoughtfulness rather than in the life of practical action. This is so even if the same basic ("premodern") idea also recognizes the fundamental duty to morality as the primary condition of any decent life in human society as well as of the attainment of the life rooted in genuine thoughtfulness: "the traditional conception of contemplation," once "restored" on a modern basis by Spinoza, certainly allows for the greater urgency of morality and the common political life (what Maimonides dubs "the first perfection" in *Guide* 3.27), but even so it still results for Spinoza in "the [higher] dignity of speculation." Strauss recognized in Spinoza a version of basic Maimonideanism cleverly adapted—although, to be sure, not untransformed in the process—to the changed conditions of modern life.[1] It is in this sense, then, that Strauss recognized he was not compelled to abandon

Spinoza's modern practical teaching in the process of his rediscovering Maimonides' greater theoretical profundity—there remains a certain continuity between the two thinkers.

Of course, Spinoza cannot follow Maimonides in all matters: he certainly seems to reject revelation in its root and principle, i.e., the "fundamentalist" thesis regarding how revelation occurs. But he also needs something like it, in order to make his structure "move" as something vital, as a form of human life: it morally subsists on the fruit of revelation, i.e., scripture and theology, albeit both radically revised. In other words, Strauss perceived that the thinking and the art of Maimonides reached a height never previously, and never subsequently, attained, even if this might well have been "improved" in some respects by Spinoza, relying on the comprehensive criticism provided by Machiavelli. Viewed from the ground on which Strauss stood as he admired the height attained by Maimonides, it may be epitomized as follows: He alone made it possible for us to believe that what the West is (i.e., reason and revelation somehow combined in the full integrity of both), is genuinely possible, as can be recognized in a spiritually honest state of Western self-consciousness. Maimonides remakes or completes the West as the attempt to devise a form of thought which—as this approximates to *the* truth—is a truly rigorous form of thinking, is still in need of a fierce dialectical tension for its thought to thrive, and requires of us (as the descendants in modern array of a Maimonidean Spinoza) in our adapted form both reason, i.e., modern science, *and* revelation, i.e., the Hebrew Bible. Hence, Strauss diverged from the historical construction of Harry A. Wolfson, who maintained that the attempt to bring about the harmony of scripture and science which defines the West was first fully established by Philo Judaeus of Alexandria in the 1st century CE and was decisively destroyed by Spinoza in the 17th century. As Strauss seems to have been of the opinion, this construction was not so much historically wrong as philosophically superficial: Philo did not comprehend as deeply as Maimonides the potential implications of the attempt to synthesize or harmonize reason and revelation. Certainly there was no corresponding attention paid to either how to read scripture with the utmost care or the reasons for the great precision with which it was originally written. Likewise Strauss was of the view that Spinoza had not forever deconstructed this possibility as thoroughly as Wolfson believed he had, since for Strauss Spinoza's method was definitely not able to "refute" revelation, as he tacitly claimed. Moreover, this same method of supposedly deconstructing revelation remained beholden to some of the key notions in Maimonides' mode of thought, which had supposedly been surpassed as obsolete. It may not be surprising then that Wolfson wrote lengthy and complex books on Philo and Spinoza, but no equivalent book on Maimonides. In Strauss's judgment, it seems something of profundity was missing in Wolfson's grand account of Western spiritual history: the unresolved dialectical tension or difference between the two sides. And this very unsettled dialectical tension, as a moral and cognitive quarrel, is the warrant for the future survival of the modern West: even though it will still be confronted by numerous enemies, it need not regard these as philosophically decisive. Its two claims to truth still stand, for they have not been able to refute, defeat, and swallow one another.[2] For the numerous enemies of the modern West (e.g., Nazis, communists, Islamists, etc.), in spite of their diversity, are mostly able to mount serious criticisms in which the West is arraigned on assorted charges by their studying in the philosophic school of Nietzsche and Heidegger: these two elaborated the most serious criticisms used by left and right alike. Strauss believed he had compellingly grasped and persuasively shown, in the wake of his study of Maimonides, that the philosophic integrity, moral substance, and theological-political solidity of the modern West with regard to its fundamental principles can be sustained against these criticisms. For Strauss, Maimonides anticipated most of Nietzsche's (more or less ancient) criticism of the biblical legacy, and if properly comprehended, his "reform" can be perceived to have already reset the biblical legacy in a revised form capable of responding to the most forceful Nietzschean (or post-Nietzschean) challenges.

To be sure, it was not until the 20th century that Maimonides began to be rediscovered in a philosophically serious, and relatedly positive, light. This may have something to do with the constant decay besetting the house built by Spinoza, accompanied by its occasional collapse and difficult reconstruction, often precariously persisting in the wake of criticism by a host of "postmodern" (i.e., post-Heideggerian) opponents. The achievement of Spinoza's dream in a project of such ambiguous, often falling fulfillment has led to doubts about its solidity and about the philosophy that bolsters it. These doubts have perhaps helped to spur a reconsideration of the figure whose thought Spinoza seemed most vigorously to oppose, Maimonides, showing this opposition to often be philosophically misguided or superficial, even if historically defensible. Much of the beginning of this reconsideration of Maimonides as a serious thinker may be primarily attributed to the German Jewish philosophic thinker Hermann Cohen, whose comments often acted as an aggressive spur to Strauss.

He doubted the definitive character of Cohen's defense of Maimonides, which reconceptualized his thought by morally grounding it in an anticipatory neo-Kantian form. Besides his modern philosophic neo-Kantianism, Cohen made an earnest and concerted attempt to explore, and finally even to rely on, what he was the first to recognize as Maimonides' medieval *Platonic* (rather than, as conventionally asserted, merely *Aristotelian*) thought, or cast of mind. He did so in order to validate, on a quasi-traditional basis, his own modern rationalistic, i.e., neo-Kantian, interpretation of the sources of Judaism as a religion of reason, which was itself calculated to advance the cause of modernity.

In certain respects, no doubt Cohen's scheme bore a distinct resemblance to Maimonides' scheme; but Strauss perceived that this also required a clear divergence from Maimonides, sufficient for him to recognize the resemblance as on the surface only. It would have been necessary for Cohen to pay greater attention to the philosophically political as well as to the priority of thinking in Maimonidean thought as what determines its trajectory in its author's mind, which Cohen refused to consider, since it would imply a compromise of its "pure" morality. To be sure, Strauss acknowledged in Cohen a greater awareness of the Western tradition of political philosophy than in all of the major 20th-century philosophers who followed him (and rarely recognized what he had contributed even on such matters): "As regards the philosophers, it is sufficient to contrast the work of the four greatest philosophers of the last forty years—Bergson, Whitehead, Husserl, and Heidegger—with the work of Hermann Cohen in order to see how rapidly and thoroughly political philosophy has become discredited."

"The last forty years" is judged from the perspective of 1954–55, in which academic year the lecture was originally delivered in Jerusalem from which those remarks on Cohen derive. Whether or not he wished to say in this statement that Cohen's awareness of the tradition of Western political philosophy was deeper than all of them put together is not as evident; he certainly never seemed to judge Cohen one of the great political philosophers. Yet he seemed to imply that Cohen vigorously responded to this tradition as if it still represented a serious challenge to thought and a vital repository from which wisdom might be obtained, which view held true among philosophers until the onset of World War I in the 20th century.[3] Indeed, Strauss was, in fact, highly impressed by Cohen's philosophic system, even though he was not ultimately persuaded by it. This was also and especially true with regard to Cohen's account of Maimonides, which Strauss viewed as worthy of being admired for its motives, even if essentially flawed. Not only did Strauss reject the modern method of interpreting the medieval texts of Maimonides employed by Cohen, but Strauss also was not able to recognize the thought of Maimonides in the content of those texts, at least as they had been explicated by Cohen. However, as a result of Strauss's reconsideration of Cohen's attempted vindication of Maimonides, as well as by his critically reviewing Spinoza's well-established critique of Maimonides, he did start to discern in Maimonides certain theological and political features of his thought which, strangely enough, seemed to him to be of greater philosophic persuasiveness than almost anything available to him in the arguments presented by the full array of modern Jewish thinkers.

Consider the passing comment that Strauss made about Maimonides, which raises the issue of what his ultimate intent was, insofar as this explains some of the peculiar features in his work: "This is the defense of philosophy which was required always and everywhere," i.e., to satisfy the city that the philosophers are "good citizens and even the best of citizens." But the two-sidedness of this endeavor was already stated in his first work on Maimonides, for that work stressed the need to balance two imperatives:

> Maimonides is not setting up a pedagogic program by virtue of sovereign philosophy. He himself had in his own life followed this advice given to the young. He also was brought up as a Jew, before he turned to philosophy. As a Jew, born, living and dying with Jews, he pursued philosophy as a Jewish teacher of Jews. His argumentation takes its course, his disputes take place, within the context of Jewish life, and for that context. He defends the context of Jewish life which is threatened by the philosophers in so far as it is threatened by them. He enlightens Judaism by means of philosophy, to the extent that Judaism can be enlightened. He elevates Judaism by means of philosophy once again to the height it originally attained, so far as Judaism had descended from that height as a result of the disfavor of the times; Maimonides' philosophy is based in principle and throughout on Judaism.

Even if it might be necessary to qualify and supplement the first and last phrases, there is nothing else in this statement that could not have been repeated by Strauss at any stage in the development of his own thought. However far he advanced, Strauss never forgot the dialectical double-sidedness of the Maimonidean project, and he was taught by him never to forget the need to balance those same two imperatives: it makes sense for one to pursue and unfold the esoteric teaching only if one is grounded in the exoteric teaching.

Indeed, one is capable of properly bringing to light the former only if one respects, remains fully attentive to, and adequately derives one's guidelines for proceeding from the latter. According to the school of ancient and medieval philosophy, which he was trying to renovate and in whose vital elements he was trying to ground himself, piety is mostly consistent with philosophy, however they may be hierarchically related to one another. Thus, Catherine Zuckert curiously suggests that Strauss imitates Maimonides' piety by calling a halt to his own "introductory essay," as an interpretation of the *Guide*, with the first seventy chapters, which focus almost entirely on biblical exegesis. This literary device allowed him to avoid the need to *directly* confront the great speculative issues, such as whether the world is created or eternal; these issues *can* properly be confronted only obliquely. For a comment by Maimonides himself along these lines, consider the following: "For my purpose is that the truths be glimpsed and then again be concealed, so as not to oppose *that divine purpose which one cannot possibly oppose* and which has concealed from the vulgar among the people those truths especially requisite for His apprehension." Hence, what must be focused on is why it "*cannot*" be opposed: it is scarcely a matter of merely obeying the law. Even if one traces the steps by which Strauss uncovered what he would begin to regard as the forgotten literary depths in Maimonides, this would ultimately yield the still highly relevant original teachings of Maimonides that preserve, elaborate, sift, and advance—if on different grounds—the two sides of his thought focused on both philosophy and the Hebrew Bible. This original teaching Strauss was moved to defend, in spite of its supposedly "medieval" character, by attempting to reclaim its deepest impulses of thought and its most exacting insights as a defense of *both* reason *and* revelation, which according to Strauss are not limited by its medieval context. From Maimonides Strauss believed he learned truths that enabled him to resist what he was most critical of in contemporary philosophy. Thus, to state it in somewhat perplexing, but still accurate, terms, Strauss thought the medievals were keener critics and sharper assessors of what is most relevant in the thought of Maimonides even to present-day students. Hence, he was more impressed by the medieval critique of Maimonides and its grounds—i.e., philosophy is apparently opposed to divine law, rather than obviously in harmony with it—than he was by the modern critique of Maimonides. According to the modern critique, Maimonides *either* compromises philosophic reason in the name of theology *or* is too near to philosophic reason and too far from theology, implying he is too elitist, too intellectualist, and too naturalistic. Similarly, Strauss was less drawn to the modern appreciation of Maimonides and its grounds. According to what Maimonides' modern admirers praise him for, *either* his philosophy favors supreme and autonomous morality as opposed to the desire for knowledge *or* his views culminate in negative theology, this being a still-defensible form of religious thought that modern theology cannot transcend or surpass. But Strauss was drawn to what Maimonides' medieval advocates appreciated in his thought not because of its medievalism, but rather because of how it may be of aid in addressing modern concerns: philosophy and divine law are conjoined in a moral and speculative training to cultivate the supreme desire for knowledge, while their conjunction also prepares adequately enlightened leaders and teachers. To put it in even terser terms still, Strauss was able to rediscover the perennial philosophic argument in which Maimonides' medieval notion of law was grounded. As a result, Strauss was also able to articulate an accurate restatement of the philosophic argument of Maimonides, which Strauss was convinced had been rejected mainly because it had been deliberately misconstrued and misrepresented by its original modern critics, especially Spinoza, but also his numerous modern "students" who in his wake merely thought to carry further various aspects of his criticism.[4]

This was at least in some measure due to Strauss's full awareness of the "crisis" of modernity and of modern thought, which amounted to a full-scale attack on modern reason as well as on traditional revelation. This crisis had been provoked by Nietzsche's and Heidegger's radically critical thought about modernity, a radically critical thought that Strauss believed goes to the heart of what modernity is and challenges that heart fundamentally. Strauss maintained that, as of yet, no previous modern Jewish thinker had adequately come to terms with this crisis, or even faced it fully.[5] And it was precisely this same modern predicament that induced Strauss to examine Maimonides again, since he started to think that perhaps in this medieval thinker something of original and essential rationalism had been better preserved, which was better able to be reconciled with needed revelation than anything which the moderns had on offer, especially since authentic revelation was required and was to be preferred, against the ersatz as well as deficient versions put on offer by Nietzsche, by Heidegger, and by their numerous postmodern heirs. Though the moderns (like Spinoza) treated reason as their point of departure and as their special possession, Strauss started to wonder whether in what he discovered about Maimonides' thought, i.e., how he wrote, and what he taught, it did not make him something higher or purer as a devotee to reason and to critical thinking, while never forced to abandon revelation as the biblical legacy, and yet maintaining his commitment to intellectual excellence, cognitive integrity, and uncompromised honesty. Indeed, once Maimonides had been reconsidered, Strauss dramatically asked whether he was not "the 'classic of rationalism' in Judaism," if not "the true natural model, the standard" of rationalism per se,[6] "to be carefully protected from any distortion, and thus the stumbling-block on which modern rationalism falls."[7] And yet in the end it is not so simple to say *precisely what*, for Strauss, made Maimonides the standard of rationalism in every time and place, which became a matter of conviction in Strauss's thought.

The effort to determine whether Strauss finally judged Maimonides to be quite such a uniquely fundamental figure in the entire history of Western thought as it might at first seem requires a substantial and prolonged reflection by serious readers, since some critics believe that this is not so much Maimonideanism as revived Platonism (or Farabianism) unencumbered by revelation in one form or another. But judged from the perspective of Strauss's devotion to studying Maimonides during his entire scholarly career, no doubt Strauss never ceased trying to "awaken a prejudice in favor" of Maimonides as a "true natural model," as a "standard of rationalism," in Judaism and in philosophy itself. Simultaneously, though with even greater and no doubt undiminished conviction, Strauss never ceased trying to "arouse a suspicion" against the powerful opposing prejudices, insofar as such prejudices were directed against Maimonides by his most wounding modern critic, Spinoza, or generated in his favor by his most ardent modern defender, Cohen. Reflecting on the character of Strauss's achievement and the moment in which it received its definitive form and direction, one may refer to the "Introduction" of *Philosophy and Law* as meriting the term "monumental," representing also what was achieved in the entire book. Further consideration of this book and of other contemporary works by Strauss, seen in light of recent discoveries of his letters and previously unknown writings thanks to the very useful detective and deciphering work done by Heinrich Meier, has made it possible to better trace the details in the unfolding of Strauss's thought. Yet in spite of this careful research and the vigorous discussion by serious and able scholars which it has spawned, it is not clear that it compels of us a fundamental change in our view of what his thought represents in the bigger sense. It does not require one to withdraw, diminish, or qualify that adjective as a judgment on this key work in the unfolding of his thought. It is noteworthy that he had already made his discovery of esotericism in this book—even if I do not in any sense wish to claim that he had grasped immediately just how far reaching were the consequences of what this discovery was to eventually imply for him. Heinrich Meier has characterized the entire book as "revolutionary." This is not to suggest that one of his works (i.e., "Literary Character"), which has received due and deserved recognition for its transformative impact, is to be diminished; it is merely to acknowledge the work which formed the essential argument and defined the directional moment. Thus, Kenneth Seeskin writes: "No one doubts that Leo Strauss's essay 'The Literary Character of the *Guide of the Perplexed*' revolutionized the study of Maimonides." Yet in the same spirit of fixing the high point in Strauss's voyage of rediscovery toward Maimonides, Hillel Fradkin and Alfred Ivry both point to "How To Begin To Study *The Guide of the Perplexed*" as undoubtedly Strauss's most significant contribution. My point in mentioning these contrasting opinions about the peak of Strauss's search is merely that the subsequent rediscovery of forgotten, neglected, or ignored hidden depths in Maimonides' *Guide*, or *Mishneh Torah*, made by Strauss through his other great works—as this entailed the discovery of previously undetected hidden depths in the mind and character of Maimonides himself—would not have been possible if not for the revolution in Strauss's thinking which occurred with the composition of *Philosophy and Law* and was already evident in it, so as to prepare the unfolding transformative moments of discovery, as reflected in his letters to Jacob Klein and to Nahum Glatzer.[8]

In the end, Strauss devoted himself to the careful exposition of Maimonides' *Guide* for about fifty years, which he characterized as "frequently interrupted but never abandoned study." In the work which for some crowned this careful reading of the *Guide* and the teaching of others how to proceed in the same fashion, Strauss focused on the style of study of Maimonides that had been launched by him about twenty-five years prior to the date on which he made the aforementioned statement, i.e., about 1938. But this point is also worth stressing: Strauss's study of and fascination with Maimonides, in whatever style or according to whatever premises, was a passion that had continued unbroken almost from his early youth. This is a fact that needs to be reflected on, however significant a role the Maimonides of a certain type had played in the thought of the later, mature Strauss.[9] This means that for most of his life, he remained fascinated with "his beloved Maimonides," to whom he "returned repeatedly."[10] His repeated returns amounted to fresh confrontations and yielded progressive deepenings of his comprehension, in the process of which he was willing to reconsider, revamp, and modify his views. The notion of "progressive deepenings" in Strauss's changes of thought might be seen in the following light. The subsequent stages built, more or less continuously, on those that preceded them. Hence, even if significant changes still occurred, this was not decisive enough to make for a complete discontinuity, at least since the great break of the late 1930s and early 1940s. Whatever the number (never mind the dates) of such breaks as may have occurred, these are not enough to alter one fundamental constant from the beginning of Strauss's rediscovery of Maimonides to its end: the claim about Maimonides' cognitive superiority both to his wide-ranging critics and to his far-flung students, which makes Maimonides' thought as "modern"—in the sense of not merely historically conditioned—as Plato or Thomas Aquinas are capable of being to their most dedicated contemporary students. To be sure, the notion of an essential continuity in Strauss's thought about Maimonides has been criticized by Michael Zank. He thinks that this sort of revolution at the very beginning either is impossible or was not actually the case; he prefers to think that as Strauss moved from one stage to another, this movement represented a development by which he was compelled to cast away the entire old basis and proceed on a radically new basis. According to Zank, "Platonic political philosophy" is not only "irreconcilably opposed to a belief in revelation," but is also expressly adverse if not antagonistic to "the assumption of its believability" as based on "informed philosophical judgment." This assertion is presumably based on the premise that philosophers know, rather than merely believe, that revelation is impossible; as a result, the view in favor of continuity holds only insofar as Strauss's apparent seriousness about revelation is either "an exoteric defense of orthodoxy" or "a substantial alternative to postmodernist answers to the 'crisis of modernity.'" The position in favor of a radical discontinuity in the thought of Strauss is, in my opinion, a reversion to a sort of modernized "Latin Averroism," which Strauss distinguished carefully from the genuine article. However, Joel L. Kraemer has recently asserted that Strauss viewed Maimonides as an "Averroist," which he is careful not to qualify. As he significantly adds, this was "in line with the best of his medieval Jewish commentators." But he avoids the dilemma which arises between the blatantly announced medieval philosophic (i.e., "Averroist") dogmas of "the best of his commentators" and what Strauss teaches about Maimonides' concealed opinions. For if Maimonides, unlike most of his commentators, resorted in his works to sharply diversionary language rooted in the logic of contradiction (i.e., esotericism), he did so as Strauss argues because he was convinced it was necessary for him to conceal what he "believed" regarding the truth.[11] One of the reasons for this concealment, Strauss suggests, is that Maimonides was less certain, and more skeptical, about the possibility of demonstrated knowledge of the highest truths of physics and metaphysics than he appears to be.

In order to prove the value and ensure the acceptance of philosophy in Jewish society, he needed to assert the demonstrated character of such truth as fact.

Moreover, it is not clear whether Kraemer thinks that even this series of philosophic "beliefs" about the truth is grounded in anything other than what Strauss occasionally refers to as "the religion of the philosophers" (also known as "Latin Averroism"). If those selected medieval commentators interpreted Maimonides as an "Averroist," it is not altogether impossible or preposterous (once Strauss has been taken into account) to think that they did this in error, because their exegesis largely followed their convictions, which were already rooted in "Averroist" teachings; they neither gave Maimonides' own views their due nor considered his deep esotericism binding on them. In other words, they almost uniformly diverged from him on this most fundamental point, at least as Strauss presents Maimonides to his modern readers. Strauss allowed that the philosophic position depends on a claim to knowledge of the whole (often remade by the moderns as genealogical knowledge), which it desires to possess but is not able to attain, and yet on which it depends to prove that its way of life is knowable as the best human life by nature. This position, which Strauss equated with philosophy pursued in the spirit of Socrates—a much thinner thread than any Averroism—may possess comprehensive knowledge of a "part," the human being, which as such is fairly persuasive. But ultimately this position rests on the plausibility of attaining human perfection through fulfilled knowledge of the whole, which is something it cannot—or so far, has not been able to—achieve. Certainly the Maimonides that Strauss rediscovered did not present a claim to base his position on comprehensive knowledge achieved, even if his Maimonides allowed for the legitimacy of the effort to strive for this sort of knowledge. Strauss discerned in Maimonides' endeavor to legitimate the search for comprehensive knowledge that this is much preferable to the acceptance of merely apparent knowledge as if it were genuine knowledge. Hence, what Strauss discovered earlier and confirmed later in his writings is that Maimonides fully accepted man's "natural desire for knowledge," which led him to "warn not against the desire for comprehensive knowledge, but against seeming knowledge." In this Maimonides affirms the pursuit of knowledge or wisdom as man's true end. But he also regards it as a promise not yet fulfilled. And as a result Strauss seemed to perceive Maimonides warning the honest searcher to beware of prematurely affirming its true fulfillment—however vulnerable such lack of fulfillment leaves the searcher to the charge of futility, which is likely to be made by moral and religious critics of the search as man's proper way of life.

Proceeding tenaciously along such lines, Strauss produced a substantial number of groundbreaking essays and lectures on Maimonides that revolutionized the manner in which Maimonides' *Guide*, and the "Sefer ha-Madda" of the *Mishneh Torah*, are read in the present, and with whose help students of Maimonides' thought will continue to study these works in future. These essays and lectures will undoubtedly continue to be mined for their still-unexploited insights by future generations of students and scholars—not to mention argued about for their controversial premises, methods of study, and results. In each of these essays and lectures he probed Maimonides' thought for its hitherto unfathomed profundity and drove his comprehension and leading ideas several steps further, each manifesting a higher level of artfulness which some faulted for a depth which seemed to be impenetrable in its shadowy remoteness. Indeed, the last fully elaborated essay, "How To Begin To Study *The Guide of the Perplexed*"—his introduction to the English translation by Shlomo Pines—reached a point of complexity of thought, and subtlety in construction, which parallels, and perhaps deliberately reproduces or even surpasses, the difficulties which most readers meet with in studying the *Guide* itself. Some regarded the aforementioned essay as a guide to how to begin to study Maimonides' great book—only for a couple of scholars who were beginning on almost the same level as himself! Consider the comment by Allan Bloom on Strauss's last or most mature works in general:

> Those [works] of the third period are ignored. They seem too far away from the way we look at things and the way we speak. But these books are the authentic, the great Strauss to which all the rest is only prolegomena.

In a similar vein, Alexander Altmann commented specifically on Strauss's late works on Maimonides, which he compared with the late works of Beethoven:

> So much had he immersed himself in the attempt to disentangle Maimonides' presumed esotericism that he discovered strange keys and often abstruse answers. The comparison with Beethoven's last quartets may not be completely out of place. One finds a similar willfulness of exegesis in his lecture *Jerusalem and Athens*.

In contrast with both of these judgments on Strauss's own literary art and its history, i.e., the "authentic" or "great" Strauss versus the "abstruse" interpreter and "willful" exegete, it is also useful to consider Stanley Rosen's assessment:

Strauss was for the most part a practitioner of standard academic prose, with certain striking exceptions at the beginning and toward the end of his academic career. With all due acknowledgment of these exceptions, one can fairly say that Strauss's literary style was in general straightforward and professorial. In this respect, it reflected the sobriety of his thinking. From time to time, he would rise from the level of sobriety to the polemical, as for example when denouncing the defects of the communist regime in Russia, or defending religion against the unsatisfactory criticism of the modern Enlightenment. I can best express my perception of Strauss as a writer or public lecturer by saying that he was never raucous and even his wit reminded me of Aristotle rather than Plato.

However one may account for the different emphases of these judgments on Strauss as a literary artist at different points in his career, they no doubt show he did conspicuously and purposefully renovate his own style, even though this is not to clarify the significance that is to be attributed to such renovations.[12] However, the highlighting of Strauss's style as a skilled writer in these judgments demonstrates one of the chief lessons that Maimonides had taught him: the "revolution" in the study of Maimonides of which he was the cause was actually the result of a revolution which Maimonides had effected in him. This lesson may be stated as follows: if a writer assumes the task of conveying to selected readers a deeply dialectical subtlety in thought which also represents a profundity of challenge to convention, thus radically transforming their comprehension about the most serious things, it is also his duty to do so while simultaneously helping to preserve moderateness in their discernment, attitudes, and conduct. This requires a writer—even if a historical scholar—to strive for the utmost perfection of literary art, and especially of that art which he judges best suited to engendering in his readers a mind-vivifying but still morally conservative reception of his multifaceted and often radical message. Whether Strauss achieved his goal in these renovations is a separate matter; what it is enough to establish is that this experimenting with academic styles and rhetoric had a powerfully "Maimonidean" intention, closely connecting what he was trying to teach with how he was trying to teach it.

While this "revolution" brought about by Strauss has still not been duly acknowledged or perhaps even commensurately pursued by every scholar of Maimonides, in actuality it is generally accepted, insofar as virtually everyone concerned with studying Maimonides continues, willingly or unwillingly, Strauss's pioneering legacy. Indeed, the *magna opera* of Herbert Davidson,

Moses Maimonides: The Man and His Works (2004), and of Joel Kraemer, *Maimonides: The Life and World of One of Civilization's Greatest Minds* (2008)—which appeared in print in proximity to one another—represent quite nicely the two poles in the scholarly attitude toward Strauss. To be sure, they both cannot help putting him, implicitly or explicitly, in the center of their discussions, although in their treatment of his work they are almost opposite as to sympathy and orientation. They complete and summarize the efforts of an entire scholarly generation to absorb the impact made by Strauss's innovations. Since at the very least things are not yet settled, and since the presence of Strauss's approach continues to provoke, this makes it an unlikely expectation that future generations of Maimonidean scholars will be able to readily escape his achievement's enormous gravitational power, whether they are "for" or "against" it. His essays and lectures on Maimonides will, I venture to predict, continue to challenge, fascinate, and exercise a powerful influence. In fact, most current Maimonidean scholars still cultivate the ground which Strauss first cleared, whether to correct his errors or clarify what remains obscure or respond to his challenge. Indeed, however much pointed criticism is certainly not likely to cease, Strauss's scholarly critics are also unlikely to be able to bury his achievement by dismissing this as a phase that has passed.[13]

But it is not adequate to reduce the almost unrelenting argument about Leo Strauss and Maimonides to a merely academic debate, of whatever great consequence may have been the scholarly issue in which those disputes had their origins. They merely raise the higher question of whether Strauss was endeavoring a venture at a Maimonidean theological-political revolution. This becomes the focus of discussion based on Strauss's unyielding and perplexing conviction that Maimonides was a deeper thinker than his modern rivals, critics, and students, however much credit he assigns to Spinoza as the political philosopher who devised liberal democracy. The attempt at an adequate answer leads less to the Maimonidean works than to the Strauss-Kojève philosophico-political debate on tyranny and the end of history, with which it may be more aptly compared. To be sure, the ostensible ground of this debate was a minor scholarly difference on what it is that Xenophon argued or achieved as a thinker, how he wrote, and what he taught. However, what emerges is that this is a philosophic debate about Plato as representative of the ancients versus Hegel as representative of the moderns. In that dispute, Strauss and Kojève each make a compelling case for their separate sides. One can imagine a similar case being made against Strauss's view of Maimonides, perhaps offered by an adherent of a rationally compelling historicism who has absorbed the lessons of its radical branch (i.e., Heidegger) but not been swallowed by it, if this is what Kojève attempted, as it seems he did. By rediscovering such "simple" facts about Maimonides (as about Xenophon) as how subtle his books are and with what immense deliberateness he wrote them, Strauss permanently changed the conception of who Maimonides was and why he wrote his books. He made it virtually impossible to either return to a "naive" perspective on Maimonides (whether modern or medieval) or reduce his significance by diminishing him to "merely" the organizer of the law or the dogmatizer of belief. In this sense, a closer analogy for the revolution that Strauss effected concerning Maimonides is perhaps a revolution in modern science: once one has uncovered certain forces in nature as proven causes, it can transform one's view of what nature is and what it can do.[14]

Others, who claim to reject root and branch Strauss's approach to Maimonides and its consequences, still have to spend a great deal of effort so as to be able to argue against Strauss's hard evidence, which is not so easy to dispose of. And if they are intellectually honest, they cannot avoid the expectation that they will justify this rejection by showing how the evidence he uncovered may be discounted, and its implications dismissed. With regard to the multiple challenges issued by Strauss's work on Maimonides, at the very least it has to be said that this makes him (in the word of George Steiner) "unavoidable" (*incontournable*).[15] David Novak makes the lead point in a review essay that in spite of the diversity of studies in Maimonidean thought (he was reviewing works by Eliezer Schweid, Marvin Fox, Oliver Leaman, and Kenneth Seeskin), their unity is manifested, in one way or another, by the need to meet the challenge of Strauss: this is the core of every contemporary effort. They are trying either to build on his approach (whether they revise or refine it), or to deal it a lethal blow. In other words, almost everyone among serious contemporary scholars or thinkers whose study is dedicated to the accurate comprehension of Maimonidean thought is ultimately compelled to give substantial thought to Strauss's achievement, and especially to his claim to have rediscovered a Maimonides who was so completely different from what conventional wisdom, both traditional and modern, had attributed to him: it continues to elude those who try to make it smaller than it is. Alan Verskin, on the other hand, takes a different approach. He doubts whether the achievement of Strauss is about anything scholarly. Instead, he views Strauss as employing Maimonides in order to advance a project that is far larger than any simple historical rediscovery. Even if Strauss pursued the study of Maimonides with proper scholarly scruples, this was merely a rhetorical strategy for a certain segment of readers that his scholarly works were aimed at. That "personal project," which was philosophico-theologico-political in nature, parallels almost in reverse the similar project of Spinoza. According to this view, one of Strauss's chief aims was to influence Enlightenment-disillusioned Jews to take Judaism seriously again by allowing Maimonides, as reconfigured by Strauss, to seem to give as much esoteric weight to the conflict between reason and revelation as Spinoza did. This would supposedly allow Strauss to show how Maimonides was able to remain loyal to both, but on different levels and for different reasons, as a model of loyalty to Judaism in modernity, precisely with the aim of spiritually fortifying such Enlightenment-disillusioned Jews. However, one of the chief flaws in that perspective is the question of why Strauss would establish such a scheme as characterized by Verskin, which he never fully answers. Basically it seems to reduce Strauss's intensely detailed exegesis of Maimonides to a sort of Spinozism with a human face. No doubt this is an original and interesting explanation, but it seems to me that it cannot account for some of the key currents flowing through Strauss's actual work on Maimonides: it elucidates both too much and too little. At the furthest reaches, Verskin asserts: "Strauss claims that Maimonides secretly agreed with Spinoza's belief that these truths [of prophecy] are infra-rational and consequently that they are not truths at all." While Verskin pursues a reading which is very clever ("it is reasonable to apply to [Strauss's] own writings the hermeneutic which he applies to others"), this approach is a little too hasty, if not cavalier, since it rushes to doubt the historical or textual accuracy of Strauss's scholarly readings of Maimonides, even if Verskin regards what he dubs their hermeneutical "errors" as deliberate. That Strauss wished, as Verskin contends, to repair the "break with tradition" first made by Spinoza is certainly worth considering as an element in the motives for his work. But the requirements of this motive, supposedly dominant, need not have led him to force his readings of Maimonides.[16] Strauss was not compelled to deny any "concept of truth in revelation" for Maimonides. Although this is the position held by Spinoza, for him it is so as the only position compatible with rational honesty. In marked difference from this, revelation is a concept that Strauss, along with Maimonides, seemed to consider at the very least philosophically "possible." By this logic, he also requires that anyone who is thinking philosophically abstain from dogmatism about what is truly knowable. Whatever philosophers like Spinoza may want to believe about the necessary condition for philosophy itself, Strauss contrasted this with what philosophers can truly demonstrate, and hence what reason is sufficient to know, which is to be opposed to boastful and embellished claims. This is the modesty of reason which becomes it, insofar as it is unseemly for it to exaggerate what it can genuinely know. The philosophers, for Strauss as for Maimonides, do not know the answers to every essential question about the fundamental nature of things. This seems to have been a truth that, however similar Maimonides and Spinoza may appear at several key points, continues to divide the two thinkers.

Strauss showed the manner in which the *Guide* should be read if it would be comprehended accurately, inasmuch as the way of reading which Strauss brought to light can claim to follow the author's own expression of his intention. Not only did Strauss follow the instructions of the "great eagle" for carefully reading books which Maimonides himself considered most carefully written (like Farabi), but Strauss also followed Maimonides' example in reading "most carefully books which are most carefully written" insofar as this is exemplified in Maimonides himself, who indicates about his own book that it was itself written "most carefully." It may be worthwhile to note that among those selected books which Maimonides judges to be the "most carefully written" (the Torah, Aristotle, Farabi, and his own *Guide*) are some of those books which Strauss immersed himself in and to whose serious reading he dedicated enormous and repeated efforts. Of course, Strauss surpassed the reading list set by Maimonides; indeed, his own list embraced most of the highly significant books in the Western philosophic canon. Yet some of the inspiration for drafting this highly selected list as the key to the "Western mind" may have derived from his reading of Maimonides. Strauss seems to suggest that he got the clue from Maimonides himself that he did not always reveal his true assessment of numerous books, if this was not in his immediate agenda: one of his specific aims was to elevate certain authors and to demote other authors. In connection with this, Stanley Rosen made a shrewd and oft-repeated comment on the strangeness of Strauss's procedure, which constitutes itself as an openness about what is supposed to have been closed, in the authentic conception of Maimonides himself, to everyone but an elite (i.e., the "esoteric")—and to which Strauss himself lends expression candidly, emphatically, and repeatedly! Rosen concludes that if Strauss revealed what is supposed to have been concealed, this is unassailable proof that Strauss was conscious of himself fully as a "modern" rather than an "ancient." In this sense, it is enlightening to compare Strauss's comments on studying Spinoza's book with those which Maimonides composes as directions for reading his own book:

> A man learns to write well by reading well good books, by reading most carefully books which are most carefully written. We may therefore acquire some previous knowledge of an author's habits of writing by studying his habits of reading. The task is simplified if the author in question explicitly discusses the right manner of reading books in general, or of reading a particular book which he has studied with a great deal of attention.[17]

Maimonides' counsel for the method of reading his own book is most similar to the method by which to uncover what is concealed in the Torah, if not in the entire Hebrew Bible.

> If you wish to grasp the totality of what this Treatise contains, so that nothing of it will escape you, then you must connect its chapters one with another; and when reading a given chapter, your intention must be not only to understand the totality of the subject of that chapter, but also to grasp each word that occurs in it in the course of the speech, even if that word does not belong to the intention of that chapter. For the diction of this Treatise has not been chosen at haphazard, but with great exactness and exceeding precision, and with care to avoid failing to explain any obscure point. And nothing has been mentioned out of its place, save with a view to explaining some matter in its proper place.

As this suggests, in light of what Strauss gleaned from Maimonides, we may see that the *Guide* "is an imitation of the Bible," if not indeed "of the Torah," thus seemingly asserting the right of certain human authors to aspire to imitate these revealed books in their own books. However, Strauss adds, "Maimonides read the Torah as a book, every word of which was of divine origin and, consequently, of the greatest importance." By implication, Strauss tacitly raises the issue of how Maimonides presumed to imitate the Torah, the divine book par excellence. Further, since according to Maimonides it is possible for a human being—albeit someone of the highest intellectual perfection—to imitate the authorial style and deliberateness in composition of the sole book "of divine origin," Strauss makes us wonder what it implies about Maimonides' view of the Torah itself: can it be "of divine origin" and yet still somehow written by a man and so also still somehow conceived in and by the human mind? What precisely is the relation between the "divine origin" and the human author who, as it were, records or conveys the divine word but is not a mere "secretary" who receives a dictation? What is the process by which the one is translated to the other, or the one is received from the other? If Maimonides assumes as his model to imitate what is true about the divine book, what is he implying especially about the truly competent thinker? Strauss once referred to "the law of logographic necessity": just as he makes bold to claim that "nothing is accidental in a Platonic dialogue," so he seems ready to apply this same law to any carefully written work. The consummate thinker who makes himself an author must be a consummate artist, which is what the divine author teaches us: as an architectonic mind, he must choose everything which appears in his book, and he will leave nothing to chance.[18]

As Strauss was wont to emphasize (and as he was disposed to emulate), Maimonides aimed his directions for reading his book especially at its most serious students. This is not only because of the emphasis Strauss put on the need to consider the specifically "esoteric" manner of literary expression in Maimonides' *Guide*. It is also because of the type of philosophical and historical premises that Strauss laid down as the basis for any adequate approach to the interpretation of medieval philosophy in general. These premises cover an enormous range. Of course, Strauss's passion for books and their authors differed from those who specialized in hermeneutics, as he tended to begin by asking such seemingly simple questions as "What is a book?" or "What is an author?" As a result, he addressed the problem of why philosophers choose to write books, how those books differ from one another in type, and why the choice about book type or writing style is significant (e.g., why did Plato write dialogues?). Strauss proceeded so far along this line of thought as to wonder if the *Guide* is properly called a "book" at all in the true sense, according to the terms that Maimonides himself employs to characterize the purpose and thrust of his own written work.

> How then can the *Guide* . . . be a book? It is noteworthy that Maimonides himself in the *Guide* never calls it a book, but consistently refers to it as a *maqala* (*ma'amar*). *Maqala* (just as *ma'amar*) has several meanings. It may mean a treatise . . . but it may also mean—and this is its original connotation—a speech. Maimonides, by refraining from calling the *Guide* a book and by calling it a *maqala*, hints at the essentially oral character of its teaching. . . . The *Guide* is, in a sense, not a book at all.

Strauss suggests that the *Guide* seems to have been closer to a conversation between friends, and as such, this "book" should be read almost as one would approach a Platonic dialogue: in terms of characters, setting, historical situation, dramatic plot, type of work (comedy, tragedy, etc.), theme, etc. It is thus no surprise that Strauss argued for the seemingly pedantic need to pay careful attention to the peculiarities of medieval philosophic terminology as well as to its uses and transformations by each specific author, who employed it as needed in deliberately chosen, but significantly different, styles and contexts. This is not for the reason which the philosophy of language asserts, i.e., because thought is supposed to be derivative from and dependent on language. Instead, it is because certain medieval philosophers concealed their true level of thought or teaching beneath their ordinary language. Hence, what they actually think often has to be distinguished from what they say on the surface. To uncover what they truly think requires digging beneath what is written on the surface. For example, it requires paying careful attention to the philosopher's terminology and the consistent use of terms, or in the occasional but momentous irregularity of such terms. This uncovering can be done only by starting from significant deviations or discrepancies that can be observed occurring in their language on the surface; one gets clues or pointers to what is concealed especially, although not solely, by a study of these key terms in their manifest form. Interpretation is for the purpose not of showing the historical condition of thought in the past and how it is to be seen in light of the present, but of attempting to penetrate and bring it to light, precisely through the explication of a carefully written text. The point of this inquiry is to consider whether what the author says is true. This, of course, also means that if it is possible that it was true then, it is also possible for it still to be true now.[19]

It is interesting to note that Strauss's scholarly explorations of Maimonides have exercised perhaps their greatest influence among Israeli scholars, irrespective of whether they follow his general philosophic approach. They were probably impelled toward a more or less common scholarly approach to the contemporary study of Maimonides by Shlomo Pines, who was both a friend and a colleague of Strauss's. With respect to the approach to Maimonides' *Guide*—both how to read it and how to translate it—Pines was also Strauss's "student." Following Strauss, Pines also designated the political as well as the literary as essential in order to make sense of Maimonides. Approaching the *Guide* from the unconventional angle of such questions, Pines acknowledged that this likewise raises the fundamental problem of what he was aiming at in his book. This requires a fresh view of almost everything that we thought we knew about Maimonides. Of course, Pines's monumental English translation of the *Guide* also contains Strauss's epic introductory essay, which, as it happens, is also cleverly difficult and for some almost impenetrable, and thus rather ironically titled "How To Begin To Study *The Guide of the Perplexed*." However, Pines's rigorous search for Maimonides' "philosophic sources" may be juxtaposed with Strauss's essay with its difficulty and its irony, which is anything but a work for beginners: the former might be viewed as the first commentary or at least primer on the latter and serves well as its adept guide. This is not even to mention Pines's translation of the *Guide*, which put the study of Maimonides in the English-speaking world on its first solid ground: it is based on Strauss's notion of how to translate, and hence how to properly study, the book. As Strauss himself suggests about the Pines translation, it is perhaps the only modern aid to Maimonides' original Arabic text that is equal to Ibn Tibbon's medieval Hebrew translation.[20] Nevertheless, it has not yet had the desired effect of making most Maimonidean scholars convinced of the need to read the *Guide* differently from what has been prevalent since Salomon Munk in the 19th century.[21] To make what might seem a self-evident point according to Strauss's approach (but which seems obvious only thanks to his highlighted emphasis), careful and precise thinkers are, as a rule, careful and precise writers, and Maimonides was a most attentive reader of the Hebrew Bible as well as of the philosophers.[22] In fact, this point has still not been absorbed by a substantial number of scholars, who instead still prefer a Maimonides measured by modern historical standards, in the sense of what he contributed to contemporary thought (e.g., negative theology), rather than a Maimonides who can serve as a basis for a critique of contemporary thought. Indeed, it is for this purpose that Strauss turned to him at least after *Philosophy and Law* (1935). What Israeli scholars, in the wake of Pines, seem capable of apprehending in Maimonides' *Guide* is that it is a book not neatly accommodated to the modern mind, even if it surprises by how well it still speaks to the modern, and especially the post-Nietzschean, mind. As a result, Strauss defends the seemingly pedantic function of the scholar, who can substantially aid the philosopher *if* he pays attention to supposedly petty details and highlights fine terminological differences. This stress on such subtle interpretive devices should not be regarded as excessive, since only through them, Strauss contends, can one bring to light significant distinctions which, even if not expressed with clarity, were intended by the author and yet have tended to become lost. As Strauss puts it, no contemporary scholar should be "ashamed to be a micrologist," or concerned with minute details: to comprehend the thought of the past, and especially of a writer like Maimonides, what is needed primarily is "the reconstruction of an adequate terminology." Obviously such a scholar will have to have a keen sense of the philosophic issues that are prospectively raised by and involved in this exercise of nonpedantic "micrology"; i.e., according to what Strauss contends, the scholar will actually have to be or to become a philosopher in order to make proper sense of what the author was thinking and saying.

Certainly what has emerged most obviously from Strauss's fifty years devoted to the study of Maimonides' *Guide* is that he has been able to make Maimonides requisite for anyone seriously engaged in the pursuit and study of contemporary philosophy, never mind political science and the study of religion, the history of literature, and hermeneutics in its biblical origins. This has compelled students of Western thought to add him, as it were, to the basic curriculum, i.e., to the privileged "canon" of essential Western thinkers—even though, prior to Strauss, it had been the tendency of most modern thinkers and philosophers to reject him as a "parochial" Jewish theologian. Thanks to Strauss, Maimonides (and especially his *Guide*) has moved from the obscure periphery of modern intellectual life (to which he was consigned by Spinoza, and from which he was never quite saved by Cohen) almost to the very center. Hence, Maimonides is again recognized as a philosopher of great profundity, whose mind was free and courageous, and whose thought was never merely determined by dogma. In order to penetrate the mind of Maimonides through his compactly written work, Strauss made the fundamental distinction between thought and teaching. This not only follows from the awareness of esotericism, but also leads to it and makes it possible: the commonsense awareness that no thinker worth the name reveals everything which he thinks in what he says, writes, lectures, or promulgates. This is certainly not unique to Maimonides, since Strauss noticed that Plato in his *Seventh Letter* boldly claimed to have never actually discussed in his literary works *any* of the issues that were of deepest concern to him. This would make the reticence to which Strauss pays high tribute neither an idiosyncrasy of Maimonides' personality rooted merely in his historical setting nor a peculiarity grounded in a eccentric facet of his thinking, but a fundamental aspect of the human condition with which the philosopher, thinker, or poet must deal.[23] He is again likely to be judged—even by those who have not much use for his actual thought—as one of *the* truly exemplary figures in the history of Western thought. Strauss's revolutionary rehabilitation of Maimonides is no little achievement. But of course, as has been stressed hitherto, Strauss's achievement with respect to Maimonides, although a great scholarly event in the 20th century, is not merely a great scholarly event. He certainly made it problematic to continue the dismissal of Maimonides that Spinoza initiated in the 17th century. In fact, once Strauss was able to disprove Spinoza's characterization of Maimonides as an apologist for religious orthodoxy and medieval theocracy, he simultaneously revealed the difficulty of following Spinoza's complete philosophical project as the only efficacious and humane route to a decent society. For if Spinoza's confident explanation of what the free mind is, how it is made, and what life it requires is not truly accurate and can misapprehend such giants of thought as Maimonides, it renders questionable his theological, political, and pedagogical program, which was designed to ensure the production of free minds. At the very least, it certainly shows that this program is not foolproof. To be sure, in the spirit of Maimonides Strauss is not doubting the end which Spinoza sets and pursues, i.e., the production of free minds in a decent society, only the total claims which he makes for his means to achieve it.

It should be noted that while Spinoza's criticism made the greatest impact, this was not the only view of Maimonides held by modern thinkers. At least prior to the late 18th and early 19th centuries, with the victory of German idealism in Western philosophy (which based itself on Spinoza), there were several thinkers who were still great admirers of Maimonides: Hugo Grotius, Leibniz, Lessing, and Solomon Maimon. Even the writer Petrus Cunaeus, who was not especially fair-minded toward the Jews, was able to recognize the enormous significance of Maimonides' thought. As he states in his *The Hebrew Republic* of 1617:

> There is an excellent author, esteemed by the world, named Rabbi Moses ben Maimon; he successfully collected the Talmud's teachings—and left out its trifles—in that divine work he calls *Mishneh Torah*. I could never say anything so grand about this author that his virtues would not outshine it. For he was, by some quirk of fate, the first and only member of his nation who correctly understood what it is not to say anything foolish. In this book I will often call on him to testify, as he is the most distinguished of witnesses.

The positive aspect of Cunaeus's opinion was confirmed by Leibniz, while he directly dismisses its prejudice:

> Rabbi Maimonides (whose merit is not sufficiently recognized in the statement that he is the first of the Rabbis to have ceased talking non-

sense) also gave wise judgment on this question of the predominance of good over evil in the world.

Indeed, Leibniz prefaces his "observations" on the *Guide* with the following remarks:

> This book of Rabbi Moses Maimonides entitled *The Teacher of the Perplexed* seems quite remarkable and more philosophical than I had supposed. It deserves careful reading. The author was distinguished in philosophy, mathematics, and the art of medicine as well as his understanding of sacred scripture. . . . He promises to reveal the true sense of the parables of the law. He had feared to write, he says, since "These are things of which none of our people in this captivity has written until now."

As for those who would dismiss the esoteric reading of the *Guide* as a peculiarity of Strauss's mind, or as the result of a "perverse" mode of reading, it is useful to consider the words spoken by a character in a 16th-century dialogue about religion and philosophy written by Jean Bodin, perhaps the first great student of Machiavelli, in his *Colloquium of the Seven about Secrets of the Sublime* [*Colloquium heptaplomeres*] (1588):

> *Salomon*: Senamus' complaint is against the sophists, not against the wise men and surely not against those who veiled the teachings of sacred wisdom in very obscure writings. Rabbi Moses, son of Maimon, implores his readers by his sacred writings not to allow hidden secrets to be made common or polluted by profane men.

Finally, it is to Maimonides (or at least to his students and his legacy) that Nietzsche seems to point in this rare tribute:

> Furthermore, in the darkest medieval times, when the Asiatic cloud had settled heavily over Europe, it was the Jewish freethinkers, scholars, and doctors, who, under the harshest personal pressure, held fast to the banner of enlightenment and intellectual independence, and defended Europe against Asia; we owe to their efforts not least, that a more natural, rational, and in any event unmythical explanation of the world could

finally triumph again, and that the ring of culture which now links us to the enlightenment of Greco-Roman antiquity, remained unbroken.

Although Nietzsche might perhaps have been reflecting on medieval Jewish thinkers other than Maimonides, it is difficult to imagine anyone else whom it fits better. If these writers considered altogether were not Strauss's direct predecessors, since he had to surmount the negative judgment against Maimonides unaided and on his own, they were at least of the same opinion about Maimonides with regard to his great power as a thinker. Those who hesitate about the far-reaching and comprehensive favor which Strauss shows toward Maimonides may want to recall the numerous other modern writers for whom Maimonides also was not confined in a medieval straitjacket. They too acknowledged him as someone capable of transcending his era, and hence who has much to contribute to modern thinkers confronting the dilemmas and impasses of modern thought.[24]

As a result of Strauss's "revolution," the study of Maimonides' thought is often considered requisite for any contemporary discussion in philosophy, politics, and religion insofar as these are concerned with considering afresh the issues which he examined so paradigmatically: as we have been shown by him, it is at the very least essential to consider how and why philosophers or thinkers write in the way they do, suddenly aware as he has made us that this is a deliberately chosen manner of literary art, with its own unique motives. Likewise this is entirely separate from the role that Maimonides has played in the advancement and deepening of Strauss's own thinking, which may in fact be essential for grasping the philosophic thought of one of the most powerful thinkers in the recent past. So much is this the case that Strauss has made Maimonides not just a figure of great historical interest again, but also suddenly a most vital figure for the present: just as most believe Plato *cannot* be reduced to a Greek philosophical poet and author of dialogues written in dramatic form peculiar to polytheistic, ancient Athens, so Strauss made most acknowledge Maimonides as a great philosophic figure who *cannot* be reduced to 12th-century Jewish religious apologist and legalist of medieval Muslim Spain and Egypt. In other words, Maimonides has been brought to life again as a thinker by Strauss's own efforts as a thinker, just as he has been rejuvenated as a historical force by Strauss's labors as a scholar. However, in order to grasp properly the implications of Strauss's revolutionary contribution to the study of medieval philosophy and its philosophic resuscitation, I believe it is also imperative to explicate the development of Strauss's own philosophic thought, on which Maimonides made an impact of great significance. It should be done in order to unfold its "latent reasoning," which followed a discernible order in the process of discovery by which Strauss gradually uncovered hidden layers of Maimonides' thought and of his actions as a thinker. The term "latent reasoning" (which originated in modern psychology) was first employed by Harry A. Wolfson to achieve quite a different historical purpose. I borrow it for use about Strauss but do not utilize it as Wolfson did. His aim was to discover the philosophic "sources" in the historical past of the thought of a philosophic author, sources of which the author himself may have been thoroughly unaware. My use of the term is not meant as an attempt to reconstruct Strauss's philosophic "unconscious" as drawn from the past, employing a psychological model for historical research, and claiming to know him better than he knew himself. Instead, my aim is to trace the stages of his conscious cognitive development as a series of ever-deepening discoveries; hence, I utilize, if anything, a sort of archaeological model of the conscious mind. To put it imaginatively: my use of the term "latent reasoning," which I try to "de-sediment" (borrowing Husserl's term, as also deployed by Stanley Rosen to penetrate Strauss's mind), is designed on analogy with an archaeologist's pinpointing how the discovery by a civilization of one tool revealed the possibilities of other tools' being devised. This invention meanwhile allowed the further exploration of deeper aspects of the world which were previously unknown to it, unfolding "logically" from the original discovery.[25] As I have been trying to make clear thus far, alongside recounting what he contributed as a scholar, Strauss's own philosophic development as a thinker was decisively influenced by his ever-repeated encounter with and his ever-deepening penetration into the massive and labyrinthine edifice of Maimonides' thought in his *Guide*. For Strauss regarded the *Guide* as mapped by its author through a series of paths and byways, in which "secret" or "hidden" key words play a leading role, and in which a paradoxical "method of contradiction" soundly and consistently guides the student or reader who is himself in search of enlightenment through Maimonides' *Guide*. It is this gradually expanding insight about Maimonides' enlightening project that is at least reflected in the progressive stages of Strauss's own thought.

However, first some mention must be made of the philosophical context in which Strauss's thought arose. Strauss's beginnings as an original thinker truly began with his shattering—and yet also bracing, and even energizing—realization that contemporary rational philosophy is morally and intellectually bankrupt. This is not to suggest that every form and aspect of modern philosophy is necessarily ruined; it only portends a specific dissatisfaction with the legacy of modern philosophy on behalf of the most powerful thinkers of our era, which generally encompasses all contemporary thought inasmuch as it is almost entirely beholden to Nietzsche, whose destructive but trenchant questions have to be answered. Indeed, he regarded contemporary philosophy as having simply surrendered to what he called "radical historicism" (which Nietzsche offered in alternative to the pretensions of modern reason), especially via the thought of Heidegger.[26] As Strauss perceived it, this surrender further led to the victory of the dominant forms of irrationalism and antirationalism which we can observe all around us, and which merely masquerade as philosophy (or science). This surrender is often obscured from view by an astounding tendency: the numerous liberal democratic idealizations of the compromise with "radical historicism" that leads to an unwitting participation in what even the Marxist Georg Lukacs called "the self-destruction of reason" (albeit on a safe "postmodern" basis).[27] Strauss's view of the threats to liberal democracy, a political system in which he firmly believed, of course caused him to be deeply affected as a Jew by the destruction during the 1930s by Adolf Hitler and his Nazis of the Weimar Republic in Germany, its first liberal democracy. Strauss was especially shaken by the fact that this occurred in a seemingly legal, quasi-electoral popular victory of Adolf Hitler and his Nazis, and that this victory issued in a preannounced destruction of liberal democracy, which was scarcely resisted by the German people and which was heralded by the intellectuals and professors as a great liberation. All of this led Strauss to proclaim the excellence of liberal democracy only if properly maintained: it cannot "evolve" beyond the constraints of reason and traditional morality. But one may say with some confidence that it was precisely for this purpose that Strauss defends and tentatively "returns" to the ancients and medievals: because the defense of liberal democracy requires the true defense of reason, and this cannot be achieved entirely on a modern grounds. As Strauss states,

> The same effect which Heidegger produced in the late twenties and early thirties in Germany, he produced very soon in continental Europe as a whole. There is no longer in existence a philosophic position, apart from neo-Thomism and Marxism crude or refined. All rational liberal philosophic positions have lost their significance and power. One may deplore this, but I for one cannot bring myself to cling to philosophic

positions which have been shown to be inadequate. I am afraid that we shall have to make a very great effort in order to find a solid basis for rational liberalism.[28]

Even though Strauss did not regard Heidegger's radical historicism as philosophy proper, but rather viewed this as antiphilosophical "thought" (as in accord with Heidegger's own assessment of himself as a "thinker" rather than a "philosopher"), he did believe that it issues nonetheless in a powerful challenge to philosophy. He has delivered a challenge, to which philosophy itself *must* respond and with which it *must* wrestle, especially if it is to survive (or rather, to be revived), since it is at present in a more or less moribund or desiccated state. For it was against the Western philosophic tradition *tout court* that the "thought" of Heidegger was designed to administer the coup de grâce, since he believed this tradition had been built on a nihilist ground ("forgetfulness of Being") from its very beginnings with Plato. Strauss, by contrast, regarded Heidegger as himself playing the lead role in this descent to nihilism, which fate he observes only with regard to most of recent *modern* Western philosophy. The story Strauss tells about Heidegger is lent support by his startlingly correct characterization of our actual situation in the West, i.e., by his astonishingly accurate prognosication of the direction in which Western philosophy would move in the forty or so years that has followed Strauss's demise. In anticipation, as it were, he raised the dilemma with which Western philosophy is faced: what is to be done? Being a thinker himself (and not a Hegelian disposed to rely on history), Strauss perceived that this crisis in philosophic thought will only be settled by a resolution in philosophic thought. Yet the fate of modern Western civilization is bound, Strauss seems to also obliquely suggest, to the fate of philosophy, implying that anyone who is in favor of the modern West must support the defense of this form of thought.

Strauss's turn to Maimonides and the medievals was then—to put it with a simple, if perhaps a little too paradoxical but still not erroneous phrase—a return to reason based on a recovery of nature but engaged in the study of history to do so. Strauss's logic was that, if there is still such a thing as reason which can be defended, and if nature is not something entirely dominated and shaped by man's will, so the medievals must, like Maimonides, know something about the true character of each which we as moderns do not know or have been led to forget—perhaps in a certain measure due to our unreasonable rejection of the medieval as well as the ancient legacy of philosophy. Certainly this is so for our recent "philosophers," else they would not have been so readily captivated by irrationalism and antirationalism, as the best medieval philosophers certainly were not, despite the supposed immersion of those medievals—who trained their minds on Aristotelian philosophy and politics as it confronts revealed religion—in a mystical form of neo-Platonism, a supposition which Strauss emphatically rejected.[29] What was perhaps most unbelievable to Strauss was the notion that these free, vigorous, and critical medieval philosophic thinkers naively allowed this neo-Platonism to determine their view of philosophy, as if they could not see in what a badly distorting light it cast philosophy, which is supposed to be based on the premise of nature and its rational comprehension, other than as it may be comprehended as a tactical surface, or an "exoteric teaching."[30] Moreover, Strauss saw that modern rationalism, in its various and sundry manifestations, undoubtedly did not seem to provide recent "philosophers" with the resources to resist the siren-like appeal of such an antiphilosophical, if vividly imaginative, teaching as Heideggerian radical historicism.

For the insight occurred to Strauss that this deeper rationality of Maimonides and selected medievals might help to explain why they were able to resist the great appeal to medieval antiphilosophical teachings, to one of the many versions of either dogmatic or mystical theology: because theirs was also a return to revelation, as they claimed to authentically comprehend it. Such an apparently deeper rationality appealed to him, since its seriousness about revelation (as the leading form of what, in modern thought, would have to be consigned to irrationalism) seemed instead clearer sighted about its challenge to reason than its modern substitutes. Strauss's logic was that something in the human soul (be it only man's passionate and imaginative nature) resists reason, and this "something" which resists is either reasonable or unreasonable. This may verge on being reasonable because philosophy is always tempted to claim too much for itself as to what it can actually know, even if it attempts to justify this claim by the defensive measures that the life of reason needs to employ in order to preserve itself. However, maybe the medieval strategy of Maimonides was more reasonable and less irrational, in the sense of provisionally accepting revelation (mainly but not solely in the form of law) as not adverse to the life of reason rather than rejecting it completely and almost a priori, with such provisional acceptance based on both its evident usefulness and its manifest wisdom. If revelation so conceived can perform the social action he envisages for it, linked with both morality and philosophy, it is because it always comprises both law and belief, although how these two are distributed will be negotiated or decided by a historical tradition. The very tentative acceptance of revelation, which had to be faced as a compelling challenge, allowed medievals like Maimonides to keep clearer in their minds the precise limits of reason and its need for nonrational things in order to survive, even if they (not unlike Spinoza) also acknowledge the need and assert the right to "correct" revelation if it wanders too far from its substantially rational base, although it must be allowed to do its business, by which it accommodates the irrational needs of the human soul in a fashion helping to rationalize or at least moderate those psychic needs and their social articulation. In other words, the rational man might be wiser to allow himself to accept the seemingly "irrational" blandishments of authentic biblical revelation, because he could discern that by its means, eminently rational ends were achieved.

Indeed, the modern forms of irrationalism have proved themselves ill suited to attaining the control and the harnessing of the irrational in the cause of the rational. As a result, certain discoveries formed themselves in Strauss's mind, as a result of his studying Maimonides. First, that reason needs revelation precisely in order to remain reasonable, however paradoxical this may at first sound. And second, that revelation accepted as its leading challenger (in the form of prophetically revealed scripture) is a better way for reason to deal with its perennial challengers than the forms of modern "irrationalism" (often themselves devised by philosophers) are able to provide. Indeed, this is precisely the opposite of what has happened in modern thought. By getting rid of revelation, by in effect banishing it, or rather repressing it (although such "getting rid" was made to appear in the guise of a philosophy and science which claimed to be able to refute it), the "irrational" returns with even greater force and destructiveness. It might appear paradoxical to assert that Strauss's effort to rehabilitate philosophy seemed to lead him to defend biblical revelation, in view of the long-standing rivalry between reason and revelation, considering that he himself did not emphasize this defense in his own writings as a product of his concern with reason. But Maimonides taught Strauss that this opposition about the one truth may energize and revitalize both—which, whatever it may indicate, itself appears paradoxical. Although Strauss did not celebrate paradox, he did seem to regard its use as imperative or at least unavoidable on fundamental issues, as Socrates, Kierkegaard, and Nietzsche also maintained. All three assert that there is a clarifying spirit present in dialectical thinking, the first fruit of which is not always a lucid result. "Paradoxes only become dangerous when they are transformed into platitudes." In assessing the impact made by Strauss's own thought, it is certainly possible to speak of a paradox, namely, the effort to revive both philosophy and biblical thought, especially in their original form, as the project of a self-consciously modern thinker. Even if it cannot be ascertained with sureness whether this was a deliberate cognitive dualism (and might amount to a cognitive dissonance), it is curious that perhaps *the* essential conflict in interpreting Strauss himself among students of his thought centers on what one camp contends is Strauss's atheism and another camp maintains is his piety and patriotism as follows from a cognitive theism, i.e., the unwavering belief in the *possibility* of knowing the truth. Is it plausible that contained in this conflict about Strauss's legacy is expressed an ambiguity about the nature of philosophy itself. If so, then the ambiguity might be best apprehended through Strauss's notion that any discussions of this matter must be framed by a dialectical awareness of the political context in which the discussions are occurring. Seen in this light, the relation between reason and revelation is also determined by the priority of the political even in philosophic debate, the awareness of which priority, as Strauss contends, animated Maimonides' thought. This would help to explain Strauss's curious reiteration of his notion of "Jerusalem and Athens" in the preface to a lecture on Thucydides, in which he defends his notion of the Western tradition as sustained in life by the *unresolved* tension between Jerusalem and Athens. This unresolved tension is a problem that admits of no solution free of contradiction, or at least in a way which is consistent with the Western tradition itself. For "the Western tradition" is itself a political notion not capable of being disentangled in such a manner as to be consistent with the loyalty to both of the elements by which it is constituted. As Strauss contends,

> I must leave it open whether the very principles underlying the Western tradition, i.e., whether philosophy and theology, would allow us to speak of "the Western tradition" in the terms which I have used. Permit me to declare that it is impossible to do so in the last analysis. But it is foolish even to try always to speak in terms which could stand the test of precise analysis. Most of the time our maxim must be that expressed in the words of a Greek poet [Euripides, as referred to by Aristotle, *Politics* 1277a19-20]: "I do not want these highbrow things, I want what the city needs." As long as we speak politically, i.e., crudely, we are indeed forced to speak of the Western tradition more or less in the terms which I have used.[31]

So long as Strauss spoke or wrote as a mature thinker, he did so "politically," i.e., with a keen awareness of the consequences of his spoken words as a teacher, or his written words as a scholar. To be sure, this keen awareness somehow did not cramp his style or diminish his vivacity as teacher or scholar. Once he had rediscovered Maimonidean wisdom, it seems that he never ceased to measure how precise an analysis is to be allowed, which compelled him to make the defense of the Western tradition ever constitutive of his thought in presenting it publicly to students and readers, and even privately to friends.

In comprehending Strauss's effort to trace how the moderns were misled by their own attempt to secure the supreme position of reason while employing the biblical legacy in a subordinate capacity for moral purposes, we must reconsider their attempt to fully banish the "irrational" and to blame its continued dominance mainly on revelation. Yet previously the "irrational" had been fairly well contained, absorbed, and redirected by revelation (as diverted in a corrective direction by great teachers of revelation like Maimonides)—although of course authentic revelation acts as something much greater than a mere corrective or cathartic channel for the irrational, or a mere educative conveyance of the rational. This reappearance with a vengeance of the irrational, which had been repressed—or rather, redirected—in revelation is, of course, the very opposite of that which was promised by the modern philosophers like Spinoza, who had misjudged man's soul and its need for things which had been prospectively discarded with the mostly dismissive term, the "irrational" (or the "superstitious"), although it embraces some of the deepest needs of the human soul, which can only be put in remission, or refined and elevated, but never eliminated.

For dealing with this chronic modern dilemma, Strauss believed that he benefitted from recurring to Gotthold Ephraim Lessing, one of his favorite modern authors, who somehow seems to have escaped the worst dilemmas about reason and revelation in which modern thought had become permanently caught. According to Strauss, he taught a critical view on reason and revelation which, even if not perfect, is wiser than most modern alternatives, and the study of which can be advantageous for those who are likewise attempting to get around this dilemma. He achieved a higher perspective precisely because he did not strive for a total resolution, although he did offer a way to fruitfully mediate the contenders. Especially worth considering is a dramatic comment made by Lessing in a letter to his brother Karl of 2 February 1774, which reflects one side of his wise attitude. I would further suggest that it is very much in the judiciously "enlightening" spirit of Maimonides, whose works Lessing seems to have known well:

> With orthodoxy, thank God, things were fairly well settled. A curtain had been drawn between it and philosophy, behind which each could go his

own way without disturbing the other. But what is happening now? They are tearing down this curtain, and under the pretext of making us rational Christians, they are making us very irrational philosophers. I beg of you, my dear brother, inquire more carefully after this point and look less at what our new theologians discard than at what they want to put in its place. We are agreed that the old religious system is false, but I cannot share your conviction that it is a patchwork of bunglers and half philosophers. I know of nothing in the world in which human sagacity has been better displayed and cultivated. The real patchwork of bunglers and half philosophers is the religious system which they now want to set in place of the old, and with far more influence on reason and philosophy than the old ever presumed.

Lessing's comment mounts a criticism of modern-style theology, i.e., 18th-century "liberal" theology, which was beholden to the modern Enlightenment, and which was only slightly transformed by its 19th- and 20th-century heirs, in contrast with what Lessing calls "the old religious system," i.e., premodern theology. The new religious system subverts or at least enfeebles revelation in the name of defending it by trying too much to modernize it, so squandering what made it great, namely, its ability to "display and cultivate human sagacity" so well. But along with this is the other side of his "Maimonidean" attitude, which perceived that a key element in the greatness manifest by the original sources and teachings—both religious and philosophic—is that they should remain separate from one another, for this is the only way in which each can retain its unique spiritual power, as this is required for their proper confrontation. In his last years Lessing recognized in original revealed religion, as well as in ancient and medieval philosophy, genuine sources of wisdom, each in its own fashion, which he had unwittingly disposed of by a once too enthusiastic embrace of modern thought. In helping to get rid of old prejudices, modern thought had merely substituted new ones for them; as a result, it seems to have neutralized the ability to think. Consider some key passages from a letter to his friend Moses Mendelssohn of 9 January 1777:

> Is it really good to contemplate and to concern oneself seriously with truths which one has lived and, for the sake of peace, must continue to live in constant contradiction? ... Among them are some which I have for a long time ceased to regard as truths. Still, it is not since yesterday that I have been concerned that while discarding certain prejudices I might

have thrown away a little too much, which I shall have to retrieve. It is only the fear of dragging all the rubbish back into my house which has so far hindered me from doing this. It is infinitely difficult to know when and where one should stop, and for the vast majority of men the object of their reflection lies at the point at which they have become tired of reflecting.

I would suggest that for Strauss this is what impressed him about Lessing, just as it also did about Maimonides: the robustly dialectical spirit which animates their mature minds and which serves the cause of doing justice to the truth. In other words, the true thinker must remain vivid and animated in his reflection and never let his fatigue determine what his position will be, as a mere position of convenience or rest. If Lessing was capable of radically amending his conviction about scripture and classical philosophy (inasmuch as these seem to comprise the teachings which he once threw away as "prejudices," if not "rubbish") while not simple-mindedly rejecting modern philosophy, he has achieved the state of the free mind, which state Strauss discovered Maimonides to have also attained. The genuinely open-minded thinker is willing to consider as possible truths that his current "faith" disallows (if modern thought may be defined as a "faith"). Lessing epitomized this genuine open-mindedness in the 18th century, just as Maimonides represents it in the 12th century (however far-fetched and implausible such a possibility was to most contemporary readers). Indeed, this very contention shows Strauss's commitment to thinking for himself in that he can assert such a thing about Maimonides even though most modern scholars and philosophers have rejected the notion that Maimonides was, or even could have been, this type of thinker. It is, as I argue, to this open-minded and vivid thinking, as an essentially dialectical approach to the truth, that Strauss maintained fidelity, as he believed Plato had likewise done. He thought its vital elements could survive and arise irrespective of history, as a permanent human possibility: it is the authentic philosophic life, which precedes all philosophic teachings. Precisely as it is possible that this properly dialectical spirit of true thinking and the free mind can become actual and even be taught in every era, it is never merely the product of any single period but transcends every historical situation, however unique may be its conditions.[32]

But why, according to Strauss, did a man like Lessing "preach" the humane virtue of tolerance and the cognitive-moral need for modern Enlightenment from his peculiar "pulpit" (as he liked to characterize his theatrical plays, such as *The Jews* and *Nathan the Wise*), while a man like Maimonides elevated the superhuman virtue of prophecy for the few based on intellectual excellence, and valorized cognitive enlightenment for as many as possible in the very process of codifying the Law? No doubt Strauss conceived that some of these specific, historically situated teachings may still be relevant and valid in part or whole, but this was not his main concern. What fundamentally counted for Strauss were not so much these teachings on their own as the spirit of mind which animated the thinkers who propounded them. Lessing seems to have regarded himself as duty bound to use his subtle but powerful literary arts not only to elevate the minds of those with the potential for higher things so as to help them get closer to what they are made for, but he also sensed himself obligated to enlighten and to educate all decent human beings insofar as his ability allowed him. The ground for this sense of duty in the great-souled (or magnanimous) man seems to be that not only is he driven toward intellectual perfection, which might be construed as a private virtue, but his very drive also elicits in him a love for the unity of all human excellence, which manifests itself across a broad human field. These virtues somehow have to be cultivated together, and their inculcation in and execution by younger souls full of potential somehow depends on noble public action by the highest human types, usually older souls who love and want to be loved by those with the potential for the great and the higher things. Obviously most of this argument for the natural "duty" elicited by love (however roughly conceived) of the higher man toward the inculcation of excellence in other human beings needs to be judged on its merits as to whether it actually appears in and naturally imposes itself on certain human beings. In other words, is love so powerful and compelling a spiritual force in the truly superior human being? Strauss speaks—in answering the question Why do philosophers write books?—not about the will to power, but of "the love of the mature philosopher for the puppies of his race, by whom he wants to be loved in turn."[33] He curiously points to Plato's *Republic* and *Apology* in order to justify his language or rather his logic. The argument receives perhaps its best proof not from the authority of any book, but rather from the great teachers, leaders, thinkers, writers, and lawgivers who seem to spontaneously appear among human beings, who manifest surpassing human virtue, who dedicate enormous labor to their task, and who despite adversity, grave difficulty, and resistance guide segments of humanity in a better direction. Thus, it requires a sacrifice in personal terms that this human type seems to willingly make for the sake of his fellow human beings. Indeed, the difficulty and the resistance are often generated by antagonism to the action by which those superior human beings as a type teach, lead, think, write, or legislate—but it rarely prevents them from doing what they sense themselves called to do. Maimonides discussed it in terms of the natural (if also divinely stirred) human type known as the "prophet." If it is not proof, it is at least a sort of confirmation of a human possibility that seems to naturally recur as an inexorable force, however rare. And it seems to be most fully materialized as a historical actuality in selected great figures, of which Maimonides is a classic paradigm or archetype. As a natural quality of a superlative or "perfected" human type (in the language of Maimonides), which recurs among human beings in all times and places, it shows itself—certainly as he presents it—as a superfluity of surpassing virtue, i.e., somewhat like Aristotle's magnanimous man, whose "overflow" requires the love which brings him to act for others on the basis of his intellectual excellence, crowning his panoply of supporting virtues.[34] It is not too much of a stretch to apply it, with appropriate adjustment, to a reticent figure like Leo Strauss. One may say that this is the case at least insofar as he is considered to be a teacher with great reach, ambition, and impact.

However, the drawing-forth produced by love is not just productive of external conflict, as in the struggle of the great historical type to fulfill his mission or task through an act of love for others, with regard to what he is called to do from without. It is also internal, and it concerns the spiritual struggle and heroic effort within to penetrate to the truth, which is in a certain measure known through one's own virtue; according to Maimonides, the struggle and effort are called forth by the love of God. However one chooses to frame it, the higher type wants to know whether the true gift he has received is something merely internal or is from some external source. It is most difficult to know what the source of truth is, but an awareness of it and its possible origins is a key element in the search to know himself as well as what is beyond himself. It is at the very least the beginning of the discernment of how it is possible to appreciate both reason and revelation as rivals who struggle together—and against one another—for the same ultimate purpose: the search for truth. If, with Maimonides and Lessing, Strauss was able to acknowledge "nothing in the world in which human sagacity has been better displayed and cultivated" than in the ancient religious and philosophic books, then there is also in this recognition the basis for justifying a common life that can be established between reason and revelation, even if it may also imply or require tension and argument as an aspect of their aspirant life together.

Strauss brought to light, in a substantial measure aided by his rediscovery of the subtlety, depth, and freedom in Maimonides' thought, that these stark challenges and seemingly permanent perplexities are not so readily resolved as the great moderns had led us to believe, but he contended that this resourceful thought promises to harmonize them better by keeping the two opponents and competitors for the truth in civilized, even if often paradoxical, conversation. Thanks to Strauss's bold reflections and transformative researches, this moves all who are compelled by the course of modernity to reassess most of the issues raised and the results reached by modern philosophy to a greater willingness to reconsider the thought of a deep medieval thinker like Maimonides, who may still have a very great deal to teach us even if, and perhaps especially if, we are to be and to remain fully modern.

ABBREVIATIONS

GENERAL WORKS

Albo, *Ikkarim* (*Roots*)
Joseph Albo, *Sefer ha-Ikkarim* (*Book of Roots* or *Book of Principles*), ed. and trans. Isaac Husik (Philadelphia: Jewish Publication Society of America, 1930).

"Book of Knowledge"
Maimonides, "Book of Knowledge" in *Mishneh Torah*, trans. Ralph Lerner, in *Maimonides' Empire of Light: Popular Enlightenment in an Age of Belief*, by Ralph Lerner (Chicago: University of Chicago Press, 2000), pp. 141–53.

Cambridge Companion to Leo Strauss
The Cambridge Companion to Leo Strauss, ed. Steven B. Smith (New York: Cambridge University Press, 2009).

"Epistle to Yemen"
Maimonides, "Epistle to Yemen," trans. Joel L. Kraemer, in *Maimonides' Empire of Light: Popular Enlightenment in an Age of Belief*, by Ralph Lerner (Chicago: University of Chicago Press, 2000), pp. 99–132.

Falaquera, "Epistle of the Debate"
Shem-Tov ben Joseph Ibn Falaquera, "Epistle of the Debate," trans. Steven Harvey, in *Maimonides' Empire of Light: Popular Enlightenment in an Age of Belief*, by Ralph Lerner (Chicago: University of Chicago Press, 2000), pp. 188–208.

Green, *Jew and Philosopher*
Kenneth Hart Green, *Jew and Philosopher: The Return to Maimonides in the Jewish Thought of Leo Strauss* (Albany: State University of New York Press, 1993).

Guide
Maimonides, *The Guide of the Perplexed*, trans. Shlomo Pines, with an introductory essay by Leo Strauss (Chicago: University of Chicago Press, 1963).

"Introduction"

Maimonides, "Introduction," in *Mishneh Torah*, trans. Ralph Lerner, in *Maimonides' Empire of Light: Popular Enlightenment in an Age of Belief*, by Ralph Lerner (Chicago: University of Chicago Press, 2000), pp. 133–41.

Lerner, *Maimonides' Empire of Light*

Ralph Lerner, *Maimonides' Empire of Light: Popular Enlightenment in an Age of Belief* (Chicago: University of Chicago Press, 2000).

"Letter on Astrology"

Maimonides, "Letter on Astrology," trans. Ralph Lerner, in *Maimonides' Empire of Light: Popular Enlightenment in an Age of Belief*, by Ralph Lerner (Chicago: University of Chicago Press, 2000), pp. 178–87.

Meier, *Leo Strauss and the Theologico-Political Problem*

Heinrich Meier, *Leo Strauss and the Theologico-Political Problem* (New York: Cambridge University Press, 2006).

"Treatise on Resurrection"

Maimonides, "Treatise on Resurrection," trans. Hillel Fradkin, in *Maimonides' Empire of Light: Popular Enlightenment in an Age of Belief*, by Ralph Lerner (Chicago: University of Chicago Press, 2000) , pp. 154–77.

WORKS BY LEO STRAUSS

The City and Man

The City and Man (Chicago: University of Chicago Press, 1977).

Early Writings

The Early Writings: 1921–32, ed. and trans. Michael Zank (Albany: State University of New York Press, 2002).

Hobbes Politische Wissenschaft und zugehörige Schriften—Briefe, vol. 3 of *Gesammelte Schriften*

Hobbes Politische Wissenschaft und zugehörige Schriften—Briefe, vol. 3 of *Gesammelte Schriften*, ed. Heinrich Meier (Stuttgart: J. B. Metzler, 2001).

Introduction to Political Philosophy

An Introduction to Political Philosophy: Ten Essays, ed. Hilail Gildin (Detroit: Wayne State University Press, 1989).

Jewish Philosophy and the Crisis of Modernity

Jewish Philosophy and the Crisis of Modernity: Essays and Lectures in Modern Jewish Thought, ed. Kenneth Hart Green (Albany: State University of New York Press, 1997).

Liberalism Ancient and Modern

Liberalism Ancient and Modern (New York: Basic Books, 1968; reprint, Chicago: University of Chicago Press, 1995).

Natural Right and History
Natural Right and History (Chicago: University of Chicago Press, 1953).

On Maimonides
Leo Strauss on Maimonides: The Complete Writings, ed. Kenneth Hart Green (Chicago: University of Chicago Press, 2013).

On Tyranny
On Tyranny, ed. Victor Gourevitch and Michael S. Roth (Chicago: University of Chicago Press, 2000).

Persecution and the Art of Writing
Persecution and the Art of Writing (Glencoe, IL: Free Press, 1952; reprint, Chicago: University of Chicago Press, 1988).

Philosophie und Gesetz: Frühe Schriften, vol. 2 of Gesammelte Schriften
Philosophie und Gesetz: Frühe Schriften, vol. 2 of *Gesammelte Schriften*, ed. Heinrich Meier (Stuttgart: J. B. Metzler, 1997).

Philosophy and Law
Philosophy and Law: Contributions to the Understanding of Maimonides and His Predecessors, trans. Eve Adler (Albany: State University of New York Press, 1995).

Rebirth of Classical Political Rationalism
The Rebirth of Classical Political Rationalism: An Introduction to the Thought of Leo Strauss; Essays and Lectures, ed. Thomas L. Pangle (Chicago: University of Chicago Press, 1989).

Die Religionskritik Spinozas und zugehörige Schriften, vol. 1 of Gesammelte Schriften
Die Religionskritik Spinozas und zugehörige Schriften, vol. 1 of *Gesammelte Schriften*, ed. Heinrich Meier (Stuttgart: J. B. Metzler, 1996; rev. ed., 2001).

Spinoza's Critique of Religion
Spinoza's Critique of Religion, trans. Elsa Sinclair (New York: Schocken, 1965; reprint, Chicago: University of Chicago Press, 1997).

Thoughts on Machiavelli
Thoughts on Machiavelli (Glencoe, IL: Free Press, 1958; reprint, Chicago: University of Chicago Press, 1978).

What Is Political Philosophy?
What Is Political Philosophy? And Other Studies (New York: Free Press, 1959; reprint, Chicago: University of Chicago Press, 1988).

NOTES

EPIGRAPHS (P. VI)

Philo Judaeus, *The Special Laws*, trans. F. H. Colson (Cambridge, MA: Harvard University Press, 1937), II, 44, 46-47, pp. 334-37. Cf. Pierre Hadot, *Philosophy as a Way of Life*, ed. A. I. Davidson, trans. M. Chase (Oxford: Blackwell, 1995), pp. 265-76. Cf. also Maimonides, *Guide*, 3.51, pp. 623-24, 627-28.

Abu Nasr al-Farabi, "Philosophy and Religion," chap. 17 of *The Perfect State*, ed. and trans. Richard Walzer (Oxford: Clarendon Press, 1985), pp. 280-83. Its original title is *The Book of the Principles of the Opinions of the People of the Virtuous City* (*Kitab mabadi' ara' ahl al-madina al-fadila*).

Maimonides, *Guide* 1. Introduction, pp. 16-17.

Nietzsche, "Preface," in *Beyond Good and Evil*, trans. Walter Kaufmann (New York: Vintage, 1966), pp. 2-3.

Strauss to Jacob Klein, 20 January 1938, in *Hobbes Politische Wissenschaft und zugehörige Schriften—Briefe*, vol. 3 of *Gesammelte Schriften*, p. 545. His actual German words were "Maimonides . . . war ein wirklich freier Geist." For an effort to trace the phases of discovery in Strauss's thought, focused on the figure of Maimonides, as unfolded by and reflected in his letters to Jacob Klein, see Laurence Lampert, "Leo Strauss's Recovery of Esotericism," in *Cambridge Companion to Leo Strauss*, pp. 63-92.

CHAPTER ONE

1. For two unusually bold statements, see app. 4A in *On Maimonides*; and *Philosophy and Law*, p. 21. Cf. also "On a Forgotten Kind of Writing," in *What Is Political Philosophy?*, pp. 221-32, especially p. 230.

2. See "Introduction" to *Philosophy and Law*, pp. 21-39, as well as 102-3. See also Steven Lenzner, "Leo Strauss and the Problem of Freedom of Thought: The Rediscovery of the Philosophic Arts of Reading and Writing" (Ph.D. dissertation, Harvard University). Cf. *Guide* 1.31-35, pp. 65-81.

3. See "Review of Julius Ebbighaus, *On the Progress of Metaphysics*," in *Early Writings*, p. 215. See also *Philosophie und Gesetz: Frühe Schriften*, vol. 2 of *Gesammelte Schriften*, p. 438.

4. For a curious transitional work by Strauss which as a lecture was never finalized in essay

form, see "Cohen and Maimonides," chap. 3 in *On Maimonides*. Heinrich Meier dates the lecture to 1931, based on Strauss's designation on the manuscript; he also detects evidence that this comprises smaller sections of what was originally designed to be a larger work.

　　5. See Strauss and Hans-Georg Gadamer, "Correspondence Concerning *Wahrheit und Methode*," ed. and trans. George Elliot Tucker, *Independent Journal of Philosophy* 2 (1978): 5–12, and especially p. 6. In this dialogue with Gadamer, Strauss specifically mentions his recent "experience" of interpretation, i.e., with Maimonides. As Strauss asserts, Maimonides himself in authoring a new book based on his reading of an old book thoroughly "reflected on his hermeneutic situation." See also "How to Study Medieval Philosophy," chap. 1 in *On Maimonides*; and Strauss, "On a New Interpretation of Plato's Political Philosophy," *Social Research* 13, no. 3 (September 1946): 326–67, and especially p. 331.

　　6. See "Cohen's Analysis of Spinoza's Bible Science" and "On the Bible Science of Spinoza and His Precursors," in *Early Writings*, pp. 139–72, 173–200; "Maimonides' Statement on Political Science," "Introduction to Maimonides' *Guide*," and "How To Begin," chaps. 9, 10, and 11 in *On Maimonides*. Cf. *Guide* 3.51, pp. 618–20. Consider Albo, in *Ikkarim* (*Roots*), vol. 1, chap. 24, pp. 191–93; Ralph Lerner, *Maimonides' Empire of Light*, p. 20; and Kalman Bland, "Moses and the Law according to Maimonides," in *Mystics, Philosophers, and Politicians: Essays in Jewish Intellectual History in Honor of Alexander Altmann*, ed. J. Reinharz and D. Swetschinski (Durham: Duke University Press, 1982), pp. 49–66.

　　7. For Strauss's "Maimonidean" critiques of Spinoza and of Cohen, see Kenneth Hart Green, "Editor's Introduction," in *Jewish Philosophy and the Crisis of Modernity*, pp. 9–15, and 17–25.

　　8. See Michael Nutkiewicz, "Maimonides on the Ptolemaic System: The Limits of Our Knowledge," *Comitatus* 9 (1978): 63–72; and David Blumenthal, "A Lesson from the Arcane World of the Heavenly Spheres according to Maimonides," *Hebrew Annual Review* 9 (1985): 79–89. Cf. "Letter on Astrology," pp. 179–80, with Machiavelli, *Discourses on Livy*, trans. Harvey Mansfield and Nathan Tarcov (Chicago: University of Chicago Press, 1996), bk. II, chap. 2, pp. 131–32. See also Steven Lenzner, "Author as Educator: Strauss's Twofold Treatment of Maimonides and Machiavelli," Claremont Institute, http://www.claremont.org. Also Lenzner, "A Literary Exercise in Self-Knowledge: Strauss's Twofold Interpretation of Maimonides," *Perspectives on Political Science* 31, no. 4 (Fall 2002): 225–34. For Maimonides on "necessary" versus "true" beliefs, see *Guide* 3.28, pp. 513–14; and *Guide* 1.71, pp. 178–79, for how to determine correct opinions. See also Shlomo Pines, "Spinoza's *Tractatus Theologico-Politicus*, Maimonides, and Kant," *Scripta Hierosolymitana* 20 (1968): 3–54; Warren Zev Harvey, "A Portrait of Spinoza as a Maimonidean," *Journal of the History of Philosophy* 19 (1981): 151–72; Rémi Brague, *The Wisdom of the World: The Human Experience of the Universe in Western Thought* (Chicago: University of Chicago Press, 2003), especially pp. 87, 94, 110–11, 173; C. S. Lewis, *The Discarded Image* (Cambridge: Cambridge University Press, 1964); Menachem Kellner, *Maimonides' Confrontation with Mysticism* (Oxford: Littman Library of Jewish Civilization, 2006). Cf. *Guide* 3.32, pp. 525–31. With regard to Maimonides' "modernity," he refused to embrace or conceal any "superstitions" in religion, even if he often only subverted them with his use of irony, or also with what Strauss in a letter dubs "parody": see *Hobbes Politische Wissenschaft und zugehörige Schriften—Briefe*, vol. 3 of *Gesammelte Schriften*, p. 553. Strauss prefers to stress Maimonides' subtle use of parody in referring to the stench of animal sacrifices in the Temple (as had to be perfumed away), which humor supports his view of them as pagan relics. Curiously the great historian of Hebrew literature Israel Davidson obliquely traces the venerable medieval Jewish tradition of literary parody to Maimonides through one of his 13th–14th-century Hebrew translators, Judah al-Ḥarizi: see *Parody in Jewish Literature*

(New York: Columbia University Press, 1907), pp. 5-7. Is it possible that this is another sign of the multifarious impact made by Maimonides?

9. See "Progress or Return?" and "Jerusalem and Athens," in *Jewish Philosophy and the Crisis of Modernity*, pp. 104-7, 377-405. Cf. Daniel Tanguay, "The Conflict between Jerusalem and Athens," in *Leo Strauss: An Intellectual Biography*, trans. Christopher Nadon (New Haven: Yale University Press, 2007), pp. 144-92. Consider Matthew Arnold, "Hebraism and Hellenism," and "Porro Unum Est Necessarium," chaps. 4 and 5 in *Culture and Anarchy*, ed. Stefan Collini (Cambridge: Cambridge University Press, 1993), pp. 126-52. See Isaac Husik, "Hellenism and Judaism," in *Philosophical Essays: Ancient, Mediaeval, and Modern*, ed. Leo Strauss and Milton C. Nahm (Oxford: Basil Blackwell, 1952), pp. 3-14; Lev Shestov, *Athens and Jerusalem*, trans. Bernard Martin (Athens: Ohio University Press, 1966); original Russian version: *Afiny i Ierusalim* (Paris: YMCA Press, 1951); Louis Feldman, "Hebraism and Hellenism Reconsidered," *Judaism* 43, no. 2 (Spring 1994): 115-26; David R. Lachterman, "Torah and Logos," *Graduate Faculty Philosophy Journal* 17, no. 1-2 (1994): 3-27; Sergei Averintsev, "Ancient Greek 'Literature' and Near Eastern 'Writings': The Opposition and Encounter of Two Creative Principles," trans. Richard Pevear and Larissa Volokhonsky, in *Arion* 7, no. 1 (1999): 1-39; and 7, no. 2 (1999): 1-26. Strauss's assessment of Husik appears in *Jewish Philosophy and the Crisis of Modernity*, pp. 235-66, especially pp. 246-58.

10. To reiterate, the "most common error" in modern thought for Strauss is the claim of modern philosophers to lay to rest the biblical challenge by attempting to ground themselves in the mere assumption that this challenge has been adequately dealt with, whether by their attempts to swallow it, to encompass it, to synthesize it, or to refute it. But in none of these attempts have they ever actually been able to achieve completely their goal, their multiple claims to the contrary notwithstanding. Yet even if it is needful to speak of "error," it is also not to be read one-dimensionally. This is because it is vital to notice in Strauss's thought that he speaks—occasionally, but most significantly—of "fruitful errors," a notion which is intended to express something highly dialectical and even Platonic. The phrase "fruitful error" seems to derive from Vilfredo Pareto, *The Mind and Society*, ed. Arthur Livingston, trans. Andrew Bongiorno and Arthur Livingston, 4 vols. (London: Jonathan Cape, 1935), even if his notion seems not quite the same as Strauss's. For what Strauss recognized about Nietzsche, see *Jewish Philosophy and the Crisis of Modernity*, p. 379; *Studies in Platonic Political Philosophy* (Chicago: University of Chicago Press, 1983), pp. 178-81.

11. Strauss refers most directly to the presence of Maimonidean thought among the Christian scholastics in his review of J. O. Riedl's 1944 translation of the treatise of Giles of Rome, *Errores philosophorum*: the twelfth chapter in Giles's book consists of a "refutation" of Maimonides. See *Church History* 15, no. 1 (March 1946): 62-63. See also Isaac Husik, *History of Mediaeval Jewish Philosophy* (New York: Macmillan, 1916); Etienne Gilson, *History of Christian Philosophy in the Middle Ages* (New York: Random House, 1955); Lenn E. Goodman, "Maimonides and Leibniz," *Journal of Jewish Studies* 31 (1980): 214-24 (with a translation of Leibniz's "observations" in Latin on the *Guide*: pp. 225-36); Friedrich Niewöhner, *Maimonides: Aufklärung und Toleranz in Mittelalter* (Wolfenbüttel: Lessing-Akademie, 1988); Niewöhner, *Veritas sive varietas: Lessings Toleranzparabel und das Buch "Von den drei Betrügern"* (Wolfenbüttel: Lessing-Akademie, 1988).

12. See "Progress or Return?," in *Jewish Philosophy and the Crisis of Modernity*, p. 99; Strauss, "Farabi's *Plato*," in *Louis Ginzberg Jubilee Volume* (New York: American Academy for Jewish Research, 1945), pp. 357-58, 392-93. Compare with his "The Law of Reason in the *Kuzari*," in *Persecution and the Art of Writing*, pp. 95-98, 135-41. See also Kenneth Hart Green, "Religion, Philosophy, and Morality: How Leo Strauss Read Judah Halevi's *Kuzari*," *Journal of the American Academy of Religion* 61, no. 2 (Summer 1993): 225-73.

13. See Francis Bacon, *The New Atlantis*, ed. Jerry Weinberger (Arlington Heights, IL: AHM Publishing, 1980), pp. 35-81, and editor's "Introduction," pp. xiii-xxix; and see Richard Kennington, "Bacon's Humanitarian Revision of Machiavelli," in *On Modern Origins: Essays in Early Modern Philosophy*, ed. Pamela Kraus and Frank Hunt (Lanham, MD: Lexington Books, 2004), pp. 57-77, especially pp. 65-68.

14. For "the return of the repressed" as Freud fitted the theme to the history of religion, see *Moses and Monotheism*, trans. Katherine Jones (New York: Alfred A. Knopf, 1939), and especially pp. 158-76. Contrast the surprise that the continued vitality of religion provokes in much of the journalistic and academic world, which prefers to deal with it as "the sacred," and whose opinion of it conforms with Allan Bloom's image: "Our old atheists had a better grasp of religion than does this new respect for the sacred. Atheists took religion seriously and recognized that it is a real force, costs something, and requires difficult choices. These sociologists who talk so facilely about the sacred are like a man who keeps a toothless, old circus lion around the house in order to experience the thrills of the jungle." See *The Closing of the American Mind* (New York: Simon and Schuster, 1987), p. 216. The farther-reaching lesson of this parable, perhaps beyond what Bloom would seem to imply by it, is that a lion can suddenly come to life again and maul its complacent host fatally. Thus, even a man who keeps a "toothless, old circus lion" around the house had better go to the trouble of comprehending lions and what they are capable of doing.

15. For the priority of the rational in human nature, see *Guide* 1.1-2, pp. 21-26; and *Mishneh Torah*, vol. 1: *Sefer ha-Madda*, "Hilkhot Yesodei ha-Torah," 4.8-9. But this fact is no guarantee that it can be actualized by most human beings: see *Guide* 1.34, pp. 72-79. If the movements of the heavens are "the greatest proof through which one can know the existence of the deity," human rationality is no guarantee that this is genuinely knowable by man: *Guide* 1.70, p. 175; 1.71, p. 183; 2.18, p. 302; 2.25, p. 327. For Spinoza's faulting of Maimonides for precisely these things, as they appear in *Guide* 2.25, pp. 327-28, see Spinoza, *Theological-Political Treatise*, trans. Martin D. Yaffe (Newburyport, MA.: Focus, 2004), chap. 7, pp. 97-100. For Strauss's contrasting of Machiavelli with Maimonides, compare *Thoughts on Machiavelli*, pp. 294-95, with *On Tyranny*, p. 184. Cf. "How to Study Medieval Philosophy" and "Note on Maimonides' *Letter on Astrology*," chaps. 1 and 14 in *On Maimonides*. See also "How To Begin." For the passage from Maimonides to which Strauss refers, see his "Letter on Astrology," in Lerner, *Maimonides' Empire of Light*, pp. 179-80.

16. See *Guide* 1.34, pp. 72-79.

17. Maimonides encountered a medieval version of the modern "radical Enlightenment" in Abu Bakr Muhammad ibn Zakariya al-Razi (865-925). For Maimonides as awake to the challenge of "free thought" as it appears in Razi, see his letter to Ibn Tibbon, in *Guide* 3.12, pp. 441-42; and Shlomo Pines, "Translator's Introduction," in *Guide*, pp. cxxxi-cxxxii. For research on Razi, see Paul Kraus, "Raziana I," *Orientalia*, n.s., 4 (1935): 300-334; "Raziana II," *Orientalia*, n.s., 5 (1936): 35-56, 358-78. (Kraus happens to have been Strauss's friend and brother-in-law.) These were mostly reprinted in Razi, *Rasa'il Falsafiyyah* (Cairo: Imprimerie Paul Barbey, 1939). Cf. also Paul Kraus, *Alchemie, Ketzerei, Apokryphen in frühen Islam: Gesammelte Aufsätze*, ed. Rémi Brague (Hildesheim: Georg Olms Verlag, 1994). For a recent study of Razi, see Paul E. Walker, "The Political Implications of al-Razi's Philosophy," in *The Political Aspects of Islamic Philosophy: Essays in Honor of Muhsin Mahdi*, ed. Charles E. Butterworth (Cambridge, MA: Harvard University Press, 1992), pp. 61-94.

18. Strauss was aware that notions like "human perfection" and "the fulfillment of human nature"—as the human *telos*, and hence as the ground of philosophy—are difficult if not impossible to maintain in the context of modern science. This is because modern science believes it has definitively done away with teleology and final causes in the interpretation of nature which em-

braces human nature—or at least, it has done away with the need for them as explanatory devices for dealing with human beings. Whether final causes might somehow still be evident in biological nature, i.e., whether teleology has actually been refuted or not, is of no interest to modern science, because it has been rendered superfluous in the spirit of Ockham's Razor, and hence it is regarded as a disposable notion, or as simple excess. See *Natural Right and History*, pp. 7-8.

19. "Philosophy is to fulfill the function of both philosophy and religion." See *Thoughts on Machiavelli*, p. 297. For Strauss's most complete and most direct contrast between ancients and moderns as between Plato and Machiavelli, consider pp. 288-99.

20. Strauss lets the greater question of man's desire for eternity reverberate through most of his thought; he settles it only insofar as he suggests that like it or not this deeply human problem has to be resolved, and will be whether consciously or willy-nilly, by every human being in order to lead a human life.

> Modern thought reaches its culmination, its highest self-consciousness, in the most radical historicism, i.e., in explicitly condemning to oblivion the notion of eternity. For oblivion of eternity, or, in other words, estrangement from man's deepest desire and therewith from the primary issues, is the price which modern man had to pay, from the very beginning, for attempting to be absolutely sovereign, to become the master and owner of nature, to conquer chance.

See "What Is Political Philosophy?," in *What Is Political Philosophy?*, p. 55.

21. Maimonides' most famous, and also most controversial, discussion of how the repression of religion will not work is in *Guide* 3.29 and 3.32, pp. 514-22, 523-31. ("For a sudden transition from one opposite to another is impossible [in human nature]. And therefore man, according to his nature, is not capable of abandoning suddenly all to which he was accustomed.") Thomas Jefferson (in the U.S. Declaration of Independence) echoes the same wisdom about human nature: "Prudence, indeed, will dictate that governments long established should not be changed for light and transient causes; and accordingly all experience has shown, that mankind are more disposed to suffer, while evils are sufferable, than to right themselves by abolishing the forms to which they are accustomed." As for the choice which apparently has to be made between God and gods, and cannot be either denied or evaded, it eventually led Strauss to open his mind to "the full impact of the all-important question which is coeval with philosophy although the philosophers do not frequently pronounce it—*quid sit deus*." See *The City and Man*, p. 241.

22. See "What Is Political Philosophy?," in *What Is Political Philosophy?*, p. 40, for the statement on "variability"; "Restatement on Xenophon's *Hiero*," in *What Is Political Philosophy?*, pp. 102-3, for the parallel between Machiavelli and Maimonides; *Thoughts on Machiavelli*, p. 294-98, for Strauss on Machiavelli and human nature.

23. Consider Nietzsche, *Beyond Good and Evil*, trans. Walter Kaufmann (New York: Vintage, 1966), pt. 3, sec. 54: "What is the whole of modern philosophy doing at bottom? Since Descartes . . . all the philosophers seek to assassinate the old soul concept. . . . For, formerly, one believed in 'the soul' as one believed in grammar and the grammatical subject." Nietzsche's emphasis in this passage is on the word "believed." See also secs. 12 and 45, and the "Preface," for "the soul superstition," as well as "Plato's invention of the pure mind and of the good in itself." For Rosen's view, see his "Leo Strauss and the Quarrel between the Ancients and the Moderns," in *Leo Strauss's Thought: Toward a Critical Engagement*, ed. Alan Udoff (Boulder, CO: Lynne Rienner, 1991), p. 162.

24. For the evidence of human beings as may be observed around us, and as is not such as to require us to believe in the march of reason in history and its victory against every challenge, we must consider those facts about human life which may make us wonder if we are not in need of

thinking through again what Maimonides teaches about the grandeur of human rationality as well as about its unavoidable limits.

> If concrete historical reality is all that the human mind can know, if there is no transcendent intelligible world, then for there to be philosophy or science reality must have become rational. . . . If Hegel is right that history fulfills the demands of reason, the citizen of the final state should enjoy the satisfaction of all reasonable human aspirations; he should be a free, rational being, content with his situation and exercising all of his powers, emancipated from the bonds of prejudice and oppression. But looking around us, . . . every . . . penetrating observer sees that the completion of the human task may very well coincide with the decay of humanity, the rebarbarization and even reanimalization of man.

See Allan Bloom, "Editor's Introduction," in *Introduction to the Reading of Hegel*, by Alexandre Kojève, trans. James H. Nichols (New York: Basic Books, 1969), pp. vii–xii. For two serious efforts—each quite different from Strauss's and yet each beholden to his deepened view—to grasp the entire "mind" of Maimonides as it was shaped by and yet endures beyond the historical epoch of its emergence, see David Novak, "The Mind of Maimonides," in *The Second One Thousand Years: Ten People Who Defined a Millennium*, ed. Richard John Neuhaus (Grand Rapids, MI: Eerdmans, 2001), pp. 15–27; and Joel L. Kraemer, *Maimonides: The Life and World of One of Civilization's Greatest Minds* (New York: Doubleday, 2008).

25. A eulogy reflects those dialectical qualities of soul esteemed most highly in Strauss's thought: "He did not permit his mind to stifle the voice of his heart nor his heart to give commands to his mind." See "Memorial Remarks for Jason Aronson," in *Jewish Philosophy and the Crisis of Modernity*, pp. 475–76.

26. For the great-souled man of Aristotelian virtue contrasted with the man of humility in biblical virtue, see "Progress or Return?," in *Jewish Philosophy and the Crisis of Modernity*, pp. 107–8. For the tension touched on in Maimonidean thought, see Raymond L. Weiss, *Maimonides' Ethics* (Chicago: University of Chicago Press, 1991), pp. 38–46, 111–13, 193–95. For how to adequately judge the nature of a great thinker, see already "Cohen's Analysis of Spinoza's Bible Science," in *Early Writings*, p. 141. For his statement of the fundamental principle as he employed it in his reading of the great thinkers, "It is safer to try to understand the low in the light of the high than the high in the light of the low. In doing the latter one necessarily distorts the high, whereas in doing the former one does not deprive the low of the freedom to reveal itself fully as what it is," see "Preface to *Spinoza's Critique of Religion*," in *Jewish Philosophy and the Crisis of Modernity*, p. 138. As he also shows, the effort to make the high entirely derivative from the low also has the effect of distorting the low: "A social science that cannot speak of tyranny with the same confidence with which medicine speaks, for example, of cancer cannot understand social phenomena for what they are." See *On Tyranny*, p. 177. This leads to Strauss's postulate that it is man's "thinking," rather than his "recognition" by others, which "constitutes the humanity of man." It is harmonious with the Maimonidean thought about man that Strauss attempted to make historically modern. See *Guide* 1.2, and 3.54, pp. 23–26, 632–38, and compare it with *On Tyranny*, pp. 209–10, but especially p. 212 (or *Jewish Philosophy and the Crisis of Modernity*, pp. 471–72).

27. A close approach to the one I have suggested (although I do not believe Strauss was quite so autobiographical or confessional) is by Lenzner, "A Literary Exercise in Self-Knowledge" (n. 8 above).

28. Testifying to the impact which Strauss made on him as a teacher not only with regard to political philosophy, but especially with regard to Judaism, Werner Dannhauser stresses that this

had perhaps its keenest focus in his presentation of Maimonides: "I simply wish to record that he astounded me by the care with which he studied books by Jews like Maimonides, thus showing me that one could not afford to treat the whole tradition of Jewish learning as relics in one's mind. In this unobtrusive way he caused me to revise—to broaden and deepen—my whole understanding of Judaism." See "Leo Strauss as Jew and Citizen," *Interpretation* 17, no. 3 (Spring 1991): 433–47, and especially p. 446.

29. For Maimonides as identifying precisely *how* revealed religion changed the fundamental natural situation in which philosophy arises among human beings, which Strauss was perhaps the first to notice as original to him, cf. *Guide* 1.31, pp. 66–67, with "'Religiöse Lage der Gegenwart'" (1930), in *Philosophie und Gesetz: Frühe Schriften*, vol. 2 of *Gesammelte Schriften*, pp. 386–87. See also "Introduction to Maimonides' *Guide*" and "How To Begin."

CHAPTER TWO

1. See "Progress or Return?," "Preface to *Spinoza's Critique of Religion*," "On the Interpretation of Genesis," and "Jerusalem and Athens," in *Jewish Philosophy and the Crisis of Modernity*. See also Strauss's absorbing, subtle, and provocative lecture "Reason and Revelation," in Meier, *Leo Strauss and the Theologico-Political Problem*, pp. 141–80. I suggest that in the lecture Strauss was still thinking through the issue and did not believe he had satisfactorily resolved it. Meier contends that in this lecture Strauss claimed to have discovered the philosophic ability to refute revelation through the method of historical genealogy, i.e., how in order to rationally satisfy requisite, otherwise unfulfillable needs in political life, adaptive thinkers had arrived at the notion of revelation. But as Strauss would have been the first to observe about any such claim by philosophers, historical genealogy (even if radically historicist) provides "natural" causes derived in a certain sort of fashion from history for what is claimed by religious tradition to have a supernatural cause, i.e., revelation as of supernatural origin. These are the limits of every genealogy as a disproof of God: who can prove that God did not design and set in motion this genealogy as an aspect of His plan for man and the universe? Thus, revelation as a possibility has still not been refuted and certainly cannot be refuted by genealogy, precisely insofar as it is an effort to "refute" the supernatural on historical, or (adapted) "natural," grounds. The circularity is not avoided by resorting to history instead of nature, even if it is the history of ideas in religion.

2. In a highly significant passage, Strauss makes so bold as to characterize Maimonides as "the greatest analyst of [the] fundamental difference" between Jerusalem and Athens; he enlarges on this point by maintaining that Maimonides most definitely "knew the true roots" of the fundamental difference. See "Progress or Return?," in *Jewish Philosophy and the Crisis of Modernity*, pp. 110–12.

3. Strauss attributed enormous historic significance to the continued debate of reason and revelation, which is best summarized in the following statement: "It seems to me that this unresolved conflict is the secret of the vitality of Western civilization." This reasoning can, it appears to me, only be dismissed as so much rhetoric by enemies or even by so-called friends of Strauss's thought (who reject the tacit defense of revelation contained in it) if they have proven in a decisive manner that Strauss was in no substantial or serious way concerned with the fate of Western civilization.

4. See "How To Begin," chap. 11 in On *Maimonides*. See also Green, *Jew and Philosopher*, p. 222, n. 15. Heinrich Meier notes that in the original manuscript of this essay, composed between May and August of 1960, Strauss wrote "36 years" but changed it to "25 years." However, if this is the correct chronology as discovered by Meier, it may suggest that the serious study of

Maimonides' *Guide* began for Strauss in his own mind around 1924, perhaps while he prepared "Cohen's Analysis of Spinoza's Bible Science." See *Philosophie und Gesetz: Frühe Schriften*, vol. 2 of *Gesammelte Schriften*, p. XXII, n. 26. See "Cohens Analyse der Bibel-Wissenschaft Spinozas," in *Die Religionskritik Spinozas und zugehörige Schriften*, vol. 1 of *Gesammelte Schriften*, pp. 363–87; "Cohen's Analysis of Spinoza's Bible Science," in *Early Writings*, pp. 140–72.

5. For the reason why the two sides must confront one another, see "Progress or Return?," in *Jewish Philosophy and the Crisis of Modernity*, pp. 116–17: "No one can be both a philosopher and a theologian, or, for that matter, some possibility which transcends the conflict between philosophy and theology, or pretends to be a synthesis of both. But every one of us can be and ought to be either one or the other, the philosopher open to the challenge of theology, or the theologian open to the challenge of philosophy." This is a seemingly unequivocal statement about intention that is often rather ambiguous in the execution. Strauss himself is in no sense unambiguously clear about which side of the divide he stood on—and the same thing may be suggested about his Maimonides, whose position at the pinnacle (or the root) of his view often remains obscure in Strauss's treatment. The ambiguity seems quite deliberate.

6. Of course, Strauss raises an issue of an opposite order: whether Maimonides and those like him who pursued a similar line of thought (traceable to Plato), which attempted to harmonize the two sides—philosophy and revelation—was in fact "too successful." See *On Tyranny*, p. 206. By this suggestion (espying an almost grander historical narrative than that of his Hegelian dialogue partner, Alexandre Kojève), Strauss stood very much against the modern consensus of historians who have long held the view, ever since Spinoza leveled his damning criticism against Maimonides, that Maimonidean thought was a complete failure. Strauss's suggestion seems to have descended from Nietzsche's criticism, even if he is not sanctioning it; he only says, "one sometimes wonders" about it, but he never declares it true. This is because Strauss is chiefly concerned about an awareness that thinkers like Maimonides used to know, but which seems to have been misplaced. For Nietzsche, however, his concern is with something else: not only Western religion, but also Western philosophy is "Plato for the people." To "popularize" in this Platonic fashion (followed by Maimonides and those like him) was for Nietzsche a turn in the wrong direction that both philosophy and religion have been misled by.

7. See "Progress or Return?," in *Jewish Philosophy and the Crisis of Modernity*, pp. 105–10; "Preface to Isaac Husik, *Philosophical Essays*," in *Jewish Philosophy and the Crisis of Modernity*, p. 253. See also "How to Study Medieval Philosophy" and "Literary Character," chaps. 1 and 8 in *On Maimonides*. For Scholem's counterargument about Kabbalah, consider Gershom Scholem, *Origins of the Kabbalah*, trans. Allan Arkush (New York: Jewish Publication Society, 1987), pp. 7–12. Recent scholars have begun to rethink the relations between Maimonides and Kabbalah. See Moshe Idel, "*Sitre 'Arayot* in Maimonides' Thought," in *Maimonides and Philosophy*, ed. Shlomo Pines and Yirmiyahu Yovel (Dordrecht: Martinus Nijhoff, 1986), pp. 79–91; Idel, *Kabbalah: New Perspectives* (New Haven: Yale University Press, 1988), pp. 250–56; Idel, "Maimonides and Jewish Mysticism," in *Studies in Maimonides*, ed. Isadore Twersky (Cambridge, MA: Harvard University Center for Jewish Studies, 1990), pp. 31–81; Idel, *Maimonïde et la mystique juive* (Paris: Les Éditions du Cerf, 1991); Idel, "Maimonides' *Guide of the Perplexed* and the Kabbalah," *Jewish History* 18 (2004): 197–226; Elliot R. Wolfson, *Abraham Abulafia—Kabbalist and Prophet: Hermeneutics, Theosophy, and Theurgy* (Los Angeles: Cherub Press, 2000); Wolfson, "Beneath the Wings of the Great Eagle: Maimonides and 13th-Century Kabbalah," in *Moses Maimonides (1138–1204): His Religious, Scientific, and Philosophical "Wirkungsgeschichte" in Different Cultural Contexts*, ed. Görge K. Hasselhoff and Otfried Fraisse (Wuerzburg: Ergon Verlag, 2004), pp. 209–37; and Wolfson, "Via Negativa in Maimonides and Its Impact on 13th Century Kabbalah," *Maimonidean Studies* 5 (2008): 393–442. In these works neither Idel nor Wolfson attributes his rethinking of Scholem

on Maimonides to any ideas or suggestions derived from his reading of Strauss, although they show both awareness of his thought and evidence of familiarity with his books and essays.

8. For Strauss's acknowledgment of elements in Spinoza's thought which contributed significantly to his thinking through of the argument between reason and revelation, see "Progress or Return?," in *Jewish Philosophy and the Crisis of Modernity*, p. 130.

9. This is also close to the gist of the argument that David Novak makes in his recent consideration of whether "Maimonideanism" is still relevant. See "Can We Be Maimonideans Today?," in *Maimonides and His Heritage*, ed. Idit Dobbs-Weinstein, Lenn E. Goodman, and James Allan Grady (Albany: State University of New York Press, 2009), pp. 193-209, and especially p. 205. A not entirely dissimilar argument was made by Marvin Fox, *Interpreting Maimonides: Studies in Methodology, Metaphysics, and Moral Philosophy* (Chicago: University of Chicago Press, 1990), pp. 323-42. This should lead one to ask whether these general arguments and numerous others like them, in favor of Maimonidean thought (which most moderns, following Spinoza, had once declared obsolete), were not in the decisive respect prepared by Strauss's decades-long recovery of the immediate relevance of Maimonides *as a thinker*.

10. Sarah Stroumsa, *Maimonides and His World* (Princeton: Princeton University Press, 2009), pp. 73-76, 177-79, 183-88, compares Maimonides' *Guide of the Perplexed* with Averroes' *al-Kashf 'an Manahij al-Adilla* [*Exposition of the Method of Proof*], which is most pertinent; she even imaginatively conceives of the former as a reaction or response to the latter. Yet in proceeding along this novel historical line she seems not to pay due attention to the philosophic thrust of Strauss's argument about the art of writing, in which he contends that the form of Maimonides' work is *essential* to the superiority of his achievement. Miriam Galston seems to reach a position closer to Strauss's notion of what Maimonides was doing in his *Guide*: "The Moral Status of Teaching and Writing," in *Enlightening Revolutions: Essays in Honor of Ralph Lerner*, ed. Svetozar Minkov (Lanham, MD: Lexington Books, 2006), pp. 3-21, especially pp. 8-10, 12-14.

11. See "Some Remarks on the Political Science of Maimonides and Farabi," chap. 5 in *On Maimonides*.

12. Strauss was concerned over and above everything with those "capable of truly independent thinking": see "Persecution and the Art of Writing," in *Persecution and the Art of Writing*, p. 23.

13. Ibid., p. 24, for "the discovery of a terra incognita," the evidence for which had hitherto merely been ignored, though it was standing visible and waiting to be noticed.

14. See the letter to Jacob Klein of 23 July 1938, in *Hobbes Politische Wissenschaft und zugehörige Schriften—Briefe*, vol. 3 of *Gesammelte Schriften*, p. 553. The vexed question What is Strauss's relation to Nietzsche? has received such contradictory and partisan answers for and against both figures—seemingly depending on whether one likes or dislikes Strauss, and whether one likes or dislikes Nietzsche—that it is probably best to let this debate lie for a while (as with sleeping dogs), until polemical passions have subsided.

15. See "The Three Waves of Modernity, in *Introduction to Political Philosophy*, pp. 81-98.

16. It is on this ground, i.e., the assumption of the "free mind" as the needed basis of all genuine and deep thinking (whether philosophic or not) that Strauss was eventually able to begin to see even the Bible in a completely novel, almost Maimonidean, light. In other words, he seems to perceive in the biblical authors an astonishing freedom of thought, though related to their fundamental premises. See "On the Interpretation of Genesis," in *Jewish Philosophy and the Crisis of Modernity*, pp. 359-76.

17. See *Hobbes Politische Wissenschaft und zugehörige Schriften—Briefe*, vol. 3 of *Gesammelte Schriften*, pp. 549-50. The previously unknown, decades-long correspondence between Glatzer and Strauss is currently being transcribed, edited, and translated by Susanne Klingenstein (see

Weekly Standard 16, no. 6 [16 October 2010], http://www.weeklystandard.com/articles/greeks-and-jews_508813.html). For the comment on Maimonides as a "radical philosopher," see the letter to Julius Guttmann of 30 May 1949, the most relevant section of which is reproduced in Meier, *Leo Strauss and the Theologico-Political Problem*, n. 32, pp. 23–24. And for the "historian with a sense of decency," see "Literary Character." In general, we must be grateful to Heinrich Meier for deciphering, annotating, and subsequently publishing these letters. However, those who wish to interpret the letters as finished texts must exercise great care in doing so. So far the best effort to begin thinking about these issues, and to appreciate the Meier edition of the letters, is Werner Dannhauser, "Leo Strauss in His Letters," in Minkov, *Enlightening Revolutions*, pp. 355–61; for his doubts about the letters as a source, see especially pp. 359–60. See also Heinrich Meier, "How Strauss Became Strauss," in Minkov, *Enlightening Revolutions*, pp. 363–82. It contains useful comments on the phases in Strauss's discovery of Maimonides, as reflected in the letters and his other works (some unpublished until Meier's edition) of the 1920s and 1930s. Those letters which, as it seems to me, are most directly relevant or helpful for a grasp of various points in his growing, and deepening, comprehension of Maimonides, are as follows. Those sent from Strauss to Gerhard Krüger: 7 May 1931 (p. 385); 1 June 1931 (p. 388); 28 June 1931 (p. 389); 17 November 1932 (pp. 404–5); 16 December 1931 (p. 417); 25 December 1935 (p. 450). Those sent from Strauss to Jacob Klein: 6 May 1935 (pp. 538–39); 20 January 1938 (pp. 545–46); 16 February 1938 (pp. 549–50); 23 July 1938 (pp. 553–54). Those sent from Strauss to Karl Löwith: 23 June 1935 (pp. 648–50); 17 July 1935 (p. 655–57); 15 August 1946 (pp. 661–64); 20 August 1946 (pp. 666–70); 19 July 1951 (pp. 675–76); 11 July 1964 (pp. 691–93); 12 March 1970 (pp. 695–96). Those sent from Strauss to Gershom Scholem: 3 November 1933 (pp. 703–4); 7 December 1933 (pp. 706–9); 14 February 1934 (pp. 711–12); 2 August 1934 (p. 713); 14 December 1934 (p. 714); 2 October 1935 (pp. 715–16); 10 May 1950 (pp. 721–22); 5 February 1952 (pp. 724–25); 22 June 1952 (pp. 727–28); 16 January 1953 (pp. 731–32); 27 October 1955 (pp. 735–36); 18 October 1957 (p. 737); 23 March 1959 (pp. 738–39); 11 August 1960 (pp. 740–41); 4 May 1962 (pp. 745–46); 21 November 1962 (pp. 746–47); 6 December 1962 (p. 748); 15 December 1963 (pp. 750–51); 7 August 1965 (p. 753); 5 November 1966 (pp. 754–55); 7 August 1967 (pp. 755–56); 18 December 1970 (p. 761); 17 November 1972 (pp. 764–65); 26 February 1973 (p. 767); 19 March 1973 (pp. 768–69); 7 July 1973 (pp. 769–70); 30 September 1973 (pp. 770–71); 17 October 1973 (p. 771).

18. Perhaps Strauss was aided by the counterexample of Nietzsche's and Heidegger's radical disinterring of the roots of the tradition in order to show their baneful or harmful character, while Strauss did the same in order to show the health of those roots. See "An Unspoken Prologue," in *Jewish Philosophy and the Crisis of Modernity*, p. 450.

19. See "Cohen and Maimonides" and "Maimonides' Statement on Political Science," chaps. 3 and 9 in *On Maimonides*. For Strauss on Cohen, see also *Jewish Philosophy and the Crisis of Modernity*, pp. 158–69, 251–56, 267–82, 398–99; and Kenneth Hart Green, "Editor's Introduction," in *Jewish Philosophy and the Crisis of Modernity*, pp. 17–25.

20. For Maimonides as "the great eagle," see "Maimonides' Statement on Political Science," and especially n. 27, which contains the passage from Albo, *Ikkarim* (*Roots*), p. 190, and *Guide* 3.6, p. 427, to which Strauss refers. For the boldness of Maimonides as a thinker, see his own author's "Introduction" to the *Guide*, with its comment on his aim to address the "single virtuous man," even if it "displeases ten thousand ignoramuses." For another discoverer of a lost continent, i.e., for another "Columbus," see Strauss's remarks on Machiavelli in "What Is Political Philosophy?," in *What Is Political Philosophy?*, p. 40.

21. See "Maimonides' Statement on Political Science" and "How To Begin," chaps. 9 and 11 in *On Maimonides*. See also *Philosophy and Truth: Selections from Nietzsche's Notebooks of the*

Early 1870s, ed. and trans. David Breazeale (New Jersey: Humanities Press, 1990), especially "On the Pathos of Truth," pp. 61–63, and "The Philosopher," p. 22, para. 58. For the letter to Scholem (19 March 1973), see *Hobbes Politische Wissenschaft und zugehörige Schriften—Briefe*, vol. 3 of *Gesammelte Schriften*, p. 769.

    22. See "A Giving of Accounts," in *Jewish Philosophy and the Crisis of Modernity*, pp. 462–63; "How to Study Medieval Philosophy." See also Allan Bloom, "Leo Strauss: September 20, 1899–October 18, 1973," in *Giants and Dwarfs: Essays, 1960–1990* (New York: Simon and Schuster, 1990), pp. 243–45; Ralph Lerner, "Dispersal by Design: The Author's Choice," in *Reason, Faith, and Politics: Essays in Honor of Werner J. Dannhauser*, ed. Arthur M. Meltzer and Robert P. Kraynak (Lanham, MD: Lexington Books, 2008), pp. 29–41.

    23. For *Keter Malkhut*, by Solomon ibn Gabirol, see *The Kingly Crown*, trans. Bernard Lewis (London: Vallentine-Mitchell, 1961).

    24. See especially "How To Begin." See also "Introduction," in *Persecution and the Art of Writing*, pp. 19–21; "Literary Character" and "Introduction to Maimonides' *Guide*," chaps. 8 and 10 in *On Maimonides*.

    25. Consider the golden apple and the silver filigree in Maimonides' "Introduction" to the *Guide* (pp. 11–12), as well as the comments in "How To Begin":

> The corporealistic meaning is not the only meaning, it is not the deepest meaning, it is not the true meaning, but it is as much intended as the true meaning; it is intended because of the need to educate and to guide the vulgar and, we may add, a vulgar that originally was altogether under the spell of Sabianism.... According to King Solomon, who was "wiser than all men" (I Kings 5:11), the outer is like silver, i.e., it is useful for the ordering of human society, and the inner is like gold, i.e., it conveys true beliefs (1.Intro.).

This idea of "golden apple" and "silver filigree" levels in *any* great book, which notion "is buried in the writings of the rhetoricians of antiquity" (*Persecution and the Art of Writing*, p. 24), is perhaps the main reason why Maimonides' approach is not accepted by scholars as plausible in contemporary readings of the Torah: the idea that any such ancient text can contain multiple layers is considered *historically* impossible, futile, or absurd.

    26. Strauss's thesis and approach are perhaps best tested by considering (a) whether Maimonides' use of scriptural and midrashic sources is as deliberate as he claimed, and (b) whether these contain thus far mostly undetected hidden depths. For two contemporary scholars who emphasize the need for just such considerations, and whose work seems to confirm Strauss's essential thesis and approach, see Fox, *Interpreting Maimonides*, pp. 154–55, 260–64; and likewise James A. Diamond, "Forging a New *Righteous Nation*: Maimonides' Midrashic Interweave of Verse and Text," in *New Directions in Jewish Philosophy*, ed. Aaron W. Hughes and Elliot R. Wolfson (Bloomington: Indiana University Press, 2009), pp. 286–325.

    27. Strauss seems to clarify in a passing comment why it so exhilarates the mind to study great books like the *Guide*: it involves "listening to the conversation . . . between the greatest minds." See "What Is Liberal Education?," in *Liberalism Ancient and Modern*, p. 7.

    28. See *On Tyranny*, p. 206.

    29. See "Some Remarks on the Political Science of Maimonides and Farabi."

    30. For the properly historical, i.e., "nonhistoricist," manner of reading books by both Spinoza and Maimonides, consider the comments on how to read past authors in "How to Study Spinoza's *Theologico-Political Treatise*," in *Jewish Philosophy and the Crisis of Modernity*, p. 194.

CHAPTER THREE

1. "How to Study Medieval Philosophy," chap. 1 in *On Maimonides*.

2. See "How To Begin," chap. 11 in *On Maimonides*, as he contrasts *Guide* 1.31 with 2.22 and 24. Strauss suggests that the dramatic discrepancy in Maimonides' attitude toward natural science (Can it know the celestial beings and can it know the reasons for their movements? And can it, consequently, truly demonstrate the existence of God?) is due to the needs of the argument at different junctures in his book: as the argument progresses, he starts to move toward a different result, determined by his pedagogical strategy. So Strauss hints that something is permanently truer than any available natural science for Maimonides, which guides his use of it and the variations in his argument, i.e., human science.

3. Strauss mentions Scholem's critical-historical assessment of the impact made by Maimonides and the Jewish philosophers who followed him, as likewise by the Jewish mystics: "Undoubtedly both the mystics and the philosophers completely transform the structure of ancient Judaism." In other words, once both had completed their work, Judaism was *not* the same as it had been in its original form. This is because, according to Scholem, "both have lost the simple relation to Judaism, that naïveté which speaks to us from the classical documents of rabbinical literature." Compare "How to Study Medieval Philosophy" with Gershom Scholem, *Major Trends in Jewish Mysticism* (New York: Schocken, 1995), p. 23. This assumes that the original character of Judaism (i.e., its essential teaching) was "naive," unreflective, unsophisticated, or even simpleminded, as the most accurate critical-historical judgment—which was, of course, denied by both the Jewish philosophers and the Jewish mystics themselves. In this context, it is perhaps useful to keep in mind one of Strauss's most unambiguous statements about truth and history: "*The* modern prejudice, namely, [is] the prejudice that *the* truth has not already been found in the past." See "Review of Julius Ebbinghaus, *On the Progress of Metaphysics*," in *Early Writings*, p. 214. But it happens that Scholem is fully in accord with Strauss on this judgment: see his letter to Zalman Schocken of 29 October 1937, in David Biale, *Gershom Scholem: Kabbalah and Counter-history* (Cambridge, MA: Harvard University Press, 1982), pp. 155–56 (German original) and pp. 31–32 (English translation).

4. According to Freud, it is the "intellectual" excellence of the Jewish tradition, and the pride in it, which most arouses hatred against the Jews. See Strauss's comments in "Freud on Moses and Monotheism," in *Jewish Philosophy and the Crisis of Modernity*, pp. 285–309, and especially p. 301. In this sense it may be suggested that Freud unwittingly made a genuinely Maimonidean argument.

5. In the "Introduction" to the *Eight Chapters*, Maimonides makes an unequivocal statement: "Hear the truth from whoever says it." In other words, it is not significant what the source of a statement is, or who utters it, or what it may lack or possess in the grounding of authority, even if seemingly set in the context of revelation; it is only a matter of whether it is true or not. As a result, he imposes a duty to think for oneself about the true and the false, and not merely to judge on the basis of what is revered or conforming with accepted standards. Further, to love the truth as truth—not encompassed by a single book, source, or tradition—is a lesson which he also wishes the statement to imply. The last logical consequence of this statement would seem to be that, if one aspires to know the truth, one must also be an *open-minded* searcher. See *The Ethical Writings of Maimonides*, ed. Raymond L. Weiss and Charles E. Butterworth (New York: New York University Press, 1975), p. 60.

6. Strauss was critical of the modern project at the place where the following notion emerged and became sacrosanct: the belief that there could ever be "a time when no one would suffer any harm from hearing any truth." If one has no wish to do harm to the naive or unequipped, never

mind how this harm may redound to one's detriment, one must consider carefully what the consequences of one's speech are likely to be. To be one of those who engages in thinking and who says or writes what one thinks, certain self-imposed limits seem to be called for. Of course, just how such lines are to be drawn must be adapted to the specific society of which the thinker is a member. Maimonides was the first—or if not the first, certainly the best—teacher that Strauss encountered who made this a prime consideration forthrightly discussed. But eventually he started to perceive that other thinkers had much to teach about this same issue. Indeed, he would perceive that this issue had been probed and dealt with by philosophers, poets, and writers from Aristophanes and Plato to Lessing and Goethe, if not (at least sporadically) through the 20th century. See *Persecution and the Art of Writing*, pp. 32–35.

7. See Maimonides' "Introduction" to his reading of the "account of the chariot" (*ma'aseh merkavah*), apparently the most crucial and most secret teaching in the Torah (*Guide* 3.Introduction, p. 416): he keeps the entire discussion in the realm of reasoning about the texts. First, he has arrived at what he says by "conjecture and supposition." Second, he makes no claim to "divine revelation." Third, in what he presents of "these matters," he also has not received truths transmitted by "a teacher." Fourth, he has depended instead only on reading the holy books together with "speculative premises" which he happened to possess. Fifth, he also concedes that these matters may be "different" from how he construes them: "Something else [may be] intended" than what he expresses in this section of his book about the "account of the chariot." Curiously, he hopes that his reader on this topic, the deepest in the Torah, will keep an open mind.

8. For what Farabi's position on what philosophy is may have taught Maimonides, and the enormous impact it may have made on him, consider the following comment by Strauss: "But what made [Farabi] a philosopher, according to his own view of philosophy, were not those convictions, but the spirit in which they were acquired, in which they were maintained, and in which they were intimated rather than preached from the housetops. Only by reading Maimonides' *Guide* against the background of philosophy thus understood, can we hope eventually to fathom its unexplored depths." See Kenneth Hart Green, "Editor's Preface," in *On Maimonides*, n. 4, for the full comment presented.

9. See "Restatement on Xenophon's *Hiero* [The Last Paragraph]," in *Jewish Philosophy and the Crisis of Modernity*, p. 471; also in *On Tyranny*, p. 212.

10. The phrase "questions are the piety of thinking" is Heidegger's, not Strauss's. See Martin Heidegger, *Vorträge und Aufsätze* (Pfullingen: Neske, 1967), vol. 1, p. 36; Heidegger, *On the Way to Language*, trans. Peter Hertz (New York: Harper and Row, 1971), pp. 71–72; Heidegger, "The Question Concerning Technology," in *The Question Concerning Technology and Other Essays*, trans. William Lovitt (New York: Harper and Row, 1971), p. 35. The way of Strauss might differ from the way of Heidegger on most things, but I would say that on this formulation they would mostly approach one another. Yet a major difference between them would be illuminated by it: whether the questioning that the philosopher or thinker is engaged in, or the questions to which he constantly recurs, are forms of piety, to which he returns or recurs from "piety." This questioning, at least with regard to the fundamental and eternal questions, is for Strauss the unique capacity of reason, which is the mode of *philosophic* thinking (although, to be sure, not the only form of "thinking"), and which is moved by *eros* in a much greater measure than by any form of piety. For is reason in its thinking capacity ever related to the fundamental questions as a relation of *piety*? (Recall Aristotle's saying: "I am a friend of Plato's, and I am a friend of truth, but I am a greater friend of truth.") Of course, Heidegger himself is careful to express that he intends piety "in the ancient sense: obedient, or submissive, . . . [i.e.,] submitting to what thinking has to think about." Strauss only discusses what the "ancient sense" of piety is in a single passage known to me: "Why We Remain Jews," in *Jewish Philosophy and the Crisis of Modernity*, p. 320. Strauss (in contrast

with Heidegger) lays a distinctly different stress on this term, which is not merely to be "obedient or submissive": to Strauss, it is clear that in the new situation of the Jews, the leading virtue of the modern Jew is "fidelity, loyalty, piety in the old Latin sense of the word *pietas*." Hence the divide between Strauss and Heidegger on the nature of questioning: the philosopher never asks questions because of loyalty to anyone, not even to another philosopher, however great their friendship. If there is any "piety" involved, then it is to the natural situation of man, which elicits the same questions and which his unquenchable desire to know impels him to explore (especially as to whether knowing is his task).

11. Stanley Rosen formulates the relation of Strauss to both Maimonides and Farabi in the context of modernity in the following paradoxical words: "Strauss presents us with the curious figure of a revolutionary Jane Austen." See "Wittgenstein, Strauss, and the Possibility of Philosophy," in *The Elusiveness of the Ordinary* (New Haven: Yale University Press, 2002), pp. 135-58, especially p. 145. For comments related to Strauss's "method" of reading as shaped by Maimonides, see also Rosen, "The Golden Apple," in *Metaphysics in Ordinary Language* (New Haven: Yale University Press, 1999), pp. 62-80; and the discussion in Rosen, "Hermeneutics as Politics," in *Hermeneutics as Politics* (New York: Oxford University Press, 1987), pp. 87-140, but especially pp. 118-20, 130-32, offers his view on the questionable character of Strauss's position insofar as it leaves the definition of philosophy at mere "awareness of the problems."

12. See "How to Study Medieval Philosophy": "The historian of philosophy must then undergo a transformation into a philosopher or a conversion to philosophy, if he wants to do his job properly, if he wants to be a competent historian of philosophy." On Socrates and philosophy, see *Rebirth of Classical Political Rationalism*, pp. 103-83; Strauss, "The Origin of Political Science and the Problem of Socrates: Six Public Lectures," *Interpretation* 23, no. 2 (Winter 1996): 127-207.

13. Cf. *Guide* 1.1 and 3.54. The first chapter of the book deals with "image," and the last chapter with "wisdom" (or rather, "the word 'wisdom'"): both concern themselves with man, not only as created in the image of God, but also as the being who makes images of God. In the best case, the "images" are shaped by "wisdom." See "Literary Character," chap. 8 in *On Maimonides*; cf. also "How To Begin." Since Strauss took number symbolism as a legitimate, or at least a not entirely frivolous, clue to the significance of what certain authors hint in their books, we may give it a voice in our considerations. See "Maimonides' Statement on Political Science," chap. 9 in *On Maimonides*: "We must consider the significance of the number 7 in Maimonides' own thought. Considerations of this kind are necessarily somewhat playful. But they are not so playful as to be incompatible with the seriousness of scholarship. . . . It is of the essence of devices of this kind that, while they are helpful up to a certain point, they are never sufficient and are never meant to be sufficient: they are merely hints." A different sort of hint is provided by how an author decides to locate a chapter in a book: the middle is most significant, or at least most concealed. (His assumption: negligent readers tend to read first and last chapters.) As for what would seem to be the middle chapter of the *Guide*, according to one reading (i.e., which counts the three introductions as chapters), the center would be 2.13; according to another reading (i.e., which does not count the three introductions as chapters), the center would be 2.15. Cf. for further discussion "Introduction to Maimonides' *Guide*," chap. 10 in *On Maimonides*, n. 57.

14. See "On the Interpretation of Genesis," in *Jewish Philosophy and the Crisis of Modernity*, pp. 359-76, but especially pp. 366-67, 373. See also "Progress or Return?," in *Jewish Philosophy and the Crisis of Modernity*, p. 115. In Strauss's explanation of biblical thought, "the [fundamental] dualism chosen by the Bible, the dualism as distinguished from the dualism of male and female, is not sensual but intellectual, noetic." See p. 367. It makes the Bible a book resting on a "cogni-

tive" base, in which the act of knowing plays a crucial role. Although this may well not be the same act of knowing as that in Greek philosophy (especially Aristotle), it is not entirely dissimilar (i.e., "thought" vs. "philosophy"). Strauss obliquely discusses these issues as they relate to Maimonides in the discussion period of "Introduction to Maimonides' *Guide*."

15. See "Progress or Return?," in *Jewish Philosophy and the Crisis of Modernity*, p. 131, for Strauss's doubts about the efforts of Pascal and those like him to prove the misery of the philosophic life: they "presuppose faith."

16. For the fundamental dualism of the Bible as "noetic," see n. 14 above. Although Strauss never mentions the name of Maimonides in the context of his explication of the biblical text, it is highly plausible to assume that he derived some of this "postcritical" perspective on the Hebrew Bible from Maimonides, who was keenly disposed to comprehend the Torah as a product of the highest intellectual excellence, which approximates to the divine: see *Guide* 2.30, pp. 348–59; and "How To Begin."

17. See *Guide* 2.15, p. 292.

18. Proceeding from a modern historical approach to the Hebrew Bible, Strauss curiously seems to present a non-Maimonidean view of the authentic biblical teaching: the problem of man begins with his desire for *autonomous* knowledge, which is not only a highly questionable desire, but also a knowledge which he apparently *cannot* achieve. The limit on autonomous knowledge puts a limit on genuine moral knowledge: whatever rudimentary knowledge of good and evil may be available to man, God must illuminate for him the full truth about good and evil. See "On the Interpretation of Genesis," in *Jewish Philosophy and the Crisis of Modernity*, pp. 372–73, 374. As Strauss also elucidates, Maimonides is not antagonistic to autonomous knowledge of a certain sort; he believes in the integrity of the theoretical life as the primordial "moral" imperative for man. As autonomous thinking and knowing, it precedes knowledge of good and evil; or rather, it is the original form of morality. Of course, whatever autonomy the life of the mind on the theoretical plane may possess, Strauss highlighted Maimonides' recognition of a continued argument between philosophy and religion on the practical plane. With regard to speculative matters which follow from moral concerns, it leads to the sharpest conflict on the issue of creation versus eternity, but it also concerns a difference about providence. However, for Strauss this highlighting of the "moral" difference did not compel Maimonides to describe the conflict, or to draw the line between the antagonists, as has been prescribed by much modern thought: the moderns emphasize man's capacity for autonomous morality on the everyday level. For Maimonides, it is not a difference about the ultimate goods of human nature, as primarily intellectual excellence and consequent moral virtue, but rather about what sorts of beliefs and laws are needed to best sustain and perfect those goods together, in harmony with the contrasting needs of political order. See "The Law of Reason in the *Kuzari*," in *Persecution and the Art of Writing*, pp. 135–41; Kenneth Hart Green, "Religion, Philosophy, and Morality: How Leo Strauss Read Judah Halevi's *Kuzari*," *Journal of the American Academy of Religion* 61, no. 2 (Summer 1993): 225–73.

19. For Strauss vis-à-vis the two Western ways toward "truth," and their impressively common way on the significance of and need for "wisdom" in human life, see "Jerusalem and Athens," in *Jewish Philosophy and the Crisis of Modernity*, pp. 379, 382, 398.

20. It is the possibility of Maimonides' critical awareness of historical unfolding in phases, and even of breaks in the continuity of tradition (both points opposed to what tradition formally teaches), that Strauss seems to be hinting at in this seemingly casual comment on a Maimonidean contradiction ("whatever [he] may have meant") about Ahijah the Shilonite: see "Progress or Return?," in *Jewish Philosophy and the Crisis of Modernity*, p. 125. Strauss suggests that Maimonides was not only pointing to possible discontinuities in the tradition and its ancient sources, as modern criticism emphasizes, but also signaling his alertness to such historicity, or to what Strauss

qualifiedly refers to as the "mythical" element in tradition. This shows how possible it is that the medieval thinker did not deny or ignore history, but was critically aware of it, as he already shows he was in *Guide* 3.29 and 32. As it especially demonstrates, he did not need modern thought to become aware of the "uses" of history. Cf. "Introduction to Maimonides' *Guide*."

21. Maimonides isolates written texts as obstacles to thinking for those raised in the present era, which has made it "an established usage to think highly [of texts] and to regard [them] as true." The minds of those who have been shaped in the scriptural era are limited and made prone to argumentative quarrel and conflict by an undue reverence for books, to which they have been habituated. See *Guide* 1.31, p. 67; and Maimonides, "Letter on Astrology," in Lerner, *Maimonides' Empire of Light*, p. 179. For Strauss's view that the high better reveals the low (although this statement is agnostic on whether or how much the high determines the low), see chap. 1, n. 26 above.

CHAPTER FOUR

1. *Guide* 1.34, p. 78.

2. Is this Strauss's way of recalling that oft-repeated saying of Nietzsche's: "To forget one's purpose is the commonest form of stupidity"? Nietzsche, *Human, All Too Human*, trans. Marion Faber and Stephen Lehmann (Lincoln: University of Nebraska Press, 1984), second supplement: "The Wanderer and His Shadow," aphorism 206. For Maimonides' casual disparagement of poetry in the *Guide*, consider 1.2, p. 24.

3. Strauss seems most keenly aware of the disparity between the scholar or scientist (however brilliant) and the philosopher in his lecture "Freud on Moses and Monotheism," in *Jewish Philosophy and the Crisis of Modernity*, pp. 304–5. See also "Why We Remain Jews," in *Jewish Philosophy and the Crisis of Modernity*, p. 328, for Strauss's pointing to Why science? as the most fundamental question that modern scholars or scientists usually cannot answer; indeed, this is rarely even asked, since most regard the worth of science as virtually self-evident.

4. See "Maimonides' Statement on Political Science," chap. 9 in *On Maimonides*. For Strauss's position on the significance of the "negative theology," which diverges from the views attributed to Maimonides by most modern scholars, see, e.g., "Introduction to Maimonides' *Guide*," chap. 10 in *On Maimonides*.

5. See "How to Study Medieval Philosophy," chap. 1 in *On Maimonides*; cf. "Literary Character," chap. 8 in *On Maimonides*.

6. The great modern exception for Strauss was Gotthold Ephraim Lessing, who seemed to have liberated himself from the modern prejudices, and who pursued literary, theological, and historical investigations of religion which transcended the modern limits: see Green, *Jew and Philosopher*, pp. 29–30; 97–98; 148, n. 6; 157, n. 49; 161, n. 78; 163, n. 99; 165, nn. 105, 114, and 116; 184, n. 14; 221, n. 14. It is curious that in the very first scene of Lessing's very first play (composed at around age eighteen, prior to his friendship with Moses Mendelssohn), *The Young Scholar* (1747), Damis the youthful hero is reading Maimonides' *Mishneh Torah* (i.e., *Yad ha-Ḥazakah*) in Hebrew. This at the very least suggests that a direct Maimonidean influence had been exercised on Lessing since his youth, although certainly it is not proof. Strauss seems to have regarded Lessing's theatrical magnum opus and last work, *Nathan the Wise* (1779), as a tribute to Maimonides at least as much as it was to Mendelssohn: "The recollection of the man Maimonides was probably one of the motives underlying Lessing's *Nathan the Wise*, the outstanding poetic monument erected in honor of Jewish medieval philosophy." See "Plan of a Book," in *Jewish Philosophy and the Crisis of Modernity*, p. 470. See also the discussion toward the end of chap. 7 in the present book as this further bears on Lessing.

7. See Gregory Bruce Smith, "The Queen of the Sciences: Political Philosophy or Biol-

ogy?," in *Between Eternities: On the Tradition of Political Philosophy, Past, Present, and Future* (Lanham, MD: Lexington Books, 2008), pp. 559-87.

8. See "Some Remarks on the Political Science of Maimonides and Farabi," chap. 5 in *On Maimonides*.

9. See Jonathan Cohen, *Philosophers and Scholars: Guttmann, Wolfson, and Strauss on the History of Jewish Philosophy* (Lanham, MD: Lexington Books, 2007).

10. "The Quarrel between the Ancients and the Moderns in the Philosophy of Judaism," in *Philosophy and Law*, p. 41. For a statement of purpose by a scholar of medieval Jewish philosophy which bears a superficial resemblance to Strauss's, yet which seems to carry vastly different implications and led him in a greatly different direction, consider David Neumark's remark, in *Geschichte der jüdischen Philosophie des Mittelalters nach Problemen dargestellt* (Berlin: Georg Reimer, 1907), p. 6: "The purpose of all research into the history of philosophy is philosophy itself, philosophic knowledge. We do not pursue the history of Jewish philosophy for the sake of a dogmatic historicism." [Der Zweck alles Forschens in der Geschichte der Philosophie ist die Philosophie selbst, die philosophische Erkenntnis. Nicht einem starren Historismus zuliebe treiben wir Geschichte der jüdischen Philosophie.] Even so, the idiosyncratic and even willful scholarly approach of Neumark emerged most clearly in his conflict with Husik, whose rigorously historical approach Strauss unqualifiedly preferred. See "Preface to Isaac Husik, *Philosophical Essays*," in *Jewish Philosophy and the Crisis of Modernity*, pp. 243-44. Cf. also Gershom Scholem, *Origins of the Kabbalah*, trans. Allan Arkush (New York: Jewish Publication Society, 1987), p. 8, n. 7, for a comment on Neumark.

11. Strauss apparently once received a query from a student about what he would ask Plato and Aristotle if he could speak to them today. Strauss's reply is very interesting for what it expresses about his views of both the ancients and the moderns: "'I think I would ask them whether the development from Galileo to Newton would cause them to modify in any way their teaching about the forms.'" See Laurence Berns, "Comments on K. H. Green's *Jew and Philosopher*," *Jewish Political Studies Review* 9, no. 3-4 (Fall 5758/1997): 96.

12. "Review of Julius Ebbinghaus, *On the Progress of Metaphysics*," in *Early Writings*, p. 214. "Ebbinghaus renounces *all* modern objections by abandoning *the* modern prejudice, namely, the prejudice that *the* truth has not already been found in the past." Similarly Strauss formulates his highest purpose with regard to Maimonides as oriented toward "prejudice," both for and against: "To awaken a prejudice in favor of this view of Maimonides [i.e., the view that 'Maimonides' rationalism is the true natural model, the standard to be protected from any distortion'] and, even more, to arouse suspicion against the powerful opposing prejudice, is the aim of the present work." See app. 4A, "Introduction to *Philosophy and Law*," in *On Maimonides*; also in *Philosophy and Law*, p. 21. Strauss suggests by this that our defense of Enlightenment rationalism is advanced not by our standing for or against "prejudice," which it seems can be either a good or a bad thing depending on what the prejudice is and what it is for, but rather by rediscovering Maimonides, whose thought in its forgotten depths can perhaps alone help us to recover what the true rationalism is and should be for our era.

13. See *What Is Political Philosophy?*, pp. 23-25; *Natural Right and History*, pp. 123-24. See also "Spinoza's Critique of Maimonides," chap. 2 in *On Maimonides*.

14. Besides the *Guide* itself, consider also *Persecution and the Art of Writing*, pp. 33-34, with n. 14.

CHAPTER FIVE

1. See *Thoughts on Machiavelli*, p. 294; "Preface to *Spinoza's Critique of Religion*," in *Jewish Philosophy and the Crisis of Modernity*, p. 156. Strauss mentions Freud's repetition of the same

essential pattern in "Freud on Moses and Monotheism," in *Jewish Philosophy and the Crisis of Modernity*, p. 305. For the "necessity" which "no longer possesses the evidence which it possessed while their adversary was powerful," see *Thoughts on Machiavelli*, p. 298.

2. See "Reason and Revelation," in Meier, *Leo Strauss and the Theologico-Political Problem*, pp. 178-79.

3. See "The Testament of Spinoza," in *Early Writings*, p. 222, for Strauss's last word in his 1932 reassessment of Spinoza: his praise for Spinoza revolves around the philosopher's "independence" (*Unabhängigkeit*), i.e., of mind. Yet see also *What Is Political Philosophy?*, p. 38, for the modern liberal democratic tendency not to produce "rugged individualists."

4. See "How To Begin," chap. 11 in *On Maimonides*: "Maimonides ... warns not against the desire for comprehensive knowledge, but against seeming knowledge."

5. See especially "On a Forgotten Kind of Writing," in *What Is Political Philosophy?*, pp. 229-31. The great, even if flawed, effort made by Cohen to rehabilitate Maimonides for modern thought—attempting to make him conform especially with neo-Kantian epistemological and moral teaching—is available to English-speaking readers: see "Charakteristik der Ethik Maimunis" [Essential Aspects of Maimonides' Ethics], which has been translated as Hermann Cohen, *The Ethics of Maimonides*, trans. A. S. Bruckstein (Madison: University of Wisconsin Press, 2004). In a youthful lecture responding to this effort by Cohen to modernize Maimonides, Strauss contended that Maimonides is much closer to Plato and Aristotle than he is to Kant: see "Cohen and Maimonides," chap. 3 in *On Maimonides*. One of the most curious things about modern Jewish thought and what is perhaps unique to it is that a medieval thinker, Maimonides, was the great philosophic liberator of the minds of so many outstanding modern Jewish thinkers. To name only a few, consider the biographies of Benedict Spinoza, Moses Mendelssohn, Solomon Maimon, Nahman Krochmal, and Hermann Cohen. Strauss was perhaps the first thinker to make sense of why this should have been so: Maimonides' "medieval" insights into tradition were as free and radical as those of any modern.

6. See Gershom Scholem, "Messianism—a Never-Ending Quest," in *On the Possibility of Jewish Mysticism in Our Time, and Other Essays*, ed. Avraham Shapira, trans. Jonathan Chipman (Philadelphia: Jewish Publication Society, 1997), pp. 102-13, and especially pp. 105-6.

7. See "Preface to *Spinoza's Critique of Religion*," in *Jewish Philosophy and the Crisis of Modernity*, p. 169.

8. The title of Maimonides' code of law, *Mishneh Torah*, which he had to know was most likely to be controversial, can be translated either as *Repetition of the Torah* or as *Second Torah*. With such a name, he acted with the greatest possible boldness and radicalism by already assigning his work a highest (even if not quite divine) authority, which was unlikely to have been dared by any merely traditional author. No wonder he provoked several centuries of "Maimonidean controversy"! Meanwhile, tradition did not stint in its own praise of the *Mishneh Torah*, reflecting its assessment of the value of his achievement in dubbing it *Yad ha-Ḥazakah* (The Mighty Hand), which imitates the term used for God as He liberated ancient Israel from Egyptian slavery (Exod. 3:19; 6:1; 13:9, 16; 32:11), and for Moses to characterize his deeds as the great liberator, leader, and lawgiver (Deut. 34:12), who is praised for his own "mighty hand." Was the achievement of Maimonides tacitly put on par with the great deeds of God and Moses? Hence, was Strauss not able to claim that it had not been him alone who recognized the achievement of Maimonides—which was massively untraditional even while he had simultaneously made it his purpose to re-form the tradition—for had this not already been tacitly admitted by the tradition? In this context, i.e., discussing human possibility not limited by history, one may say that Maimonides taught Strauss what Plato meant by "philosopher-king" or "philosopher-lawgiver," just as Churchill taught Strauss what Aristotle meant by "the magnanimous man." See letter to Karl Löwith, 20 August 1946,

in *Hobbes Politische Wissenschaft und zugehörige Schriften—Briefe*, vol. 3 of *Gesammelte Schriften*, p. 667. With regard to the two Hebrew letters which represent the number 14 (i.e., the number of volumes in his law code), they also signify the word *yad* (hand). In the *Guide* Maimonides discusses in "dispersed" fashion the meaning of the word *yad* in the Torah as attributed to God, yet Strauss stressed that for some surely significant reason this word is never assigned a separate chapter among the equivocal terms discussed in the first seventy chapters of pt. 1. Thus, consider the *Guide* 1.46: it is merely listed among "the organs of prehension ascribed to Him"; however, among cited or quoted proof-texts, he neither mentions the phrase "mighty hand" nor alludes to it. Strauss himself made a significant comment on "hand": he related this by "a certain numerical symbolism" to chap. 14, which deals specifically with "man." Not only did he highlight that there is, so to speak, a missing chapter on "hand," but he was then led to allusively suggest a perhaps hidden chapter on it, which has to be searched for. See "How To Begin."

9. See Strauss and Hans-Georg Gadamer, "Correspondence Concerning *Wahrheit und Methode*," ed. and trans. George Elliot Tucker, *Independent Journal of Philosophy* 2 (1978): 5–12, especially p. 11. See also Gadamer's comments on Strauss's views in "Hermeneutics and Historicism" (1965), supp. 1 of *Truth and Method*, 2nd rev. ed., trans. J. Weinsheimer and D. C. Marshall (New York: Crossroad, 1989), pp. 532–41; see also "Gadamer on Strauss: An Interview," conducted by Ernest Fortin, *Interpretation* 12, no. 1 (January 1984): 1–13. Compare Spinoza's *Theologico-Political Treatise*, chap. 7, with "How to Study Spinoza's *Theologico-Political Treatise*," in *Jewish Philosophy and the Crisis of Modernity*, especially pp. 181–96. Cf. also "On the Interpretation of Genesis," in *Jewish Philosophy and the Crisis of Modernity*, for Strauss's applying in action his different "principle" of reading.

10. See David R. Lachterman, "Laying Down the Law: The Theological-Political Matrix of Spinoza's Physics," in *Leo Strauss's Thought: Toward a Critical Engagement*, ed. Alan Udoff (Boulder, CO: Lynne Rienner, 1991), pp. 123–53.

11. For Francis Bacon's "idols of the mind": *The New Organon*, ed. Fulton H. Anderson (Indianapolis: Library of Liberal Arts/Bobbs-Merrill, 1960), bk. 1, aphorism 61. See aphorisms 39–68 for the four classes of idols delineated. Cf. also the much briefer treatment in Bacon, *The Advancement of Learning*, ed. G. W. Kitchin (London: Everyman/Dent, 1965), pp. 132–34. Cf. also Jean Bodin, Bacon's great predecessor in adapting and modifying Machiavellianism: *Universae naturae theatrum* (1596) (The Theater of Universal Nature). See Richard Kennington, "Bacon's Critique of Ancient Philosophy in New Organon 1," in *On Modern Origins: Essays on Early Modern Philosophy*, ed. Pamela Kraus and Frank Hunt (Lanham, MD: Lexington Books, 2004), pp. 17–32.

12. See Aristotle, *Posterior Analytics* 1.1. and 2.19.

13. See Strauss and Gadamer, "Correspondence Concerning *Wahrheit und Methode*," p. 6; Gadamer responded further to Strauss in "Hermeneutics and Historicism," pp. 536–37. For moderate historicism, see "Preface to Isaac Husik, *Philosophical Essays*," in *Jewish Philosophy and the Crisis of Modernity*, pp. 247–56.

14. According to Strauss, philosophy in the true sense of the word is periodically lost or forgotten, or even becomes decadent, and has to be recovered or remembered, as was done by Farabi. Strauss—although unlike Farabi employing the modern historical method—seems to regard himself as likewise engaged in an effort to restore philosophy, i.e., the original significance, life, and bearing of philosophy, for an era in which "it has been blurred or destroyed." See "Introduction" to *Persecution and the Art of Writing*, p. 12; also in *Jewish Philosophy and the Crisis of Modernity*, p. 421. For the reasons why "modifying" the original may have been required, consider Strauss on why "the Aristotelianism of Maimonides and the *falasifa*" seemed to allow neo-Platonism to exercise "such a great influence" on them: only if "the Platonizing politics of Farabi is the point of departure" is it possible to comprehend the *purpose* of "the neo-Platonism of the *falasifa*

and Maimonides." See "Some Remarks on the Political Science of Maimonides and Farabi," and "Maimonides' Statement on Political Science," chaps. 5 and 9 in *On Maimonides*; Strauss, "Farabi's *Plato*," in *Louis Ginzberg Jubilee Volume* (New York: American Academy for Jewish Research, 1945), pp. 357-62. For the three works of Strauss dedicated solely to Farabi, done at different points in his career as thinker and scholar, see "A Lost Writing of Farabi," *Monatsschrift für Geschichte und Wissenschaft des Judentums* 80 (1936): 96-106; "Farabi's *Plato*" (1945); "How Farabi Read Plato's *Laws*" (1957), in *What Is Political Philosophy?*, 134-54. For the most impressive recent treatment of Farabi done in the wake of Strauss's rediscovery of him as a great thinker and political philosopher, see Muhsin S. Mahdi, *Alfarabi and the Foundations of Islamic Political Philosophy* (Chicago: University of Chicago Press, 2001). For the role Farabi may have played in spurring Strauss's own thought ("the Farabian turn"), see Daniel Tanguay, *Leo Strauss: An Intellectual Biography*, trans. Christopher Nadon (New Haven: Yale University Press, 2007), pp. 79-98. Though Farabi deserves most credit for helping Strauss to obtain access to Maimonides' thought, the significant role played by Avicenna in Strauss's rediscovery of Maimonidean esotericism should also not be forgotten. See "A Giving of Accounts," in *Jewish Philosophy and the Crisis of Modernity*, pp. 462-63. Heinrich Meier dates what he dubs "a momentous surprise," i.e., fortuitously happening on the remark by Avicenna, to approximately 1929 or 1930. See "How Strauss Became Strauss," in *Enlightening Revolutions: Essays in Honor of Ralph Lerner*, ed. Svetozar Minkov (Lanham, MD: Lexington Books, 2006), p. 367; *Philosophie und Gesetz: Frühe Schriften*, vol. 2 of *Gesammelte Schriften*, p. XXIV; letter to Gerhard Krüger, of 26 June 1930, in *Hobbes Politische Wissenschaft und zugehörige Schriften—Briefe*, vol. 3 of *Gesammelte Schriften*, pp. 382-83; Meier, *Leo Strauss and the Theologico-Political Problem*, pp. 12-13. For an analysis and critique of Strauss's thought as it relates to the great Islamic philosophers, see Georges Tamer, *Islamische Philosophie und die Krise der Moderne: Das Verhaltnis von Leo Strauss zu Alfarabi, Avicenna, und Averroes* (Leiden: E. J. Brill, 2001). See especially chap. 6: "Leo Strauss, Alfarabi, und der Primat der politischen Philosophie," pp. 207-86.

15. See *Natural Right and History*, pp. 123-26. See also "Introduction" to *Persecution and the Art of Writing*, pp. 11-17; also in *Jewish Philosophy and the Crisis of Modernity*, pp. 420-25. For two avowedly "personal" statements which echo his comment on opinions as "soiled fragments of the pure truth," see "A Giving of Accounts"; and "Restatement on Xenophon's *Hiero* [The Last Paragraph]," in *Jewish Philosophy and the Crisis of Modernity*, especially pp. 460 and 471. For brief comments on the theological impact made by Karl Barth on the youthful Strauss, see "A Giving of Accounts," p. 460; "Preface to *Hobbes Politische Wissenschaft*," in *Jewish Philosophy and the Crisis of Modernity*, p. 453. See also Green, *Jew and Philosopher*, p. 163, n. 96.

16. See Strauss, "On Collingwood's Philosophy of History," *Review of Metaphysics* 5, no. 4 (June 1952): 559-86, and especially pp. 561-66, 575-76, 582-85; and Strauss, "On a New Interpretation of Plato's Political Philosophy," *Social Research* 13, no. 3 (September 1946): 326-67, and especially pp. 330-32, 351-53.

17. See "Introduction" to *The City and Man*, p. 1. Compare with the splendid comments of Harry V. Jaffa on Strauss's view of the relations between Jerusalem and Athens in his "A Reply to Michael Zuckert," *Review of Politics* 71 (2009): 241-50, especially pp. 247-49.

18. See "Political Philosophy and History," in *What Is Political Philosophy?*, pp. 66-68. The emphasis has been added.

19. Ibid. The emphasis has again been added. This was the view that Kant advocated. See *Critique of Pure Reason*, trans. Norman Kemp Smith (New York: St. Martin's, 1965), B370, p. 310; "How to Study Medieval Philosophy," chap. 1 in *On Maimonides*.

20. "Political Philosophy and History," in *What Is Political Philosophy?*, pp. 66-68, as well as how it continues through p. 74.

21. On the "why?" as pertains to science, see Strauss's comments at the end of his lecture "Freud on Moses and Monotheism," in *Jewish Philosophy and the Crisis of Modernity*, pp. 302–6.

22. Cf. *On Tyranny*, p. 212; also in *Jewish Philosophy and the Crisis of Modernity*, pp. 471–72; also "Political Philosophy and History," in *What Is Political Philosophy?*, pp. 56–77, and especially pp. 64, 69. See Karl Barth's remarks in the "Preface to the First Edition" of his commentary, *The Epistle to the Romans* (1918), trans. Edwyn C. Hoskyns (London: Oxford University Press, 1933), pp. 1–2. On the impact which Barth's "Preface" made on Strauss, see *Jewish Philosophy and Crisis of Modernity*, pp. 453, 460. For Strauss's relation to "dialectical theology," though viewed from a different angle, see Thomas Meyer, "Leo Strauss's Religious Rhetoric (1924–38)" (unpublished manuscript, 2012).

23. It is not unreasonable to adapt some key lines from the "Introduction" of *The City and Man*, pp. 1–12, and especially p. 11:

> We cannot reasonably expect that a fresh understanding of [medieval] political philosophy will supply us with recipes for today's use. . . . Only we living today can possibly find a solution to the problems of today. But an adequate understanding of the *principles* as elaborated by the [medievals] may be the *indispensable starting point* for an *adequate analysis*, to be achieved by us, of present-day society in its peculiar character, and for the *wise application*, to be achieved by us, of these principles to our tasks.

The emphases have been added. In the original version, he spoke of the classics, not of the medievals.

24. Refer to his programmatic statement in "How to Study Medieval Philosophy." But it was already clear at least with regard to Maimonides in the first and last paragraphs of the highly significant "Introduction" to *Philosophy and Law*: see app. 4A in *On Maimonides*. See also "A Giving of Accounts," p. 462.

25. Strauss says much the same thing about the historical study of classical philosophy, especially if it is to be *philosophically* useful, although he was fully aware of the differences between medieval and classical thought. For those differences, see also "Progress or Return?," in *Jewish Philosophy and the Crisis of Modernity*, pp. 110–12, 120–22. For the proper attitude to the historical study of classical philosophy, see Strauss, "On Collingwood's Philosophy of History," and Strauss, "On a New Interpretation of Plato's Political Philosophy."

26. See "Progress or Return?" and "Why We Remain Jews," in *Jewish Philosophy and the Crisis of Modernity*, pp. 93–98, and 331–32. Likewise in both "Introduction to Maimonides' *Guide*" and "How To Begin" (chaps. 10 and 11 in *On Maimonides*), Strauss is much impressed by what he conceives of as the concern with progress in Maimonides' thought—even though the word "progress" is not in Maimonides' own vocabulary. By that very fact, breaking his own cardinal hermeneutical rule, one wonders what point Strauss had in mind by his highlighting this idea as a major Maimonidean theme?

27. This list is not meant to obscure the fact that Strauss possessed a detailed knowledge of a host of other medieval philosophic thinkers of all three revealed (monotheistic) religious traditions. Besides his knowledge of the ancients and the moderns, and his mastery of the relevant languages, it makes for a purely scholarly achievement with regard to medieval philosophy alone which is astonishingly prodigious, ambitiously comprehensive, and impressively detailed. Yet it is not fair to neglect to mention a scholarly detractor of Strauss's achievement who, though aiming for the critical, verges on the hostile: Dimitri Gutas, "The Study of Arabic Philosophy in the Twentieth Century: An Essay on the Historiography of Arabic Philosophy," *British Journal of Middle Eastern Studies* 29, no. 1 (May 2002): 5–25. According to the story told by Gutas, the

"literature on both Strauss and Maimonides has grown out of bounds" (n. 32). Further, he contends that Strauss's approach "has no uniform criteria" (in n. 40), with this approach tending toward a "paranoiacal and obsessive nature." He also speaks about this approach as manifesting "the literary pathology of overinterpretation," determined as it is by an "ideological framework." The literature on Strauss ("grown out of bounds") has been perused enough by Gutas for him to have located in an Italian book a passage which apparently conclusively links Strauss's "hermeneutics" with "right-wing politics" (n. 32). In case he has not yet sufficiently disparaged the achievement of Leo Strauss, he adds the allegation of "the orientalist basis of Strauss's approach" (n. 39). Gutas manages to charge, try, convict, and sentence Strauss in a mere three footnotes. It is a tour de force of scholarly tendentiousness and ideological polemics, besides being a blatant display of historicist befuddlement. If these are the charges laid in the footnotes, Strauss is further condemned in the text of the article itself (pp. 19–24) for the following major sins: he developed one of the three "erroneous approaches to Arabic philosophy in the twentieth century" (p. 19); his approach is "an offshoot of the older orientalist conception of Arabic philosophy"; he "did not know Arabic well enough to read Arabic philosophy, and hence did not know Arabic philosophy" (p. 20); he "failed to see the historical context and philosophical pedigree of Maimonides' introduction [to the *Guide*]"; he "misinterpreted the introduction"; he and those who adopt his approach are guilty of "hermeneutical libertarianism, or arbitrariness." These grave charges are followed by a series of supporting historicist complaints. This series of complaints is made by someone apparently unable to comprehend that Strauss's approach begins with and is based on a critique of historicism. Hence, Gutas seems further unable to comprehend that such complaints cannot be taken seriously until he has shown himself adequately able to confront and address Strauss's critique of historicism, to give it its philosophical due, and subsequently to dispose of it based on fatal flaws that have been fully demonstrated by him. Had he been prepared to do the necessary difficult thinking which this requires, he might have been well advised to begin with some of Strauss's most serious historicist critics, like Alexandre Kojève and Hans-Georg Gadamer. He might even have considered an eminent historian of political thought, R. H. Tawney, who was persuaded enough by the essentials of Strauss's critique of historicism that he started to share this critique, even though in Tawney's case it is better to call him an adherent of a "left-wing politics." See, e.g., S. J. D. Green, "The Tawney-Strauss Connection: On Historicism and Values in the History of Political Ideas," *Journal of Modern History* 67 (1995): 255–77. Unfortunately Herbert Davidson, although he made a fuller attempt to do what is required in order to confront and address Strauss's thought and scholarly achievement, did not do much greater justice than Gutas in his similar effort to deflate, deconstruct, and dispose of Strauss's work of rediscovery in reading and thinking through Maimonides. See Davidson, *Moses Maimonides: The Man and His Works* (New York: Oxford University Press, 2004), pp. 393–402. He condemns Strauss's approach for transforming the *Guide* "into one of the most grotesque books ever written" (pp. 401–2). See also *Maimonides the Rationalist* (Oxford: Littman Library, 2011), pp. 174–75, 220, 227.

28. I think of the systematic doubts raised by Maimonides about the misconjoined Aristotelian physics and Ptolemaic astronomy. His doubts were as radical as those of any of the moderns, even if he did not, as it were, discover the heliocentric model in anticipation. For Strauss himself as curious about whether knowing the discoveries of modern science about nature would have led the ancient philosophers to change their views of man, see chap. 4, n. 11 above. A passage in *Guide* 2.24—in which Maimonides attempts to make celestial astronomy and physics serviceable for theology by connecting the disconnect of the two sciences (which disconnect Shlomo Pines called "a *skandalon* of medieval science")—has for centuries been the focus of passionate and unresolved scholarly debate rooted in very different views about who Maimonides is and what he is doing. As if to highlight the ambiguity as deliberate, it is in this same chapter that Maimonides

speaks of "the true perplexity"—a phrase of some significance first noticed by Strauss, who also highlighted its occurring only once in the book. The debate has recently been vigorously resumed and engaged by several of the most distinguished contemporary scholars in *Aleph: Historical Studies in Science and Judaism* 8 (2008): 151–319.

29. While I shall stress the differences, it would not do to stress them too much. Strauss made his respect for the modern Thomists known on at least two crucial literary occasions, which allowed him to show his respect for them even as he differed with them. First, in the "Introduction" to *Natural Right and History*, pp. 7–8 (but cf. also pp. 163–64), in which he acknowledged them as among the only serious defenders of natural right, or rather natural law, on the contemporary scene: "The issue of natural right presents itself today as a matter of party allegiance. Looking around us, we see two hostile camps, heavily fortified and strictly guarded. One is occupied by the liberals of various descriptions," i.e., those who reject natural right, and "the other by the Catholic and non-Catholic disciples of Thomas Aquinas," i.e., those who accept natural right. Second, in the "Introduction" to *Persecution and the Art of Writing*, p. 8, he contrasts the attitude of the modern Thomists toward medieval Christian philosophy with virtually all students of the medieval Jewish and Muslim philosophers. The approach of contemporary scholars toward medieval Jewish and Muslim philosophy is almost uniformly characterized by its antiquarianism, i.e., its conviction that this medieval thought is essentially irrelevant to the contemporary mind, other than as a curious and idiosyncratic anticipation of some modern ideas and positions, or as impressive for its era. "There is a striking difference between the level of present-day understanding of Christian scholasticism and that of present-day understanding of Islamic and Jewish medieval philosophy. This contrast is due to the fact that the foremost students of Christian scholasticism believe in the immediate philosophic relevance of their theme, whereas the foremost students of Islamic and Jewish medieval philosophy tend to regard their subject as only of historical interest." It is not my view that Strauss aimed to bury Christian medieval philosophy and to praise Islamic and Jewish medieval philosophy, as some accuse him of seeming to do. If this appearance has any substance to it, it is a function of two things: first, Strauss wished to recover the lost wisdom and way of the latter, which requires one to cease seeing it (and philosophy itself) in light of the former; second, in some respects the two medieval schools divided an ancient unity due to significantly different theological-political needs, as well as historical accidents of what philosophic texts were available to each. Among other things, Strauss wanted to reignite the debate between these two schools so as to bring about a future philosophic wisdom which would dialectically unify itself in the manner of the ancients. With regard to this anticipatory dialectical unity, I would suggest that Maimonides for him approached closest to the philosophic balance he was searching for.

30. Comparison is most apt between Strauss, on the one hand, and Etienne Gilson and Jacques Maritain, on the other hand. Gilson with respect to the moderns focused mainly on Descartes; Maritain focused mainly on Kant. It should also be observed that the modern Thomists pursued research into medieval Jewish and Muslim thinkers (and non-Thomist Christian thinkers) only to help them better comprehend Thomism and its truth. As this would seem to mean, they both knew from the beginning what for them is *the* truth—Thomism—and the rest of philosophy is of value either because it prepares, approximates, or illuminates Thomism or because it lacks the fullness and profundity of completed Thomism. Strauss, on the other hand, made it a point to study thinkers entirely on their own terms and open-mindedly, which meant to study them as if each one may have been the teacher of *the* truth. As a premise for studying thinkers, he held no brief in advance for any one thinker as against the rest. Hence, I do not wish my references to Strauss's "Maimonideanism" to suggest a fixed and formal belief in the thought and teaching of Maimonides, as if it constituted in its content and of right the absolute truth. He kept his mind open; he pursued what he had discovered, and thought it through for himself; he did not ever close

himself to alternative views or challenges; and he was never unwilling to revise his judgments. He recognized a certain philosophic superiority of Farabi with respect to Maimonides (i.e., in his ability to revive philosophy in an era of its disappearance), although this is not to say that for him Maimonides did not attain a certain superiority with respect to Farabi regarding a different aspect of philosophy (i.e., his grasping its needful defense in confronting its chief challenger, and his attaining a clearer self-consciousness of its own limits). Hence, Strauss's "Maimonideanism" implied a conviction about the evident superiority of a thinker and a form of thought, especially as concerns the heroic attempt to wrestle with and resolve the quarrel between reason and revelation, in the context of retaining the freedom of the thinker and of thought.

31. Compare Hans-Georg Gadamer, *Truth and Method*, trans. J. Weinsheimer and D. C. Marshall (New York: Crossroad, 1989), pp. 301-2, 333-34, 472, with Strauss's comment in Strauss and Gadamer, "Correspondence Concerning *Wahrheit und Methode*" (n. 9 above), p. 6, especially point [1], with his remark on studying Maimonides, and with the reply of Gadamer, p. 10. Gadamer is closest to Strauss in *Truth and Method*, pp. 310-11.

32. Consider the point made allusively by Stanley Rosen at the end of an essay on Strauss and Voegelin (who was not a modern Thomist): Strauss was undoubtedly "closer to historicism" than either Voegelin or the modern Thomists, because he accepted the current historical crisis as affecting our capacity to obtain access to the eternal and absolute truth—although he also did not dogmatically assume that this same crisis made all such access permanently impossible for us. See Stanley Rosen, "Politics or Transcendence? Responding to Historicism," in *Faith and Political Philosophy: The Correspondence between Leo Strauss and Eric Voegelin, 1934-64*, trans. and ed. Peter Emberley and Barry Cooper (University Park: Pennsylvania State University Press, 1993), pp. 261-66. See also n. 9 above for Strauss's letter of 14 May 1961 to Gadamer, especially p. 11. In their debate on historicism, Strauss comments on how strange it is that he should be defending Heidegger against his most impressive student on just this point, i.e., on the need for thinking to begin with radical historicism (our current "world-night," as styled by Heidegger) as the necessary starting point for any consideration of the possibility of philosophy in our era.

33. *Natural Right and History*, p. 8. See John Finnis, *Natural Law and Natural Rights* (New York: Oxford University Press 1980).

34. Strauss makes the claim that a "return" to ancient modes of thought, especially in the form of ancient social science, is tentatively pursued precisely because this form seems to have been *more scientific* (as proved by a comparison with its modern competitors and critics), and not merely because it is less historicist. In other words, it is better because it is truer, i.e., truer to the nature of man, and hence to the nature of things socially and politically considered, even in view of modern history and what it claims to teach as novel with regard to human things, especially as compared with the thought of the past. However, to speak about "the nature of things," even the nature of the human things, pure and simple, must be done with the greatest caution, recalling the warning of Strauss already presented in the previous note. (See Green, *Jew and Philosopher*, pp. 15-16; 34-40; 117-18; 155, n. 37; 157, n. 49; 163, n. 99; 211, n. 3; 233, n. 85.) Strauss maintains this paradoxical if tentative claim about the greater scientific character of ancient social science—or at least of its principles—even in the face of the charge, always ready to hand and never simply rejected by Strauss, that if one is to unconditionally embrace premodern human science (which he did not do), one has arbitrarily absolved oneself from the judgments of modern natural science and so one has put at risk the cognitive integrity of one's endeavor, since it seems to ignore how ancient science, in all of its forms both natural and human, has been rendered entirely obsolete by modern science. See Nasser Beneghar, *Leo Strauss, Max Weber, and the Scientific Study of Politics* (Chicago: University of Chicago Press, 2003).

35. "How to Study Medieval Philosophy."

36. According to Strauss, the philosopher who dominates our horizon and hence who defines our "hermeneutic situation" is undoubtedly Heidegger. What Strauss writes about "why Heidegger is truly important" may help to clarify the point I have been trying to make: "By uprooting and not simply rejecting the tradition of philosophy, he made it possible for the first time after many centuries—one hesitates to say how many—to see the roots of the tradition as they are and thus perhaps to know, what so many merely believe, that those roots are the only natural and healthy roots." See "An Unspoken Prologue," in *Jewish Philosophy and the Crisis of Modernity*, p. 450.

37. While it may not be possible to explain in full detail the "hermeneutical" issues involved in the Strauss-Gadamer controversy so as to do them proper justice, it is possible to state them fairly succinctly: whether to take seriously the truth claim of the text means also to give an account of *the* whole and its parts, which must be considered philosophically and not just hermeneutically; whether paying attention to the "hermeneutic situation" makes possible any escape from the hermeneutic circle; whether the "fusion of horizons" announced by Gadamer ever advances the comprehension of the original thinker as he thought about the issues himself; whether being "ministerial to the text," as Strauss puts it, allows the original author of a text to speak as his mind intended to express itself, and in doing so help us to move against—or rather, to potentially free us from—our modern prejudices, on which hermeneuticism (grounded in radical historicism) is based, whether Gadamer likes it or not. As for the reason Strauss prefers to accept, against Gadamer, something like the Heideggerian "world-night," i.e., our state of decline from modern heights to a certain desuetude in our higher powers and hence in our self-consciousness about what we are doing, it is because we stand at a much greater *historical* distance from the texts than Gadamer credits. And so it is also of much greater difficulty to get at their true meaning than Gadamer acknowledges, even or especially with his hermeneuticism. Gadamer was still too much tied to Wilhelm Dilthey and the merely scholarly-academic approach, which shows the residue of thoroughly modern concerns, i.e., a faith in "science" (if human science), whose status has been rendered dubious and needs to be radically reconsidered in the wake of Nietzsche's and Heidegger's criticism. See also Emil Fackenheim, *To Mend the World: Foundations of Post-Holocaust Jewish Thought* (New York: Schocken, 1989), pp. 262–64: Strauss had as deep a grasp as any Heideggerian of "the vast hermeneutical gulf" which stands between us and the ancient or the medieval tradition, and which separates us from past thought precisely as it is not beholden to the moderns—which is precisely what makes it so useful to us, if we let it speak in its own terms and for itself to us *as* moderns. See especially Richard L. Velkley, *Heidegger, Strauss, and the Premises of Philosophy: On Original Forgetting* (Chicago: University of Chicago Press, 2011).

38. See "Political Philosophy and History," in *What Is Political Philosophy?*, pp. 56–77, and the conception of "original form," which is accessible to us even if we grasp past thought according to historicism, and hence which heralds for us a possibility contrary to historicism. It is the gist of this point that is discussed in Green, *Jew and Philosopher*, p. 211, n. 3.

39. The difficulty for Strauss is perhaps best encapsulated in the phrase which has been previously mentioned: "the wisdom of the ancients." This is of course the title of a book, *De Sapientia Veterum* (1609), by Francis Bacon, one of the leading architects of modern thought. It reminds us that modern thought too was, in a certain respect, an attempt to recover ancient wisdom. Bacon perceived "philosophy" hidden beneath the surface of ancient myths, which did not require subsequent, wiser generations to locate in them deeper meanings: these hidden depths were intended by their original poetic authors, who expressed "philosophic" thought through parables. In other words, man almost from the beginning knew the difference between myth and reason: to speak paradoxically, the ancients taught Baconian science. But to discover this, Bacon curiously made use of an almost Maimonidean esotericism in order to prove that they so communicated it through

myths as parables. Strauss set this as a warning against any all-too-hasty claims to have been able to *recover* authentic ancient or medieval wisdom pure and simple, for we are always threatened by the tendency or temptation to see the thought of the past essentially in light of the thought of the present, and hence to radicalize modern thought through such a supposed "return," instead of employing it to obtain a view of things (human, natural, and divine) other than that of the present, truly transcending the present.

40. For Strauss's difference with Jacob Klein, see "A Giving of Accounts," in *Jewish Philosophy and the Crisis of Modernity*, p. 464. But for their greater accord, see the same piece, pp. 462–63, as well as Klein's essay "Aristotle, An Introduction," in *Ancients and Moderns: Essays on the Tradition of Political Philosophy in Honor of Leo Strauss* (New York: Basic Books, 1964), pp. 50–69. For Strauss on Heidegger, see my "Leo Strauss's Challenge to Emil Fackenheim: Heidegger, Radical Historicism, and Diabolical Evil," in *Emil L. Fackenheim: Philosopher, Theologian, Jew*, ed. Sharon Portnoff, James A. Diamond, and Martin D. Yaffe (Leiden: E. J. Brill, 2008), pp. 125–60.

41. For Strauss's awareness of the obstacles to a "return" to any past philosophic position, see "On a New Interpretation of Plato's Political Philosophy" (n. 16 above), as well as the statement in the "Introduction" to *The City and Man* (see n. 23 above). For a provocative and refreshing analysis of why Strauss wrote the aforementioned article, in which he criticized "in advance," as it were, a certain misconstruction of his own position, which never advocated a comprehensive, full-scale, or simple-minded reappropriation of the ancients, and or of the medievals, see Nathan Tarcov, "On a Certain Critique of 'Straussianism,'" in *Leo Strauss: Political Philosopher and Jewish Thinker*, ed. Kenneth L. Deutsch and Walter Nicgorski (Lanham, MD: Rowman and Littlefield, 1994), pp. 259–74.

42. Tarcov, "On a Certain Critique of 'Straussianism.'"

43. See Etienne Gilson, *The Unity of Philosophical Experience* (New York: Charles Scribner's Sons, 1937), pp. 318–19; Jacques Maritain, "On Human Knowledge," in *The Range of Reason* (New York: Charles Scribner's Sons, 1952), p. 9; Isaiah Berlin, in *Conversations with Isaiah Berlin*, ed. Ramin Jahanbegloo (London: Orion, 1993), pp. 31–33, 108–9.

44. It would be unjust to lay too little emphasis on Strauss's virtual rediscovery of Farabi as a great and still-vital philosophic source, irrespective of the fact that this wisdom originated in the medieval period. Instead, he recurred to Farabi as directed by Maimonides, and at least originally made a careful study of Farabi's works for the sake of properly comprehending Maimonides. Daniel Tanguay contends that this encounter of the 1930s with Farabi's thought—contrary to claims made by others that this honor belongs to Maimonides—was the decisive turning point in Strauss's philosophic life, which is what he calls the "Farabian turn": see "Prophet and Philosopher," in *Leo Strauss: An Intellectual Biography* (n. 14 above), pp. 49–98. Of course, the great 19th-century Jewish scholar Moritz Steinschneider had preceded Strauss in the scholarly exploration of Farabi. While Steinschneider could study Farabi for the major historical impact he made on medieval Jewish thought, of course he evinced no interest in Farabi's thought as of contemporary relevance. See his *Al-Farabi (Alpharabius): Des arabischen Philosophen Leben und Schriften* (1896; reprint, Amsterdam: Philo Press, 1966). In line with Steinschneider's view of the function of modern *Wissenschaft des Judentums* in general, his study of Farabi, as of Jewish philosophers like Maimonides, was to provide them with "a decent burial." This is almost the opposite of the view of Strauss, who thought that the study of medieval thinkers like Farabi was a search to rediscover in their philosophic thought a potentially still-vital source of wisdom, in aid of modern thought and its contemporary crisis: he wanted to resurrect, as it were, Maimonides and Farabi. Indeed, it has been the students of Strauss, and especially Muhsin Mahdi and Charles Butterworth, who have continued Strauss's massive "search-and-discover mission," not only by editing and translating several of Farabi's major works, but also by seriously interpreting those works and explicat-

ing Farabi's thought in order to show its contemporary relevance. For some of his key works, see Alfarabi, *The Philosophy of Plato and Aristotle*, ed. and trans. Muhsin Mahdi (Ithaca: Cornell University Press, 1969; 2nd ed., 2002); Alfarabi, *The Political Writings*, ed. and trans. Charles H. Butterworth (Ithaca: Cornell University Press, 2001). And for helpful works on Farabi informed by the exploratory researches of Strauss and his immediate students, see Miriam Galston, *Politics and Excellence: The Political Philosophy of Alfarabi* (Princeton: Princeton University Press, 1990); Joshua Parens, *Metaphysics as Rhetoric: Alfarabi's Summary of Plato's "Laws"* (Albany: State University of New York Press, 1995); Steven J. Lenzner, "Strauss's Farabi, Scholarly Prejudice, and Philosophic Politics," *Perspectives on Political Science* 28 (1999): 194–202; and especially Mahdi, *Alfarabi and the Foundations of Islamic Political Philosophy* (n. 14 above), as well as Mahdi's numerous other articles on Alfarabi. And for the impact Farabi made on Maimonides and on medieval Jewish thought, see Lawrence V. Berman, "Maimonides, the Disciple of Alfarabi," *Israel Oriental Studies* 4 (1974): 154–78; Steven Harvey, "Falaquera's Alfarabi," *Trumah: Studien zum jüdischen Mittelalter* 12 (2002): 97–112.

    45. For Strauss's "Maimonideanization" of the history of philosophy, consider Green, *Jew and Philosopher*. As for how Strauss revolutionized the study of Maimonides in the 20th century, Marvin Fox summarizes the impact he made while tacitly contrasting it with past study:

> A major development in the study of Maimonides in this century has been the work of Leo Strauss, whose studies have forced us to reject the easy certainties about Maimonides that were long accepted. No one has done more to make us aware of the complexity, the subtlety, and the inherent difficulty in understanding any of Maimonides' works, and above all the *Guide*. In his provocative and challenging studies Strauss has renewed the neglected ways and opened new ones for the serious study of Maimonides. He repeatedly emphasizes the fact that the *Guide* is an esoteric book, that is, a book whose surface doctrine hides another, very different set of teachings. In doing so Strauss has forcefully reminded us of what Maimonides himself made explicit to his readers.

See Marvin Fox, *Interpreting Maimonides: Studies in Methodology, Metaphysics, and Moral Philosophy* (Chicago: University of Chicago Press, 1990), pp. 4–5.

    46. See the elaborate critique of Guttmann in Leo Strauss, "The Quarrel of the Ancients and the Moderns in the Philosophy of Judaism: Notes on Julius Guttmann, *The Philosophy of Judaism*," in *Philosophy and Law*, pp. 41–79; and the analysis, together with the critique, of Husik in "Preface to Isaac Husik, *Philosophical Essays*," in *Jewish Philosophy and the Crisis of Modernity*, pp. 246–56. Guttmann's responses to Strauss's critique are in "Philosophie der Religion oder Philosophie der Gesetz?," *Proceedings of the Israel Academy of Sciences and Humanities* 5 (1974): 146–73 (with Hebrew translation: 188–207); in the Hebrew edition (which revised and augmented the original German version) of *The Philosophy of Judaism*, trans. Y. L. Baruch (Jerusalem: Bialik Institute, 1951), p. 394, n. 476; in the English translation: *Philosophies of Judaism*, trans. David W. Silverman (New York: Holt, Rinehart and Winston, 1964), p. 434, n. 125. See also Eliezer Schweid, "Religion and Philosophy: The Scholarly-Theological Debate between Julius Guttmann and Leo Strauss," *Maimonidean Studies* 1 (1990): 163–95; Mari Rethelyi, "Guttmann's Critique of Strauss's Modernist Approach to Medieval Philosophy: Some Arguments toward a Counter-critique," *Journal of Textual Reasoning* 3, no. 1 (June 2004), http://etext.virginia.edu/journals/tr/volume3/rethelyi.html; Leora Batnitzky, *Leo Strauss and Emmanuel Levinas: Philosophy and the Politics of Revelation* (New York: Cambridge University Press, 2006), pp. 181–86, 201–2; Steven Harvey, "The Value of Julius Guttmann's *Die Philosophie des Judentums* for Understanding Medieval Jewish Philosophy Today," in *Studies in Hebrew Literature and Jewish Culture*, ed. Martin

F. J. Baasten and Reinier Munk (Dordrecht: Springer, 2007), pp. 297–308; Benjamin Lazier, *God Interrupted: Heresy and the European Imagination between the World Wars* (Princeton: Princeton University Press, 2008), pp. 117–20.

CHAPTER SIX

1. See Andrew Patch, "Leo Strauss on Maimonides' Prophetology," *Review of Politics* 66, no. 1 (Winter 2004): pp. 83–104, and especially pp. 96–97, for how Guttmann changed in his view of Strauss. For the letters of Scholem and Strauss on Guttmann's subsequent critique of *Philosophy and Law*, see *Hobbes Politische Wissenschaft und zugehörige Schriften—Briefe*, vol. 3 of *Gesammelte Schriften*, pp. 764–65. For a notion of the radical rationalism in Maimonides, with which Strauss would have been familiar, see the essay by Aḥad Ha'am in n. 6 below.

2. See the letter of 3 October 1931 to Gerhard Krüger, in *Hobbes Politische Wissenschaft und zugehörige Schriften—Briefe*, vol. 3 of *Gesammelte Schriften*, pp. 392–93; Eugene R. Sheppard, *Leo Strauss and the Politics of Exile* (Lebanon, NH: University Press of New England, 2006), pp. 33–34, and p. 147, n. 100; *Hobbes Politische Wissenschaft und zugehörige Schriften—Briefe*, vol. 3 of *Gesammelte Schriften*, p. 567. Cf. "The Secret Teaching of Maimonides," in "Appendix," in *On Maimonides*; Rémi Brague, "Leo Strauss and Maimonides," in *Leo Strauss's Thought: Toward a Critical Engagement*, ed. Alan Udoff (Boulder, CO: Lynne Rienner, 1991), pp. 93–114, especially pp. 94–95. For the thrill of discovery, see Strauss's letter to Jacob Klein of 16 February 1938, in *Hobbes Politische Wissenschaft und zugehörige Schriften—Briefe*, vol. 3 of *Gesammelte Schriften*, p. 550. See also Strauss, *Hobbes' Critique of Religion* (1933–34), trans. Gabriel Bartlett and Svetozar Minkov (Chicago: University of Chicago Press, 2011); also in *Hobbes Politische Wissenschaft und zugehörige Schriften—Briefe*, vol. 3 of *Gesammelte Schriften*, pp. 263–369; Strauss, *The Political Philosophy of Hobbes: Its Basis and Its Genesis*, trans. Elsa Sinclair (Oxford: Clarendon Press, 1936; Chicago: University of Chicago Press, 1952). Cf. the letter to Gershom Scholem of 2 October 1935, in *Hobbes Politische Wissenschaft und zugehörige Schriften—Briefe*, vol. 3 of *Gesammelte Schriften*, p. 716.

3. See "Preface to Isaac Husik, *Philosophical Essays*," in *Jewish Philosophy and the Crisis of Modernity*, pp. 252–56; Green, *Jew and Philosopher*, pp. 179, n. 67; Moshe Schwarcz, "The Enlightenment and Its Implications for Jewish Philosophy in the Modern Period (in Light of the Controversy between Leo Strauss and Julius Guttmann)" [in Hebrew], *Daat* 1, no. 1 (Winter 1978): 7–16.

4. Intriguingly, Hegel's brief explanation of Maimonides' thought, however misdirected in several key respects, is in a fashion not completely unrelated to the subtle conceptions of Strauss: "a strong kabbalistic element." This appears most manifestly in Strauss's ironic—but not entirely ironic—suggestion that "Maimonides was the first Kabbalist." See "Literary Character," chap. 8 in *On Maimonides*. It suggests an alertness to his "esoteric" dimension.

5. Kenneth Hart Green, "Editor's Introduction," in *Jewish Philosophy and the Crisis of Modernity*, pp. 17–25, deals with Strauss's philosophical relation to Cohen in some detail. See Hermann Cohen, *The Ethics of Maimonides*, trans. A. S. Bruckstein (Madison: University of Wisconsin Press, 2004). This contains a translation of the momentous essay that played such a key role in the unfolding of Strauss's thought. Cf. "Cohen and Maimonides," chap. 3 in *On Maimonides*. See also Green, *Jew and Philosopher*, pp. 21–22; 52–57; 100–101; 151, n. 11; 168, n. 3; 177, n. 52; 185, n. 16; 186, n. 19; 189, n. 29; 196, n. 2; 207, n. 79; 210, n. 94; 211, n. 3. And cf. Irene Abigail Piccinini, "Leo Strauss and Hermann Cohen's 'Arch-Enemy': A Quasi-Cohenian Apology of Baruch Spinoza," *Journal of Textual Reasoning* 3, no. 1 (June 2004), http://etext.virginia.edu/journals/tr/volume3/piccinini.html#n20; Leora Batnitzky, "Hermann Cohen and Leo Strauss," *Journal of Jewish Thought and Philosophy* 13, no. 1–3 (2006): 187–212; Steven B. Smith, "Gershom Scholem

and Leo Strauss: Notes toward a German-Jewish Dialogue," in *Reading Leo Strauss: Politics, Philosophy, Judaism* (Chicago: University of Chicago Press, 2006), pp. 31–36.

6. See Aḥad Ha'am (Asher Ginzberg), "The Supremacy of Reason: Maimonides," ed. and trans. Leon Simon, in *Ahad Ha-am: Essays, Letters, Memiors* (Oxford: East and West Library, 1946), pp. 138–82; Aryeh Leo Motzkin, "On the Interpretation of Maimonides," *Independent Journal of Philosophy* 2 (1978): 39–46; also in *Philosophy and the Jewish Tradition*, ed. Yehuda Halper (Leiden: Brill, 2012), pp. 125–41.

7. G. W. F. Hegel, *Lectures on the History of Philosophy*, vol. 3, trans. E. S. Haldane and Frances H. Simon (London: Routledge and Kegan Paul, 1955), pp. 35–36.

8. See Gershom Scholem, *On the Kabbalah and Its Symbolism*, trans. Ralph Manheim (New York: Schocken, 1965), pp. 50–51. He credits Strauss by name in the context of discovering "the esoteric rationalism of the [medieval Jewish] philosophers and reformers" which appeared suddenly in the 12th century; they had borrowed it "from the philosophical tradition of the Arabs." Strauss's work had obviously helped Scholem to discern the dependence on Maimonides of the novel esotericism of the Kabbalah, which arose in the 13th century.

9. Leibniz was an exception among modern philosophers: he interpreted Maimonides' *Guide* most seriously, and he was able to perceive in Maimonides a thinker of great subtlety and profundity. For Leibniz's observations on the *Guide*, see n. 11 in chap. 1 above, and chap. 7 below. Likewise Lessing (a great admirer of Leibniz) might be counted in the same company: he seems to have known Maimonides' works from his youth, and made a point of highlighting the fact in his first play.

10. Strauss raises serious doubts about whether this was Maimonides' true position, although it is also true that Strauss never definitively answers the question: "How far Maimonides accepted the teaching of the *falasifa*, according to which a 'priestly city' is one of the bad regimes, must here remain an open question." See "Literary Character," n. 156; cf. also "Maimonides' Statement on Political Science," and "Note on Maimonides' *Letter on Astrology*," chaps. 9 and 14 in *On Maimonides*. See also *The City and Man*, pp. 33–34; *Thoughts on Machiavelli*, pp. 184–85; "Marsilius of Padua," in *Liberalism Ancient and Modern*, pp. 186–91.

11. For a much elaborated critique of Harvey's thesis, see Joshua Parens, *Maimonides and Spinoza: Their Conflicting Views of Human Nature* (Chicago: University of Chicago Press, 2012).

12. See the notorious chap. 7, as well as chaps. 1, 2, and 5, in Spinoza, *Theological-Political Treatise*, especially as translated by Martin D. Yaffe (Newburyport, MA: Focus, 2004). Yaffe makes careful note of the constant presence of Maimonides in the rest of Spinoza's *Treatise*. Further, if only by its effort to reproduce as consistently as possible in readable English Spinoza's use of Latin terms on the assumption that this repetition of language was employed in his book for deliberate purposes, Yaffe's translation makes it possible for English readers to judge for themselves just how much the argument with Maimonides runs through the entire *Treatise*. The attentive reader in search of Maimonides is also offered help by Yaffe's notes, scholarly apparatus, and introductory essay, which often bring to light Maimonidean resonances. See Warren Zev Harvey, "A Portrait of Spinoza as a Maimonidean," *Journal of the History of Philosophy* 19 (1981): 151–72.

13. See Gershom Scholem, "The Science of Judaism—Then and Now," trans. Michael A. Meyer, in *The Messianic Idea in Judaism, and Other Essays on Jewish Spirituality* (New York: Schocken, 1971), pp. 304–13; and Scholem, "Reflections on Modern Jewish Studies," in *On the Possibility of Jewish Mysticism in Our Time, and Other Essays*, ed. Avraham Shapira, trans. Jonathan Chipman (Philadelphia: Jewish Publication Society, 1997), pp. 51–71. See also Charles Manekin, "Steinschneider's 'Decent Burial': A Reassessment," in *Study and Knowledge in Jewish Thought*, vol. 1, ed. Howard Kreisel (Jerusalem: Mossad Bialik, 2006), pp. 239–51. For the remarks on Salomon Munk, see "How to Study Medieval Philosophy" and "Some Remarks on the Political

Science of Farabi and Maimonides," chaps. 1 and 5 in *On Maimonides*, as well as *Early Writings*, pp. 101-17, 124-37. Cf. *Guide* 3.51, p. 619. See also Emil L. Fackenheim, "Leo Strauss and Modern Judaism," in *Jewish Philosophers and Jewish Philosophy*, ed. Michael L. Morgan (Bloomington: Indiana University Press, 1996), pp. 97-105; Smith, "Gershom Scholem and Leo Strauss," pp. 43-64.

CHAPTER SEVEN

1. See "Esoteric Knowledge and the Vulgar: Parallels between Newton and Maimonides," *Trumah: Studien zum jüdischen Mittelalter* 12 (2002): 183-91, and especially p. 183. Cf. "Preface to *Spinoza's Critique of Religion*," in *Jewish Philosophy and the Crisis of Modernity*, p. 157. See also pp. 154-55.

2. See Harry Austryn Wolfson, *Philo: Foundations of Religious Philosophy in Judaism, Christianity, and Islam* (Cambridge, MA: Harvard University Press, 1947); and Wolfson, *The Philosophy of Spinoza: Unfolding the Latent Processes of His Reasoning* (Cambridge, MA: Harvard University Press, 1961). For the gist of Strauss's criticism of Wolfson's general approach, see "How to Study Spinoza's *Theologico-Political Treatise*," in *Jewish Philosophy and the Crisis of Modernity*, pp. 214-16.

3. See "What Is Political Philosophy?," in *What Is Political Philosophy?*, p. 17. But cf. already his lecture of 1931, "Cohen and Maimonides," chap. 3 in *On Maimonides*.

4. See *On Tyranny*, p. 206. See also "Spinoza's Critique of Maimonides" and "Literary Character," chaps. 2 and 8 in *On Maimonides*. Cf. Catherine Zuckert, "Strauss's Return to Premodern Thought," in *Cambridge Companion to Leo Strauss*, p. 104, n. 17. See *Guide* 1.Introduction, pp. 6-7 (with the emphasis added).

5. See Kenneth Hart Green, "Editor's Introduction," in *Jewish Philosophy and the Crisis of Modernity*, pp. 6-15.

6. See Hillel Fradkin, "Philosophy and Law: Leo Strauss as a Student of Medieval Jewish Thought," in *Leo Strauss: Political Philosopher and Jewish Thinker*, ed. Kenneth L. Deutsch and Walter Nicgorski (Lanham, MD: Rowman and Littlefield, 1994), pp. 129-41. In Green, *Jew and Philosopher*, p. 126, I made the suggestion that Strauss's enterprise is a virtual "Maimonideanization" of the entire history of Western thought, both philosophy and religion, since this Maimonidean form of Western thought best represents, and best helps us to comprehend, "the true natural model, the standard" of rationalism at least as it reaches its peak in Western thought insofar as it embraces philosophy, religion, morality, and politics, i.e., "Jerusalem *and* Athens."

7. See Michael Zank, "Arousing Suspicion against a Prejudice: Leo Strauss and the Study of Maimonides' *Guide of the Perplexed*," in *Moses Maimonides (1138-1204): His Religious, Scientific, and Philosophical "Wirkungsgeschichte" in Different Cultural Contexts*, ed. Görge K. Hasselhoff and Otfried Fraisse (Würzburg: Ergon Verlag, 2004), pp. 549-71, who frames his consideration of Strauss's Maimonides in terms of this phrase in the first paragraph of the "Introduction" to *Philosophy and Law*, as an announcement of the comprehensive project that Strauss will embark on—philosophical, political, theological, and moral.

8. See app. 4A in *On Maimonides*; Green, *Jew and Philosopher*, p. 8; "Introduction" to *Philosophy and Law*; "Maimonides' Doctrine of Prophecy," chap. 4 in *On Maimonides*; Heinrich Meier, "Vorwort," in *Philosophie und Gesetz: Frühe Schriften*, vol. 2 of *Gesammelte Schriften*, p. ix. See also Zank, "Arousing Suspicion against a Prejudice," pp. 549-71, and especially pp. 561-62; Kenneth Seeskin, "Maimonides' Conception of Philosophy," in *Leo Strauss and Judaism: Jerusalem and Athens Critically Revisited*, ed. David Novak (Lanham, MD: Rowman and Littlefield, 1996), p. 87; Hillel Fradkin, "A Word Fitly Spoken: The Interpretation of Maimonides and the

Legacy of Leo Strauss," pp. 55-85, as well as Alfred Ivry, "Leo Strauss on Maimonides," pp. 75-91, both in *Leo Strauss's Thought: Toward a Critical Engagement*, ed. Alan Udoff (Boulder, CO: Lynne Rienner, 1991).

9. "How To Begin," chap. 11 in *On Maimonides*; Heinrich Meier, in editor's discussion, n. 104 of "Introduction to Maimonides' *Guide*," chap. 10 in *On Maimonides*.

10. Arnaldo Momigliano, "Hermeneutics and Classical Political Thought in Leo Strauss," in *Essays on Ancient and Modern Judaism*, ed. S. Berti, trans. M. Masella-Gayley (Chicago: University of Chicago Press, 1994), p. 179. In his 1967 review of *Socrates and Aristophanes*, in *Commentary* (October 1967): 102-4, Momigliano had already spoken about "the book to which [Strauss] returned again and again during the last thirty-five years with ever loving care, Maimonides' *Guide of the Perplexed*."

11. See Kenneth Hart Green, "Editor's Introduction: Leo Strauss's Essays and Lectures on Maimonides," in *On Maimonides*; Green, *Jew and Philosopher*, p. 180, n. 76. See also Joel L. Kraemer, "The Medieval Arabic Enlightenment," in *Cambridge Companion to Leo Strauss*, p. 165. Cf. especially "Progress or Return?" in *Jewish Philosophy and the Crisis of Modernity*.

12. See Allan Bloom on Strauss's late works in general: "Leo Strauss: September 20, 1899—October 18, 1973," in *Giants and Dwarfs: Essays, 1960-1990* (New York: Simon and Schuster, 1990), pp. 247-50; Alexander Altmann, "Leo Strauss: 1899-1973," *Proceedings of the American Academy for Jewish Research* 41-42 (1975): xxxvi; Stanley Rosen, "Leo Strauss and the Problem of the Modern," in *Cambridge Companion to Leo Strauss*, p. 122.

13. Herbert Davidson, *Moses Maimonides: The Man and His Works* (New York: Oxford University Press, 2004); Joel L. Kraemer, *Maimonides: The Life and World of One of Civilization's Greatest Minds* (New York: Doubleday, 2008).

14. Curiously, two of Strauss's Canadian students, Emil Fackenheim and George Grant, moved from Hegel to Heidegger and were somehow aided by their reading of Strauss in doing so. It remains an unresolved quandary whether either Fackenheim or Grant succumbed to the tempting charms of a "theological" Heideggerianism, however atheistic his thought may be, or somehow avoided such a capitulation (as they wrestled with Heidegger) by heeding Strauss's warning.

15. See George Steiner, "Inscrutable and Tragic: Leo Strauss's Vision of the Jewish Destiny," review of *Jewish Philosophy and the Crisis of Modernity*, *Times Literary Supplement*, 14 November 1997, pp. 4-5. This is how Steiner puts it about Strauss's philosophic "presence" in general: it is "a provocation" and "an impediment" which stands against proceeding as if nothing has changed. Steiner maintains that for Strauss, Maimonides "was always close by." Hence, what he writes about Strauss's "presence" pertains with even greater force to his work on Maimonides specifically.

16. See David Novak, "Responding to Leo Strauss: Four Recent Maimonidean Studies," *Conservative Judaism* 44, no. 3 (1992): 80-86; Alan Verskin, "Reading Strauss on Maimonides: A New Approach," *Journal of Textual Reasoning* 3, no. 1 (June 2004), http://etext.virginia.edu/journals/tr/volume3/verskin.html

17. Rosen, "Leo Strauss and the Problem of the Modern," pp. 120, 135-36.

18. See "How to Study Spinoza's *Theologico-Political Treatise*," in *Jewish Philosophy and the Crisis of Modernity*, p. 182. Cf. *Guide*, "Introduction," p. 15. See also "Literary Character"; *The City and Man*, p. 60; "On the Interpretation of Genesis," in *Jewish Philosophy and the Crisis of Modernity*, pp. 373-75.

19. See "Literary Character." For Strauss on books, see especially *Jewish Philosophy and the Crisis of Modernity*, pp. 120, 181-96, 373-75, 380-82, 394.

20. See "Introduction to Maimonides' *Guide*." Cf. also "How to Study Medieval Philosophy," chap. 1, and app. 4A, in *On Maimonides*. See also Marvin Fox, *Interpreting Maimonides:*

Studies in Methodology, Metaphysics, and Moral Philosophy (Chicago: University of Chicago Press, 1990).

21. For the clearest exception to this rule, see Fox, *Interpreting Maimonides*, who is fully informed of Strauss's discoveries, even though he takes issue with him on several key points and also gives attention to what he regards as some consequent difficulties with the Pines translation.

22. See "Literary Character."

23. See "On a New Interpretation of Plato's Political Philosophy," *Social Research* 13, no. 3 (September 1946): 326–67 and especially pp. 348–55. About this section of the article-review, Strauss claimed that "the only thing I did not write only for students is the interpretation of the, in a certain sense decisive, passage of the *Seventh Letter*." See "Correspondence Concerning Modernity [with Karl Löwith]," *Independent Journal of Philosophy* 4 (1983): 105–19, and especially p. 108; *Hobbes Politische Wissenschaft und zugehörige Schriften—Briefe*, vol. 3 of *Gesammelte Schriften*, p. 663.

24. Petrus Cunaeus, *The Hebrew Republic*, trans. Peter Wyetzner (Jerusalem: Shalem Press, 2006), p. 15; Leibniz, *Theodicy*, trans. E. M. Huggard (London: Routledge and Kegan Paul, 1951), p. 287; Lenn E. Goodman, "Maimonides and Leibniz," *Journal of Jewish Studies* 31 (1980): 225; Jean Bodin, *Colloquium of the Seven about Secrets of the Sublime [Colloquium heptaplomeres]*, trans. Marion Leathers Daniels Kuntz (Princeton: Princeton University Press, 1975), pp. 93–94; Nietzsche, *Human, All Too Human*, trans. Marion Faber and Stephen Lehmann (Lincoln: University of Nebraska Press, 1984), sec. 475, p. 229. For a modern English "Cambridge Platonist," who in the present case—based on the impact which Maimonides' thought (and especially the *Guide*) made on him—might have been better named a "Cambridge Maimonidean," see John Smith, *Select Discourses*, 4th ed. (Cambridge: Cambridge University Press, 1859), pp. 166–67, 174–75, 179–81, 184–85, 187, 192–95, 204–9, 213, 216–19, 221–22, 228–31, 235, 237, 241–43, 250–54, 257, 268–69, 272–77, 279, 287, 292–93, 304–6, 310–313, 314–18. For the power of a great thinker in history, consider Nietzsche's remark: "The greatest events and thoughts—but the greatest thoughts are the greatest events." *Beyond Good and Evil*, trans. Walter Kaufmann (New York: Vintage, 1966), sec. 285.

25. For Husserl's conception of "de-sedimentation," see *The Crisis of European Sciences and Transcendental Phenomenology*, trans. David Carr (Evanston, IL: Northwestern University Press, 1970), with discussion of its relation to Strauss in Rosen, "Leo Strauss and the Problem of the Modern," pp. 120–21, 132, 133.

26. See "An Introduction to Heideggerian Existentialism," in *The Rebirth of Classical Political Rationalism*, p. 29. The course of recent thought—and hence our contemporary fate in philosophy, politics, culture, and religion—is perhaps best summarized in a chapter heading from Allan Bloom's book *The Closing of the American Mind* (New York: Simon and Schuster, 1987): "The Nietzscheanization of the Left and Vice Versa."

27. Compare Georg Lukacs, *The Destruction of Reason*, trans. Peter Palmer (Atlantic Highlands, NJ: Humanities Press, 1981), with Strauss's comments in "Relativism," in *The Rebirth of Classical Political Rationalism*, pp. 19–21.

28. On false, vain, or counterfeit forms of philosophy, as multiple species of "mutilated philosophy," see Alfarabi, *The Philosophy of Plato and Aristotle*, ed. and trans. Muhsin Mahdi (Ithaca: Cornell University Press, 1969; 2nd ed., 2002), p. 48–49; and Maimonides, *Guide* 1.5, pp. 29–31; 1.31, pp. 66–67; 1.71, pp. 177–83; 2.15, p. 292. For the forms of "pseudophilosophies" and "pseudophilosophers" by which minds are misled, see "How to Study Spinoza's *Theologico-Political Treatise*," in *Jewish Philosophy and the Crisis of Modernity*, pp. 190–91. For "restoring" philosophy once it has become "blurred or destroyed," see "Introduction" to *Persecution and the Art of Writing*, pp. 12–13; also in *Jewish Philosophy and the Crisis of Modernity*, pp. 420–22.

29. On the erroneous connections that are conventionally drawn by modern historical scholars between religious mysticism and medieval philosophic neo-Platonism, especially in relation to Alfarabi, see Muhsin S. Mahdi, *Alfarabi and the Foundations of Islamic Political Philosophy* (Chicago: University of Chicago Press, 2001), pp. 2-3, 33-36, 148-49, as well as Strauss's brief comments discussed in chap. 3, n. 8; chap. 5, nn. 14 and 44; and chap. 7, n. 28. Alfarabi regarded it also as his mission to advance the cause of philosophy, in the sense of showing how to revive its health and vitality in eras during which it has been eclipsed, or during which it has been allowed to fall ill and to languish. See Miriam Galston, "A Re-examination of al-Farabi's Neoplatonism," *Journal of the History of Philosophy* 15 (1977): 13-22; Galston, *Politics and Excellence: The Political Philosophy of Alfarabi* (Princeton: Princeton University Press, 1990). For judicious remarks on how the same issue should be resolved with regard to Maimonides, see Steven Harvey, "Did Maimonides' Letter to Samuel Ibn Tibbon Determine Which Philosophers Would Be Studied by Later Jewish Philosophers?," *Jewish Quarterly Review* 83, no. 1-2 (July-October 1992): 51-70, and especially "Appendix: Maimonides' Neoplatonism," pp. 68-70.

30. See "How to Study Medieval Philosophy."

31. See "Thucydides: The Meaning of Political History," in *The Rebirth of Classical Political Rationalism*, pp. 72-73. For the comment on paradox, see John Neville Figgis, *Studies of Political Thought from Gerson to Grotius, 1414-1625* (Cambridge: Cambridge University Press, 1907), p. 87.

32. See Henry E. Allison, *Lessing and the Enlightenment* (Ann Arbor: University of Michigan Press, 1966), p. 84; Green, *Jew and Philosopher*, pp. 148-50, nn. 6 and 7. See also *Persecution and the Art of Writing*, p. 36.

33. See *Persecution and the Art of Writing*, p. 36.

34. Cf. Nietzsche, *Beyond Good and Evil*, trans. Walter Kaufmann (New York: Vintage, 1966), secs. 212, 287, 292, 295; with Aristotle, *Nicomachean Ethics*, trans. Robert C. Bartlett and Susan D. Collins (Chicago: University of Chicago Press, 2011), bk. 4, chap. 3, pp. 75-80; and with *Guide* 2.32-48 and 3.51-54.

INDEX

Abravanel, Isaac, 93
Aḥad Ha'am (Asher Ginzberg). *See* Ginzberg, Asher (Aḥad Ha'am)
Albo, Joseph, 172n6, 180n20
Alfarabi (Abu Nasr al-Farabi). *See* Farabi (Abu Nasr al-; Alfarabi; Farabianism)
al-Ḥarizi, Judah (Yehuda), 172n8
Allison, Henry E., 203n32
Altmann, Alexander, 140, 201n12
Aquinas, Thomas. *See* Thomas Aquinas (Thomist; Thomism)
Aristophanes, 71, 83, 182n6
Aristotle (Aristotelian; Aristotelianism), 20, 22, 28, 32, 40–41, 48, 68, 71, 75, 83, 96, 100, 103, 111–12, 132, 141, 145, 157, 159, 164, 176n26, 183n10, 184n14, 187n11, 188n5, 188n8, 189n12, 189n14, 192n28, 203n34. *See also* Falasifa
Arnold, Matthew, 3, 173n9
Austen, Jane, 184n11
Averintsev, Sergei, 173n9
Averroes (Ibn Rushd; Averroism; Averroist), 32, 93, 109, 138–39, 179n10
Avicebron. *See* Ibn Gabirol, Solomon
Avicenna (Ibn Sina), 33, 93, 189n14

Bacon, Francis (Baconian), 82–83, 127, 129, 174n13, 189n11, 195n39
Barth, Karl, 86, 90–91, 190n15, 191n22
Batnitzky, Leora, 197n46, 198n5
Beethoven, Ludwig van, 140
Beneghar, Nasser, 194n34
Ben Zoma, Simeon (Shimon), 121
Bergson, Henri, 132
Berlin, Isaiah, 103, 196n43

Berman, Lawrence V., 196n44
Berns, Laurence, 187n11
Biale, David, 182n3
Bland, Kalman, 172n6
Bloom, Allan, 34, 140, 174n14, 175n24, 181n22, 201n12, 202n26
Blumenthal, David, 172n8
Bodin, Jean, 23, 82, 152, 189n11, 202n24
Borgia, Rodrigo Llançol (Pope Alexander VI), 83
Brague, Rémi, 107–8, 172n8, 198n2
Butterworth, Charles, 196n44

Catiline (Lucius Sergius Catilina), 39
Cicero, Marcus Tulius, 39
Cohen, Hermann, 1–2, 14, 22, 28–29, 72, 74, 76, 105, 110–11, 113, 120, 131–33, 136, 150, 172n7, 180n19, 188n5, 198n5. *See also* neo-Kantianism (neo-Kantian)
Cohen, Jonathan, 187n9
Cunaeus, Petrus, 151, 202n24

Dannhauser, Werner, 176n28, 179n17
Davidson, Herbert, 141, 191n27, 201n13
Davidson, Israel, 172n8
Descartes, René, 7, 22, 83, 127, 129, 175n23, 193n30
Diamond, James A., 181n26
Dilthey, Wilhelm, 195n37

Euclid, 32
Euripides, 159

Fackenheim, Emil L., 95, 195n37, 199n13, 201n14

205

Falaquera, Shem Tov ben Joseph ibn, 35
Falasifa, 22, 40, 189n14, 199n10
Farabi (Abu Nasr al-; Alfarabi; Farabianism), 28, 39, 61, 68, 75, 78, 87, 93–94, 104, 106, 136, 145, 183n8, 184n11, 189n14, 193n30, 196n44, 202n28, 203n29
Faur, José, 127–28
Feldman, Louis, 173n9
Figgis, John Neville, 203n31
Finnis, John, 194n33
Fox, Marvin, 143, 179n9, 181n26, 197n45, 201n20, 202n21
Fradkin, Hillel, 137, 200n6, 200n8
Freud, Sigmund, 8, 174n14, 182n4, 187n1

Gadamer, Hans-Georg, 83–84, 95, 99–101, 172n5, 189n9, 189n13, 191n27, 194nn31–32, 195n37
Galileo Galilei, 187n11
Galston, Miriam, 179n10, 196n44, 203n29
Gersonides, Levi, 93
Giles of Rome, 173n11
Gilson, Etienne, 100–102, 173n11, 193n30, 196n43
Ginzberg, Asher (Aḥad Ha'am), 199n6
Glatzer, Nahum N., 26, 137, 179n17
Goethe, Johann Wolfgang von, 86, 182n6
Goodman, Lenn E., 173n11, 202n24
Grant, George, 201n14
Green, Kenneth Hart, 172n7, 173n12, 177n4, 180n19, 183n8, 185n18, 186n6, 190n15, 194n34, 195n38, 196n40, 197n45, 198n3, 198n5, 200nn5–6, 200n8, 201n11, 203n32
Grotius, Hugo, 151
Gutas, Dimitri, 191n27
Guttmann, Julius, 60, 104–7, 109–10, 112, 179n17, 197n46, 198n1

Halevi, Judah (Yehuda), 87, 93, 104, 121
Harvey, Steven, 196n44, 197n46, 203n29
Harvey, Warren Zev, 115, 172n8, 199nn11–12
Hegel, Georg Wilhelm Friedrich (Hegelian), 22–23, 32, 39, 112–14, 142, 156, 175n24, 178n6, 198n4, 199n7, 201n14
Heidegger, Martin (Heideggerian; Heideggerianism), 3, 7, 58, 63, 69, 97, 99, 101–2, 105, 131–32, 135, 143, 155–57, 180n18, 183n10, 194n32, 195nn36–37, 196n40, 201n14
Hitler, Adolf, 69, 155. *See also* Nazi
Hobbes, Thomas, 109, 127, 129
Husik, Isaac, 3, 60, 104, 105, 110–12, 173n9, 173n11, 187n10, 197n46
Husserl, Edmund, 132, 202n25

Ibn Falaquera, Shem Tov ben Joseph. *See* Falaquera, Shem Tov ben Joseph ibn
Ibn Gabirol, Solomon, 34–35, 181n23
Ibn Tibbon, Samuel ben Judah (Shmuel), 149, 174n17
Idel, Moshe, 178n7
Ivry, Alfred L., 137, 200n8

Jaffa, Harry V., 190n17
Jefferson, Thomas, 77, 175n21

Kabbalah (Kabbalism; Kabbalist), 20, 112–13, 178n7, 198n4, 199n8
Kant, Immanuel (Kantian), 1, 14, 32, 61, 73, 96, 102, 110–12, 188n5, 190n19, 193n30. *See also* neo-Kantianism (neo-Kantian)
Kaufmann, David, 121
Kellner, Menachem, 172n8
Kennington, Richard, 174n13, 189n11
Kierkegaard, Søren, 22, 32, 37, 105, 158
Klein, Jacob, 26, 102, 108, 137, 171, 179n14, 179n17, 196n40, 198n2
Klingenstein, Susanne, 179n17
Kojève, Alexandre, 39, 142–43, 175n24, 178n6, 191n27
Kraemer, Joel L., 138–39, 142, 175n24, 201n11
Kraus, Paul, 174n17
Krochmal, Nahman, 188n5
Krüger, Gerhard, 179n17, 189n14, 198n2

Lachterman, David R., 173n9, 189n10
Lazier, Benjamin, 197n46
Leaman, Oliver, 143
Leibniz, Gottfried Willhelm von, 23, 151–52, 173n11, 199n9, 202n24
Lenzner, Steven, 171n2, 172n8, 176n27, 196n44
Lerner, Ralph, 172n6, 174n15, 181n22, 186n21
Lessing, Gotthold Ephraim, 22, 70, 93, 151, 160–64, 182n6, 186n6, 199n9
Löwith, Karl, 179n17, 188n8
Lukacs, Georg, 155, 202n27

Machiavelli, Niccolò (Machiavellian; Machiavellianism), 3–4, 8–12, 68, 77–78, 82, 127, 130, 152, 172n8, 174n15, 175n19, 175n22, 180n20, 189n11
Mahdi, Muhsin S., 189n14, 196n44, 203n29
Maimon, Solomon, 14, 112, 151, 188n5
Maimonides, Moses (Moses ben Maimon; Rambam), *passim*
Maritain, Jacques, 102, 193n30, 196n43
Marsilius of Padua, 87, 93, 104

Meier, Heinrich, 136-37, 172n4, 177n1, 177n4, 179n17, 188n2, 189n14, 200n8, 201n9
Mendelssohn, Moses, 1, 161, 186n6, 188n5
Meyer, Thomas, 191
Minkov, Svetozar, 179n17
modern Thomism (neo-Thomism), 94-96, 98-99, 101, 103, 155, 193nn29-30, 194n32
Momigliano, Arnaldo, 201n10
Moses (prophet), 45, 60, 76, 90, 123-24, 188n8
Motzkin, Aryeh Leo, 199n6
Munk, Salomon, 22-23, 35, 40, 105, 112, 120-21, 149, 199n13

Nazi, 69, 131, 155
neo-Kantianism (neo-Kantian), 28, 73-74, 96, 104, 105, 113, 132, 188n5
neo-Platonism (neo-Platonic), 22, 35, 40-41, 157, 189n14, 203n29
Neumark, David, 187n10
Newton, Isaac, 187n11
Nietzsche, Friedrich (Nietzschean), 3, 10-12, 25, 30, 63, 74, 76, 78, 84, 88, 97, 101, 105, 125, 131, 135, 149, 152-53, 155, 158, 173n10, 175n23, 178n6, 179n14, 180n18, 186n2, 195n37, 202n24, 203n34
Novak, David, 143, 175n24, 179n9, 201n16
Nutkiewicz, Michael, 172n8

Parens, Joshua, 196n44, 199n11
Pareto, Vilfredo, 173n10
Pascal, Blaise, 22, 185n15
Patch, Andrew, 198n1
Philo Judaeus, of Alexandria, 130-31
Pines, Shlomo, 140, 148-49, 172n8, 174n17, 192n28, 202n21
Plato (Platonic; Platonism), 11-12, 20, 28, 31-33, 35, 39, 48, 58, 68, 71, 76-78, 83, 89, 93, 100, 103-4, 132, 136, 138, 141-42, 147, 150, 153, 156, 162-63, 173n10, 175n19, 175n23, 178n6, 182n6, 183n10, 187n11, 188n5, 188n8, 189n14. *See also* neo-Platonism (neo-Platonic)
Pompey (Gnaeus Pompeius Magnus), 39

Razi, Abu Bakr Muhammad ibn Zakariya al-, 174n17
Rethelyi, Mari, 197n46
Rosen, Stanley, 12, 140, 145, 154, 175n23, 184n11, 194n32, 201n12, 201n17, 202n25
Rozenzweig, Franz, 84, 86

Savonarola, Girolamo, 9
Schocken, Zalman, 182n3

Scholasticism (Scholastic), 34, 173n11, 193n29
Scholem, Gershom, 20, 31, 75, 108-9, 120-22, 178n7, 179n17, 182n3, 187n10, 188n6, 198nn1-2, 199n8, 199n13
Schwarcz, Moshe, 198n3
Schweid, Eliezer, 143, 197n46
Seeskin, Kenneth, 137, 143, 200n8
Shestov, Lev, 173n9
Smith, Gregory Bruce, 186n7
Smith, John, 202n24
Smith, Steven B., 198n5, 199n13
Socrates (Socratic), 27, 50, 86, 109-10, 139, 158, 184n12
Solomon (king), 181n25
Spinoza, Benedict, 1-2, 13-14, 21-23, 29, 32, 40, 70-71, 73-74, 77-80, 83, 105, 114-20, 122-25, 126-31, 133, 135-36, 142, 144-45, 150-51, 158, 160, 172n7, 174n15, 178n6, 179nn8-9, 188n3, 188n5, 189n9, 199n12
Steiner, George, 143, 201n15
Steinschneider, Moritz, 120, 196n44
Strauss, Leo, *passim*

Tamer, Georges, 189n14
Tanguay, Daniel, 173n9, 189n14, 196n44
Tarcov, Nathan, 103, 196nn41-42
Tawney, R. H., 191n27
Thomas Aquinas (Thomist; Thomism), 26, 32, 93-94, 96, 102-3, 127, 138, 193nn29-30. *See also* modern Thomism (neo-Thomism)
Thucydides, 71, 159

Velkley, Richard L., 195n37
Verskin, Alan, 143-44, 201n16
Voegelin, Eric, 194n32

Walker, Paul E., 174n17
Weil, Gotthold, 120
Weiss, Raymond L., 176n26
Whitehead, Alfred North, 132
Wild, John, 103
Wolfson, Elliot R., 178n7
Wolfson, Harry Austryn, 60, 105, 121, 130-31, 154, 200n2

Xenophon, 27, 71, 142-43

Yaffe, Martin D., 199n12

Zank, Michael, 138, 200nn7-8
Zionism (Zionist), 29, 73
Zuckert, Catherine, 134, 200n4